Extractivism in the Maghreb

Centered on Algeria, Morocco, and Tunisia, this book interrogates the complex entanglements between extractivism, state power, class formation, and geopolitical reorientation in North Africa. While the global energy transition promises economic diversification and sustainable development, the international contributors to this volume show how "green extractivism" often reproduces older structures of dependency and inequality, and therefore authoritarianism consolidates.

Rather than fostering transformation, rent economies adapt, stabilize, and reconfigure themselves through new sources of rent and new modes of social control. The book makes three core contributions. First, it offers a historically grounded and theoretically informed understanding of rent economies in the Maghreb, tracing how colonial legacies of resource extraction evolved into postcolonial patterns of rentier governance. Second, it introduces a class-analytical perspective to debates on extractivism, arguing that rent not only finances authoritarian regimes but also shapes dynamic social coalitions, "state classes," and cycles of contention and co-optation. Third, the book develops a comparative approach to the political economy of green transformation, focusing on the interplay between domestic rent regimes and external pressures from global markets, international donors, and climate politics. By anchoring each case study in concrete struggles, everyday experiences, and contested claims to resources, the book reveals how global transformations are mediated, resisted, and reappropriated from the following.

The book will be vital reading for those interested in political economy, development studies, and Middle East and North Africa (MENA) studies. It will particularly appeal to scholars working on extractivism, rentier states, authoritarianism, postcolonial development, and the political sociology of class and class struggle.

Hannes Warnecke-Berger, University of Kassel, Germany.

Rachid Ouaissa, Philipps-University of Marburg, Germany.

Global Challenges in Political Economy

Taxation and Inequality in Latin America
New Perspectives on Political Economy and Tax Regimes
Edited by Philip Fehling and Hans-Jürgen Burchardt

The Political Economy of Extractivism
Global Perspectives on the Seduction of Rent
Edited by Hannes Warnecke-Berger and Jan Ickler

Global Rentier Capitalism
Theory and Development
Edited by Balihar Sanghera

The Political Economy of Elites in Latin America
Edited by Jan Ickler and Rebeca Ramos Padrón

Political Economy of Algeria
Extractivism, Rents and Populism
Ouchichi Mourad

The Political Economy of the Energy Transition in Latin America
Between Extractivism and Sustainable Development
Edited by Hannes Warnecke-Berger and Hans-Jürgen Burchardt

Extractivism in the Maghreb
Class, State and Geopolitics
Edited by Hannes Warnecke-Berger and Rachid Ouaissa

For more information about this series, please visit: www.routledge.com/Global-Challenges-in-Political-Economy/book-series/GCPE

Extractivism in the Maghreb

Class, State and Geopolitics

Edited by Hannes Warnecke-Berger and Rachid Ouaissa

Routledge
Taylor & Francis Group
LONDON AND NEW YORK

First published 2027
by Routledge
4 Park Square, Milton Park, Abingdon, Oxon OX14 4RN

and by Routledge
605 Third Avenue, New York, NY 10158

Routledge is an imprint of the Taylor & Francis Group, an informa business

British Library Cataloguing-in-Publication Data
A catalogue record for this book is available from the British Library

Library of Congress Cataloging-in-Publication Data
Names: Warnecke-Berger, Hannes editor author | Ouaissa, Rachid, 1971– editor author
Title: Extractivism in the Maghreb : class, state and geopolitics / edited by Hannes Warnecke-Berger and Rachid Ouaissa.
Other titles: Global challenges in political economy
Description: New York : Routledge, 2026. | Series: Global challenges in political economy | Includes bibliographical references.
Identifiers: LCCN 2026017032 (print) | LCCN 2026017033 (ebook) | ISBN 9781041221265 hardback | ISBN 9781041221272 paperback | ISBN 9781003730750 ebook
Subjects: LCSH: Clean energy industries—Political aspects—Africa, North | Clean energy industries—Social aspects—Africa, North | Rent (Economic theory)—Political aspects—Africa, North | Rent (Economic theory)—Social aspects—Africa, North
Classification: LCC HD9502.5.C543 A355 2026 (print) | LCC HD9502.5.C543 (ebook) | DDC 333.790961—dc23/eng/20260325
LC record available at https://lccn.loc.gov/2026017032
LC ebook record available at https://lccn.loc.gov/2026017033

ISBN: 978-1-041-22126-5 (hbk)
ISBN: 978-1-041-22127-2 (pbk)
ISBN: 978-1-003-73075-0 (ebk)

DOI: 10.4324/9781003730750

Typeset in Times New Roman
by Apex CoVantage, LLC

Contents

Contributors

Ahcène Amarouche is Professor of Economics at the University of Bouira, Algeria. His research focuses on rentier economies, macroeconomic governance, and political reforms in Algeria. He has authored several studies on the political economy of hydrocarbons and state finance.

Samir Bellal is Professor of Urban and Regional Development at the University of Tizi-Ouzou, Algeria. He works on institutional change, regional development, and the spatial dimensions of rent economies. He has also advised public institutions and development agencies.

Alessandra Bonci is Senior Researcher at the Arnold Bergstraesser Institute, Freiburg, Germany. She studies environmental conflicts, gender, and resource politics in North Africa. Her work brings a feminist political ecology perspective to extractivism studies.

Aron Buzogány is Associate Professor at the University of Natural Resources and Life Sciences, Vienna, Austria. His research focuses on environmental governance, climate policy, and the EU's external energy strategy. He has published widely on sustainability transitions and green industrial policy.

Salim Chena is Senior Researcher at the CNRS/Institute of African Worlds (IMAF), France. He specializes in Algerian political history, middle-class dynamics, and social transformation. His work bridges archival research and contemporary political analysis.

Nathalie Ferré is Associate Professor of Political Science at the Sorbonne Nouvelle University, Paris, France. Her research focuses on green transformations, public policy, and the politics of sustainability. She works especially on socio-technical imaginaries and energy transitions in Tunisia.

Anouar Hechmi is Lecturer in Geography at the University of Manouba, Tunisia. He studies territorial inequality, port infrastructure, and extractive geographies in Tunisia. He is affiliated with the Governance and Development Territorial Laboratory.

Mustapha Majidi is Professor of Political Science and Faculty of Law and Political Sciences at the Hassan First University of Settat, Morocco. He specializes in political participation, protest movements, and the political economy of post-extractivism. His research addresses state–society relations, regional marginalization, and contested governance.

Rachid Ouaissa is Professor of Political Science, Center for Near and Middle Eastern Studies (CNMS), at the Philipps-University of Marburg, Germany. He is an expert on political economy, authoritarianism, and postcolonial statehood in the MENA region. He coordinates the Merian Centre for Advanced Studies in the Maghreb (MECAM) and has published widely on rentier states and elite transformation.

Mourad Ouchichi is Professor of Political Science at the University of Bejaia, Algeria. His work focuses on political change, protest, and state–society relations in Algeria. His recent research addresses class segmentation and social movements in rentier contexts.

Mohamed Ismail Sabry is Research Fellow, Merian Centre for Advanced Studies in the Maghreb (MECAM), Tunis/CNMS, at the University of Marburg, Germany. His research focuses on energy transitions, green hydrogen, and rentier dynamics in North Africa. He holds a PhD in political economy and has published on sustainability and extractivism.

Kressen Thyen is Senior Researcher at the University of Bremen, Germany. She is a political sociologist working on protest movements, resource politics, and authoritarian resilience in North Africa. She has conducted fieldwork in Tunisia and Algeria.

Philipp Wagner is Junior Researcher at the Arnold Bergstraesser Institute, Freiburg, Germany. He specializes in critical development studies, protest, and extractive governance. His current research focuses on social contestation around renewable energy infrastructure.

Hannes Warnecke-Berger is Senior Researcher at the University of Kassel, Germany. He specializes in global political economy, development theory, and state–class relations. His work focuses on rent theory, sustainability transitions, and statehood in the Global South, with field research in Latin America and the Maghreb.

1 Extractivism in the Maghreb: Class, State, and Geopolitics

An Introduction

Hannes Warnecke-Berger and Rachid Ouaissa

The Maghreb is entering a new energy age, but it is not the one imagined in glossy strategy papers in Brussels, Berlin, or Paris. In late 2023, as Europe scrambled to replace Russian gas and accelerate its Green Deal, delegations of ministers, bankers, and corporate consortia moved through Algiers, Tunis, and Casablanca, offering memoranda of understanding, green hydrogen roadmaps, and billion-euro solar visions. Their message was simple: North Africa is the future of Europe's energy security.

On the ground, however, a very different story was unfolding. In the mining town of Jerada, where coal extraction ended two decades ago, protesters-turned-councilors struggled to rebuild a shattered local economy while navigating the legacies of an extractive social order that never truly ended; it merely mutated. In southern Tunisia, communities and unionists blocked access roads to solar plants, demanding jobs, water, and dignity as they confronted megaprojects designed primarily for export. And in Algeria, the political class, long accustomed to hydrocarbons as the backbone of national power and a promise of prosperity, confronted a paradox: the green transition promised diversification, yet it risked reinforcing the rent structures that have shaped Algeria since independence, while, at the same time, the prospect of large-scale shale exploitation has tempted decision-makers to extend a neo-fossil energy trajectory (Boudalia et al., 2022).

These tensions between global ambitions and local realities, between "green" futures and old extractive logics, lie at the heart of this volume. As we argue in this book, the Maghreb is not simply an arena of resource extraction nor is it merely a passive recipient of geopolitical designs. It is a region in which new energy frontiers collide with deeply rooted political economies of rent, producing hybrid forms of governance, selective elite renewal, and mobilizations that defy linear narratives of transition.

The Maghreb's emerging "green state class," as we propose in this volume, is not a coherent political actor but a shifting coalition of ministers, technocrats, international donors, law firms, and corporate developers who mediate the region's incorporation into new global value chains of hydrogen, solar power, and critical materials. Instead of a departure from rentierism, the result is the rise of a "green rentierism" (Bruna, 2023), embedded in European energy strategies, technological dependencies, and domestic political settlements.

DOI: 10.4324/9781003730750-1

This book takes the historical depth of these developments—from colonial infrastructures to postcolonial rent regimes—seriously, while grounding its analyses in the urgent struggles of the present perspectives. In doing so, it speaks to broader debates in global political economy: about extractivism in the age of climate crisis, about uneven energy transitions, and about the contradictions of a decarbonizing world economy.

The Maghreb is not on the periphery of the green transition. It is one of its laboratories. The conflicts unfolding there today will shape not only the future of North Africa but also the future of Europe's energy order and, ultimately, the global politics of climate change.

Energy resources from the Maghreb, particularly from Algeria, and increasingly from Morocco and Tunisia, constitute a strategically important component of Europe's energy landscape. Owing to its geographical proximity, existing pipeline infrastructure, and substantial renewable energy potential, the region offers Europe both short-term security of supply and long-term opportunities for decarbonization. Algeria has traditionally been one of Europe's principal suppliers of natural gas, with pipeline connections such as Medgaz and TransMed linking North African production directly to Southern European markets. These links have become increasingly relevant as the European Union (EU) seeks to diversify away from Russian gas and reduce its vulnerability to geopolitical disruptions.

Algeria remains North Africa's leading producer of oil and natural gas. According to the United States Energy Information Agency (2025), it is the largest natural gas producer in Africa and the region's second-largest producer of total liquid fuels. In 2024, Algeria exported about 402,000 barrels per day of crude oil and condensate, with Europe receiving the majority (295,000 barrels per day). Algeria is also a major African liquified natural gas (LNG) exporter, supplying most of its LNG to Europe through the Arzew and Skikda terminals operated by the state-owned company Sonatrach. In 2023, the country exported 1.9 trillion cubic feet of natural gas, 90% of which went to Europe.

Beyond hydrocarbons, the Maghreb holds exceptional potential for renewable energy generation, particularly solar and wind power. Ambitious national strategies, most prominently in Morocco, indicate a growing capacity not only to meet domestic demand but also to inject renewable electricity into the European market. Prospects for green hydrogen exports further underscore the region's potential to support Europe's transition to climate neutrality. As the EU moves toward a low-carbon energy system, North Africa may evolve from a conventional gas supplier to a key partner in renewable energy cooperation (Ayed et al., 2025).

Across the chapters in this volume, a remarkably consistent pattern becomes visible. First, green technologies do not displace extractivism; they reorganize it through new infrastructures, new geographies, and new forms of control. Extractivism, in this context, emerges as an explanatory concept that enriches the debate on current and historical transformations in North Africa. Second, emerging energy sectors—hydrogen, solar, and critical materials—create their own rent circuits, producing renewed elite coalitions and fresh layers of dependency. Third, global decarbonization agendas intersect unevenly with national development strategies, amplifying asymmetries between European demand and Maghrebi priorities. And fourth, within these shifting terrains, local actors—from protesters in Jerada to engineers in Tunis to phosphate workers in Safi—navigate the green transition with a mixture of ingenuity and constraint, shaping and contesting its outcomes from the following. Taken together, these four lines crystallize into a new geography of power and contestation in which the Maghreb is positioned, and positions itself, today.

Extractivism: Definition, Boundaries, and Its Relevance for the Maghreb

Although the term *extractivism* originated in Latin American debates, particularly in the context of neo-extractivism and critiques of commodity-led development (Burchardt & Dietz, 2014; Svampa, 2019), we argue that its analytical potential extends far beyond its region of origin. In our previous work, we have theoretically unpacked the concept, refining it into a framework that explains social orders structured by rents, unequal specialization, and dependent reproduction (Cerioli & Warnecke-Berger, 2025; Warnecke-Berger & Ickler, 2023b). This volume builds on that effort and demonstrates that, when properly conceptualized, extractivism offers a powerful lens for understanding contemporary transformations in the Maghreb.

Despite its long intellectual genealogy, the term *extractivism* has often been used loosely, sometimes as a synonym for extraction (Marston & Kennemore, 2019), sometimes as a critique of capitalism (Chagnon et al., 2022; Ye et al., 2020), and sometimes as a catch-all label for ecological or political violence (Dunlap & Jakobsen, 2020; Shapiro & McNeish, 2021). Recent advances in political economy have sharpened the concept analytically and distinguished it from neighboring approaches.

Contemporary developments in the Maghreb render conceptual precision indispensable. Analyses of the region within political economy and policy debates have frequently relied on frameworks that are adjacent to, yet analytically narrower than, extractivism—most notably neocolonialism (Hamouchene, 2019; Hamouchene & Sandwell, 2023) and dependency-oriented accounts that attribute the Maghreb's economic subordination primarily to its historically constituted relations with Europe (Gana et al., 2023). While these approaches offer valuable insights into external domination, unequal exchange, and postcolonial power asymmetries, they remain insufficient for explaining the durability, adaptability, and ongoing reconfiguration of extractive logics across North African political economies. In particular, they tend to privilege external relations of dependence at the expense of examining the internal institutional, territorial, and socioecological dynamics through which extractivism is reproduced and transformed. To establish a robust analytical foundation for this volume, three conceptual distinctions are therefore essential.

Extractivism as Social Order Versus Extraction as Activity

One common slip in the literature is equating extractivism with extraction. Latin American scholars, such as Gudynas (2020), define extractivism using quantitative indicators: high extraction volumes, minimal local processing, and export shares exceeding a certain threshold. These criteria are useful for empirical classification, but they remain insufficient for a political economy perspective. A focus on extraction alone cannot explain why some societies become locked into raw material dependence, why rents persist across political cycles, or why institutions evolve in ways that reinforce rather than mitigate these dynamics (Warnecke-Berger, 2023a).

Our approach improves this by drawing a sharp conceptual line between *extraction* and *extractivism*. Extraction refers to the technical and economic activity of digging, drilling, harvesting, diverting, or processing natural resources. Extractivism, by contrast, refers to a social order: a configuration of surplus structures, class relations, political coalitions, and institutional patterns shaped by the dominance of rents (Warnecke-Berger & Ickler, 2023a). It is the organization of society around the expectation of future rents, rather than the material act of extraction, that explains why extractivism persists even when volumes fall or sectors shift.

Where Gudynas (2020) and political ecology (Dunlap et al., 2024) primarily emphasize environmental degradation, territorial dispossession, and the violence of extraction, we foreground the mechanisms that make extractivism durable: the macroeconomics of specialization, the distributive politics of rent appropriation, the institutional consolidation of rent-seeking coalitions, and the material reproduction of populations dependent on rents. Without this surplus-centered view, the Maghreb cannot be adequately understood.

Extractivism Versus Imperialism or "Accumulation by Dispossession"

A second conflation arises from Marxist, dependency, and world-systems approaches, which interpret extractivism as a direct extension of imperial domination (McKay et al., 2021; Veltmeyer & Petras, 2014) and a form of accumulation by dispossession (Andreucci et al., 2023). These perspectives powerfully illuminate colonial histories of land dispossession, unequal ecological exchange, and coercive integration into global markets. But they cannot explain why extractivism changes over time, why certain countries partially escape it, or why new forms—particularly those linked to renewable energy—emerge in a multipolar world economy. Our approach builds on these insights without reducing extractivism to external coercion. The persistence of extractivism is better explained by four mechanisms: (1) the formation of economic rents; (2) technological asymmetries and productivity gaps; (3) structural underemployment in domestic labor markets; and (4) the logic of unequal specialization in global value chains. These structural forces reproduce extractivism even in the absence of overt imperial pressure. This perspective is crucial for the Maghreb, where the interplay of domestic strategies and international demand creates a terrain of continuous reconfiguration. New elite coalitions, the revalorization of land and infrastructure under European decarbonization strategies, and the incorporation of Morocco, Tunisia, and Algeria into emerging green energy markets reflect not only historical dependency but also the political construction of new rent regimes. Extractivism here is not imposed; it is co-produced.

Extractivism Versus Rentier State Theory

A third conceptual boundary must be drawn vis-à-vis rentier state theory. This approach has long been central to the study of the Middle East and North Africa (Beblawi & Luciani, 1987; Mahdavy, 1970; Moritz, 2020; Schwarz, 2008), and it remains indispensable for understanding how oil rents reshape political regimes, authoritarian practices, and state autonomy. Yet rentier state theory is analytically limited in three key respects. First, it treats rents as exogenous windfalls—as if they were gifts of nature—rather than as outcomes of global cost differentials, technological hierarchies, and structures of demand on global markets. In our conception, extractivism endogenizes rents, showing how they emerge structurally within the world economy and why they persist across sectors, including phosphates, solar power, and hydrogen. Second, rentier state theory focuses on political effects, authoritarianism, co-optation, and state autonomy, while leaving the economic foundations of persistence under-theorized (Smith & Waldner, 2021). By contrast, extractivism, following our idea, links rents to the dynamics of unequal specialization, structural unemployment, and long-term development traps. Third, rentier theory was developed in the context of hydrocarbons, particularly oil (Ross, 2012). It has limited explanatory power for the rise of green rentierism. Solar deserts, cross-Mediterranean interconnectors and energy infrastructures, and hydrogen corridors reproduce extractive logics without resembling the oil sector. Extractivism theory can account for this continuity in change; rentier theory cannot.

Applying this conceptual framework to the Maghreb yields three insights central to this volume. First, the Maghreb is not moving beyond extractivism; it is entering a new phase of it. Morocco's hydrogen ambitions, Tunisia's solar export schemes, and Algeria's repositioning of gas as a transition fuel illustrate diversification within extractivism and, hence, a transition from fossil to green rents. Second, the global energy transition intensifies existing contradictions. As multiple chapters show, renewable energy megaprojects reproduce the characteristics identified in the extractivism literature: territorial dispossession, exclusion of local communities, technocratic forms of governance, asymmetric negotiations with foreign investors, and enclave-type infrastructures. Green energy is not inherently transformative; it can easily become green extractivism. Third, extractivism links domestic politics to global transformations. Unlike narrower categories such as "oil rents" or "resource curse," extractivism captures the entire chain: global demand and price structures, domestic patterns of rent appropriation, political imaginaries of development, and evolving class and elite dynamics. As recent scholarship argues, extractivism sits at the intersection of climate change, global power shifts, and development theory (Cerioli, 2025; Cerioli & Warnecke-Berger, 2025), a conjunction more visible in the Maghreb today than anywhere else.

Defining Extractivism as a Development Model

In our conceptualization, extractivism is not the activity of extracting natural resources. Extraction occurs throughout history; it is not inherently pathological. Extractivism, by contrast, is a development model—a way of *ordering society*—characterized by three interlocking features: first, unequal specialization on raw material exports; second, a surplus structure dominated by rents; and third, a society whose reproduction depends on future rents (Warnecke-Berger & Ickler, 2023a). Extractivist societies are structurally specialized in exporting raw materials—fossil fuels, minerals, and agricultural commodities—rather than processing them or developing diversified productive capacities. This pattern is not the result of "natural endowments" but, as shown elsewhere, an outcome of unequal specialization, driven by international market structures, technological gaps, and the emergence of rents (Warnecke-Berger, 2023b). Furthermore, extractivism is shaped by Ricardian differential rents, which arise when producers with vastly different production costs sell at the same world-market price. As we show in our theoretical model (Warnecke-Berger & Ickler, 2025), rents are not temporary market anomalies but persistent features of the global economy, and they become the gravitational center of the domestic surplus structure. This insight is crucial: extractivism persists not because resources are abundant but because rents are seductive: to elites, to political coalitions, to state institutions, and, indirectly, to society at large. Finally, extractivism becomes a social order when fiscal systems, welfare arrangements, political coalitions, and everyday livelihoods depend on continued rent inflows. This dependence shapes class structures, state–society relations, and political imaginaries well beyond the extractive sector itself (Cerioli & Warnecke-Berger, 2025). In this sense, extractivism is not one sector among others; it is a totalizing development model that structures the entire political economy. This conceptualization differs from ecological or quantitative approaches to extractivism and expands classical rentier state theory by explaining why rents emerge and persist, and why new forms of "green extractivism" (Bruna, 2023; Dunlap et al., 2024) are now reshaping the Maghreb. In this sense, green hydrogen in Mauritania, solar corridors in Tunisia, and phosphate-based fertilizer strategies in Morocco are not signs of a post-extractive future but manifestations of a transformation within extractivism, driven by European decarbonization agendas, domestic elite bargains, and global technology hierarchies.

Rents, Power, and Transformation in the Maghreb

Across the chapters, rent emerges as a foundational analytical category. Whether fossil, administrative, informal, or increasingly "green," rents remain the central mechanism through which political and economic power is accumulated, distributed, and contested (Elsenhans, 2023). The region's development trajectories continue to hinge less on productive diversification than on controlling flows of revenue generated from hydrocarbons, land, water, or today solar radiation and hydrogen. The Algerian case epitomizes this dynamic. Hydrocarbon rents have long shaped the architecture of state institutions, governance practices, and social expectations, generating what contributors describe as a form of centralized resource power that structures political authority and economic strategy (Ouaissa, 2009). Reform episodes, protest cycles, and industrial modernization projects all unfold within, and are constrained by, this rent-based logic.

At the same time, new forms of rent are emerging. Large-scale solar fields, renewable energy corridors, hydrogen complexes, and related infrastructure projects in Tunisia and Morocco illustrate the rise of green rentierism. These projects reproduce key elements of extractivism—control over land and water, asymmetric negotiations between governments and foreign investors, and the exclusion of local communities—while being legitimized through discourses of decarbonization and global climate responsibility. Even post-extractive spaces, such as Jerada after the closure of its coal mines, remain structured by informal rent economies that empower local notables and perpetuate economic vulnerability. What appears as a "post-extractivist" setting often becomes a terrain where new, hybrid forms of resource dependency take shape. Taken together, these spotlights underscore that the Maghreb is not overcoming extractivism; it is recasting it through new sectors, technologies, and narratives.

Elites, Statehood, and the Selective Renewal of Power Coalitions

Political and economic elites adapt to and shape the emerging rent landscape. Across the Maghreb, transitions—whether toward green energy, administrative reform, or post-extractive development—are mediated by evolving coalitions of state actors, technocrats, business interests, and external partners. In Algeria, the logic of resource centrality is inseparable from the state's historical formation. Political authority is maintained through the capacity to allocate and redistribute rents, producing what can be described as an exteriority of state power: a disconnect between society and the state that is reinforced, not weakened, by reliance on resource revenues. Elite reproduction thus occurs through the management and manipulation of material flows rather than institutionalized mechanisms of representation or accountability. In Tunisia and Morocco, the green transition has fostered new alliances among ministries, regulatory agencies, international financial institutions, donor organizations, private law firms, and transnational corporations. These coalitions play a decisive role in drafting legislation, shaping investment regimes, and defining national energy strategies (Carboni, 2023; Kadaoui, 2023; Nicolai, 2022). Far from democratizing economic governance, green transition policies often strengthen technocratic decision-making and create new channels for elite influence, thereby promoting "democratic backsliding" (Sadiki & Saleh, 2023, pp. 1318–1319; Souilmi, 2023). Yet these evolving configurations do not erase older forms of power. Local notables, regional brokers, and informal elites retain influence, sometimes resisting reform, sometimes repositioning themselves within the new rent environment. The question is therefore not whether elites control rents, but which elites, through what mechanisms, and with what political effects. The green transition thus becomes a site not only of technological change but also of elite circulation and selective renewal, reinforcing structural inequalities even as it opens new fields of opportunity.

Ambivalent Societal Agency: Protest, Participation, and the Limits of Transformation

In this context, societal actors play an ambivalent role. Social movements, unions, local communities, and NGOs are far from passive recipients of top-down projects; they articulate grievances, mobilize collective action, and propose alternative visions of development (Gluhbegovic, 2025; Ouchichi, 2023; Rachidi & Aballagh, 2023). Yet their capacity to reshape structural conditions remains constrained by entrenched power relations (Keskes, 2025). The Jerada case vividly demonstrates this tension. Grassroots mobilization following a lethal mining accident generated new political actors, enabled electoral breakthroughs, and opened spaces for deliberation and local governance. However, the transformative potential of these efforts is constrained by institutional weakness, limited financial resources, and the continued grip of local rent networks. In Tunisia, trade unions, activist networks, and environmental groups challenge large-scale solar projects and transnational infrastructure plans. They draw on concepts such as "extractivism" and "just transition" to politicize green energy agendas and mobilize international support (Ben Jelloul, 2024). However, their influence is fragmented and often overshadowed by the well-resourced coalitions of state agencies, global firms, and donor institutions. Across the region, societal agency is therefore real but uneven, significant but insufficient to fundamentally shift the parameters of development. Protest and participation can produce openings, but these openings remain embedded in broader configurations of resource dependency and state power (Haddioui, 2025).

Europe as External Structuring Power: Green Transition, Market Logics, and Renewed Dependencies

Finally, all contributions underscore the decisive role of Europe as an external driver of energy transitions and economic restructuring in the Maghreb. The EU's decarbonization strategies, hydrogen plans, and regulatory frameworks (such as the Carbon Border Adjustment Mechanism (CBAM)) shape investment flows, policy priorities, and technological pathways across North Africa (Boafo et al., 2025). Projects like TuNur, the Elmed interconnector, and emerging hydrogen corridors are not merely technical undertakings; they represent the spatial and infrastructural materialization of Europe's search for green energy. This external demand embeds the Maghreb in a transregional energy order in which it increasingly functions as a renewable resource frontier for Europe—an echo of older extractive relations but translated into the idiom of sustainability. The normative dimension of EU influence is equally important. European standards regarding sustainability, competition, and governance set the terms on which North African states access funding, technology, and markets (Moisseron & Guesmi, 2022). While these frameworks can promote modernization, they also risk entrenching asymmetrical dependencies and sidelining domestic socioeconomic priorities. In short, the green transition is not merely a domestic process but also a geopolitically structured project that reconfigures the relations between North Africa and Europe in ways that are simultaneously enabling and constraining.

The Maghreb in a Moment of Rent-Based Transformation: Outline of the Book

This volume examines the political economy of the Maghreb through the prism of extractivism, understood as the dominant organizing principle of economic accumulation, social reproduction, and political authority in the region. It conceptualizes the Maghreb as a space in which extractive logics, historically rooted in hydrocarbons, minerals, and land, continue to structure class relations, state formations, and development strategies, even as they are rearticulated under the banner of the global energy transition. The book focuses empirically on three country cases (Algeria, Morocco, and Tunisia), which together capture both shared structural features and divergent pathways within Maghrebi extractivism. Libya is deliberately excluded from the analysis. Since the outbreak of the civil war in 2011, the country's political and economic institutions have been profoundly fragmented, rendering systematic analysis of energy transition dynamics largely impossible. While Libya constitutes a paradigmatic rentier state, based almost exclusively on oil and gas exports, ongoing armed conflict and the involvement of multiple foreign actors competing for control over energy resources have foreclosed meaningful prospects for a green energy transition. Within the selected cases, Algeria occupies a central analytical position. As a country whose exports still rely overwhelmingly on hydrocarbons, yet which simultaneously pursues ambitious projects in solar energy and green hydrogen, Algeria offers a theoretically revealing case of extractivist resilience and transformation. Its entrenched hydrocarbon-based power structures render transition processes particularly contentious, while the continued availability of fossil rents provides greater fiscal and political room for maneuver during the transitional phase than in neighboring Morocco and Tunisia. This combination makes Algeria a critical lens through which to examine the contradictions, temporalities, and power struggles inherent in extractivist transitions.

The cross-cutting themes identified across the chapters depict the Maghreb region as not transitioning out of extractivism but rather undergoing a multi-layered transformation of extractive social orders. Rents, both old and new, remain central to development trajectories. Elite coalitions adapt rather than disappear. Social actors carve out spaces of agency but confront persistent structural limits. And Europe shapes the region's green future through its own energy and geopolitical imperatives. The Maghreb's present is therefore characterized by hybridity, contestation, and overlapping temporalities: fossil pasts, green futures, and enduring material and political inequalities. These dynamics form the analytical foundation of this volume and frame the case studies that follow.

In the second chapter, *Hannes Warnecke-Berger* and *Rachid Ouaissa* provide the comparative backbone of the volume. They conceptualize Algeria, Morocco, and Tunisia as differentiated rent societies whose geopolitical relevance is continuously produced through externally anchored surplus, now reconfigured by the global energy transition. Introducing the notion of "green rents," the chapter argues that solar, wind, hydrogen, interconnectors, and phosphates do not signal a departure from rent-based development but its transformation. Tracing colonial infrastructures, postcolonial state formation, and contemporary European decarbonization strategies, the chapter frames the central question of the book: whether green rents enable structural transformation or reproduce extractivist social orders under new technological and geopolitical conditions. Chapter 3, by *Ahcène Amarouche*, offers a political economy of contemporary Algeria that links macroeconomic rent structures to social reproduction. The chapter shows how hydrocarbon rents continue to shape investment patterns, state capacity, and distributional politics, while generating structural heterogeneity and a persistent labor surplus. Rather than treating rents as exogenous windfalls, Amarouche traces the mechanisms through which rent circuits organize economic life and constrain diversification. Algeria thus emerges as a paradigmatic case of extractivist resilience, where transition pressures unfold within a deeply rent-structured economy. In the fourth chapter, *Samir Bellal* examines the institutional and actor-centered dynamics of Algeria's politics of rent. Focusing on state institutions, economic elites, and sectoral power centers, the chapter demonstrates how access to rent channels is politically mediated and institutionally stabilized. Reform agendas are repeatedly filtered through incentives that privilege control over surplus rather than productive transformation. Bellal's analysis clarifies the micro-foundations of state–class rule and shows why emerging green sectors are likely to be governed through similar mechanisms of gatekeeping and elite coordination. Chapter 5, by *Kressen Thyen*, links extractivism to protest and contention in the Maghreb. The chapter conceptualizes resource nationalism as a domestic strategy of legitimacy management rather than a purely sovereign response to external actors. Through analyses of protest dynamics and local struggles, it shows how rent-based development generates recurring cycles of mobilization, particularly in contexts of dispossession and exclusion. In the context of the energy transition, Thyen demonstrates how new green projects intensify these tensions by revalorizing land, infrastructure, and local ecologies. In Chapter 6, *Salim Chena* foregrounds the role of the middle classes in Algeria's rent society. The chapter traces how rent-based accumulation shapes middle-class formation, expectations, and political behavior, producing structurally "blocked" strata whose aspirations collide with limited productive transformation. Oscillating between co-optation, protest, and emigration, the middle classes emerge as a central axis of political stability and crisis. Chena's contribution highlights how green transitions may either widen inclusion through upgrading or deepen exclusion if they reproduce enclave logics. Chapter 7, by *Anouar Hechmi*, approaches extractivism through the lens of infrastructure, focusing on Tunisia's phosphate economy and the Gafsa mining basin. The chapter demonstrates how ports, railways, and logistical corridors materialize unequal specialization by connecting extractive enclaves to global markets while marginalizing surrounding regions. Infrastructure appears as a political technology of rent extraction and territorial control. In the context of green transitions, this analysis underscores the risk that new interconnectors and hydrogen corridors become the next generation of extractivist infrastructure. In Chapter 8, *Mourad Ouchichi* analyzes the relationship among rentier governance, state–class segmentation, and social movements in Algeria. The chapter shows how fiscal stress and institutional competition generate protest waves that interact with elite restructuring rather than simply opposing it. Selective redistribution, repression, and co-optation function as crisis-management tools, stabilizing regimes while deepening fragmentation. Ouchichi thus bridges rent theory and contentious politics, highlighting why moments of transition remain politically indeterminate. Chapter 9, by *Mustapha Majidi*, examines post-extractive governance through the case of Jerada in Morocco. The chapter demonstrates that extractivism persists beyond active extraction, leaving behind political infrastructures, distributive expectations, and informal rent networks. While protest in Jerada translated into participation and local governance, its transformative potential remains constrained by institutional weakness and fiscal scarcity. The case illustrates how post-extractive spaces risk reproducing extractivist fragilities under new developmental labels. In Chapter 10, *Mohamed Ismail Sabry* analyzes emerging pathways for green hydrogen production in North Africa. Mapping key actors, regulatory frameworks, and infrastructural constraints, the chapter shows how hydrogen strategies are shaped by export orientation and European demand. Sabry argues that hydrogen risks becoming a new enclave economy, reproducing unequal specialization within a decarbonization narrative, unless it is deliberately embedded in domestic industrial and employment strategies. Hydrogen thus emerges as a paradigmatic case of green extractivism—or a potential lever for transformation. The final chapter, Chapter 11, by *Nathalie Ferré*, *Philipp Wagner*, *Alessandra Bonci*, and *Aron Buzogány* approaches Tunisia's energy transition through the lens of contentious imaginaries. The chapter shows how competing visions of development, sovereignty, and justice shape struggles over renewable energy projects. Activists, unions, state agencies, and external partners contest not only technologies but also the meaning of transition itself. By linking discourse, governance, and material outcomes, the chapter demonstrates how green rents are legitimized and resisted, closing the volume with a focus on societal agency within structurally constrained transitions. In the final and concluding chapter, *Hannes Warnecke-Berger* and *Rachid Ouaissa* synthesize the volume's theoretical and empirical insights into a geopolitical political economy framework of green extractivism in the Maghreb. The chapter argues that the green transition transforms rent into a new organizing principle of both external alignment and domestic conflict, turning geopolitics into a central cleavage within Maghrebi societies. By systematically linking trade, investment, and debt structures to emerging green rents, the chapter demonstrates how new geopolitical competition is layered onto historically entrenched patterns of unequal specialization rather than replacing them. At the same time, it shows how this reconfiguration of rent reshapes state–class strategies, elite coalitions, and social exclusion, while opening up highly constrained conditions for new development coalitions. The chapter concludes that the Maghreb's future will be decided not by the availability of green resources but by the political capacity to neutralize the adverse effects of rent and to embed green rents in employment-centered, socially inclusive development strategies. In this sense, the Maghreb emerges not as a passive periphery of the green transition but as a critical laboratory in which the geopolitics of decarbonization, extractivism, and social transformation intersect.

References

Andreucci, D., García López, G., Radhuber, I. M., Conde, M., Voskoboynik, D. M., Farrugia, J. D., & Zografos, C. (2023). The coloniality of green extractivism: Unearthing decarbonisation by dispossession through the case of nickel. *Political Geography*, *107*, 102997. https://doi.org/10.1016/j.polgeo.2023.102997

Ayed, Y., Fortes, P., & Al Afif, R. (2025). Maghreb's renewable power future for climate mitigation: Insights from the TIMES-MAGe model. *Energy Strategy Reviews*, *62*, 101918. https://doi.org/10.1016/j.esr.2025.101918

Beblawi, H., & Luciani, G. (Eds.). (1987). *The rentier state*. Croom Helm.

Ben Jelloul, M. (2024). *What impact has the El Kamour social movement had on the establishment of a new socio-economic development model in Tataouine (Tunisia)?* (Extractivism Policy Brief No. 04/2024). University of Kassel; Philipps-University of Marburg. https://doi.org/10.17170/kobra-2024051710159

Boafo, J., Dotsey, S., & Spencer, R. (2025). Energy transition diplomacy: The EU's pursuit of Africa's critical minerals for renewable energy at whose expense? *Energy Research & Social Science*, *127*, 104213. https://doi.org/10.1016/j.erss.2025.104213

Boudalia, S., Okoth, S. A., & Zebsa, R. (2022). The exploration and exploitation of shale gas in Algeria: Surveying key developments in the context of climate uncertainty. *The Extractive Industries and Society*, *11*, 101115. https://doi.org/10.1016/j.exis.2022.101115

Bruna, N. (2023). *The rise of green extractivism: Extractivism, rural livelihoods and accumulation in a climate-smart world*. Routledge.

Burchardt, H.-J., & Dietz, K. (2014). (Neo-)extractivism: A new challenge for development theory from Latin America. *Third World Quarterly*, *35*(3), 468–486. https://doi.org/10.1080/01436597.2014.893488

Carboni, A. (2023). Non-party ministers and technocrats in post-revolutionary Tunisia. *The Journal of North African Studies*, *28*(1), 151–178. https://doi.org/10.1080/13629387.2022.2034502

Cerioli, L. (2025). Geopolitik der Energiewende und die Rekonfiguration globaler Machtverhältnisse: Lateinamerika am Scheideweg. In H.-J. Burchardt, K. Dietz, & H. Warnecke-Berger (Eds.), *Grüne Energiewende in Lateinamerika* (pp. 37–58). Nomos.

Cerioli, L., & Warnecke-Berger, H. (2025). Extractivism and international studies. *Oxford Research Encyclopedia of International Studies*. Advance online publication. https://doi.org/10.1093/acrefore/9780190846626.013.888

Chagnon, C. W., Durante, F., Gills, B. K., Hagolani-Albov, S. E., Hokkanen, S., Kangasluoma, S. M. J., Konttinen, H., Kröger, M., LaFleur, W., Ollinaho, O., & Vuola, M. P. S. (2022). From extractivism to global extractivism: The evolution of an organizing concept. *Journal of Peasant Studies*, *49*(4), 760–792. https://doi.org/10.1080/03066150.2022.2069015

Dunlap, A., & Jakobsen, J. (2020). *The violent technologies of extraction: Political ecology, critical agrarian studies and the capitalist worldeater*. Springer International Publishing. https://doi.org/10.1007/978-3-030-26852-7

Dunlap, A., Verweijen, J., & Tornel, C. (2024). The political ecologies of "green" extractivism(s): An introduction. *Journal of Political Ecology*, *31*(1). https://doi.org/10.2458/jpe.6131

Elsenhans, H. (2023). *Capitalism and rent: A destructive relationship: Why the Maghreb does not join the newly industrialising countries*. Editions Arabesque.

Gana, A., Grouiez, P., Koleva, P., & Magnin, É. (Eds.). (2023). *Capitalismes émergents et modèles de développement au Maghreb: Fondements institutionnels et performances économiques*. Centre Jacques-Berque.

Gluhbegovic, R. (2025). *Promises of development and phosphates: Between expectations and realities in Gafsa* (Extractivism Policy Brief No. 02/2025). University of Kassel; Philipps-University of Marburg. https://doi.org/10.17170/kobra-2025052711189

Gudynas, E. (2020). *Extractivisms: Politics, economy and ecology*. Fernwood Publishing.

Haddioui, O. (2025). *Decarbonization dreams in neocolonial times* (Extractivism Policy Brief No. 05/2025). University of Kassel; Philipps-University of Marburg. https://doi.org/10.17170/kobra-2025090911450

Hamouchene, H. (2019). *Extractivism and resistance in North Africa*. Transnational Institute. https://www.tni.org/en/publication/extractivism-and-resistance-in-north-africa

Hamouchene, H., & Sandwell, K. (Eds.). (2023). *Dismantling green colonialism: Energy and climate justice in the Arab region*. Pluto Press.

Kadaoui, A. (2023). A resurgence of authoritarianism in Morocco, or preservation of the status quo. *The Journal of North African Studies*, *28*(6), 1402–1424. https://doi.org/10.1080/13629387.2023.2203470

Keskes, H. (2025). *Energy sovereignty for Tunisia: A people-centered approach to transition* (Extractivism Policy Brief No. 03/2025). University of Kassel; Philipps-University of Marburg. https://doi.org/10.17170/kobra-2025090811443

Mahdavy, H. (1970). The patterns and problems of economic development in rentier states: The case of Iran. In M. A. Cook (Ed.), *Studies in the economic history of the Middle East* (pp. 428–467). Oxford University Press.

Marston, A., & Kennemore, A. (2019). Extraction, revolution, plurinationalism: Rethinking extractivism from Bolivia. *Latin American Perspectives*, *46*(2), 141–160. https://doi.org/10.1177/0094582X18781347

McKay, B. M., Alonso-Fradejas, A., & Ezquerro-Cañete, A. (Eds.). (2021). *Agrarian extractivism in Latin America*. Routledge. https://doi.org/10.4324/9780367822958

Moisseron, J.-Y., & Guesmi, K. (2022). Une évaluation des politiques européennes en direction de l'industrie au Maroc. *Maghreb–Machrek*, *248–249*(1), 43–81. https://doi.org/10.3917/machr.248.0043

Moritz, J. (2020). Re-conceptualizing civil society in rentier states. *British Journal of Middle Eastern Studies*, *47*(1), 136–151. https://doi.org/10.1080/13530194.2020.1714268

Nicolai, K. E. (2022). A green gambit: The development of environmental foreign policy in Morocco. *The Journal of North African Studies*, *27*(4), 714–740. https://doi.org/10.1080/13629387.2020.1865931

Ouaissa, R. (2009). Dynamik der Staatsklasse zwischen Konsolidierung und Segmentierung am Beispiel Algerien. In M. Beck, C. Harders, A. Jünemann, & S. Stetter (Eds.), *Der Nahe Osten im Umbruch* (pp. 78–99). VS Verlag für Sozialwissenschaften.

Ouchichi, M. (2023). *The socio-economic dynamics of Algeria's Hirak protests: An overlooked factor* (Extractivism Policy Brief No. 09/2023). University of Kassel; Philipps-University of Marburg. https://doi.org/10.17170/kobra-202310048818

Rachidi, I., & Aballagh, A. (2023). Algeria's Hirak: Fading prospects for democratisation? *The Journal of North African Studies*, *28*(6), 1515–1537. https://doi.org/10.1080/13629387.2023.2207230

Ross, M. L. (2012). *The oil curse: How petroleum wealth shapes the development of nations*. Princeton University Press.

Sadiki, L., & Saleh, L. (2023). Crisis of democratisation in the Maghreb and North Africa. *The Journal of North African Studies*, *28*(6), 1317–1323. https://doi.org/10.1080/13629387.2023.2207225

Schwarz, R. (2008). The political economy of state-formation in the Arab Middle East: Rentier states, economic reform, and democratization. *Review of International Political Economy, 15*(4), 599–621. https://doi.org/10.1080/09692290802260662

Shapiro, J., & McNeish, J.-A. (Eds.). (2021). *Our extractive age: Expressions of violence and resistance*. Routledge. https://doi.org/10.4324/9781003127611

Smith, B., & Waldner, D. (2021). *Rethinking the resource curse*. Cambridge University Press. https://doi.org/10.1017/9781108776837

Souilmi, H. (2023). A tale of two exceptions: Everyday politics of democratic backsliding in Tunisia. *The Journal of North African Studies, 28*(6), 1425–1443. https://doi.org/10.1080/13629387.2023.2207226

Svampa, M. (2019). *Neo-extractivism in Latin America*. Cambridge University Press. https://doi.org/10.1017/9781108752589

United States Energy Information Agency. (2025, June 5). *Country analysis brief: Algeria*. United States Department of Energy.

Veltmeyer, H., & Petras, J. F. (Eds.). (2014). *The new extractivism: A post-neoliberal development model or imperialism of the twenty-first century?* Zed Books.

Warnecke-Berger, H. (2023a). Renta y rentismo: Especialización desigual y trampa de desarrollo en América Latina. In H.-J. Burchardt, C. Gárgano, & L. G. Christel (Eds.), *¿De la sustentabilidad al desarrollo? Entre el extractivismo verde y la transformación socioambiental* (pp. 91–116). CLACSO.

Warnecke-Berger, H. (2023b). Trade, unequal specialization, and the persistence of extractivism. In H. Warnecke-Berger & J. Ickler (Eds.), *The political economy of extractivism: Global perspectives on the seduction of rent* (pp. 17–41). Routledge.

Warnecke-Berger, H., & Ickler, J. (2023a). Introduction: The political economy of extractivism. In H. Warnecke-Berger & J. Ickler (Eds.), *The political economy of extractivism: Global perspectives on the seduction of rent* (pp. 1–16). Routledge.

Warnecke-Berger, H., & Ickler, J. (Eds.). (2023b). *The political economy of extractivism: Global perspectives on the seduction of rent*. Routledge.

Warnecke-Berger, H., & Ickler, J. (2025). *The political economy of extractivism*. Exploring Economics. https://www.exploring-economics.org/en/discover/the-political-economy-of-extractivism/

Ye, J., van der Ploeg, J. D., Schneider, S., & Shanin, T. (2020). The incursions of extractivism: Moving from dispersed places to global capitalism. *Journal of Peasant Studies, 47*(1), 155–183. https://doi.org/10.1080/03066150.2018.1559834

2 The Maghreb at the Crossroads

A Comparative Perspective on the Region's Geopolitical and Socioecological Challenges

Hannes Warnecke-Berger and Rachid Ouaissa

Introduction

In recent years, the Maghreb has emerged as a central geopolitical arena in which security, economic, and energy-related interests of both regional and external actors converge. This development is closely linked to structural challenges such as terrorism, transnational arms and drug trafficking, and the governance of migration routes. Beyond conventional security and energy concerns, the Maghreb has become deeply embedded in European migration and climate policies. The region functions simultaneously as a transit and buffer zone within the European border regime and as a security partner in counterterrorism cooperation and the stabilization of the Mediterranean space (Herbert, 2022).

Fragile and unstable statehood in Libya and across the Sahel further exacerbates these dynamics, positioning the Maghreb as a security frontier of Europe (Ouaissa, 2023; Dirèche et al., 2023). Alongside these intraregional dynamics, the constellation of external actors engaged in the Maghreb has become increasingly pluralized. In addition to traditional European partners, China, Turkey, the Gulf states, and Russia have significantly expanded their political and economic presence. This shift reflects the gradual erosion of European—particularly French—influence, which has been weakened by political instability, economic crises, and growing neocolonial resentment within the region. As a result, the Maghreb operates within an increasingly multipolar environment that creates both new strategic opportunities and new forms of dependency. Yet these geopolitical dynamics cannot be understood without the political economy of rent: the Maghreb's strategic salience is repeatedly produced, and constrained, by its role in generating and redistributing externally anchored surplus.

The region's strategic relevance is further underpinned by its geographical position at the intersection of Europe, Africa, and the Middle East. This location shapes the foreign policy orientations of Maghreb states, which are influenced by colonial legacies, regional rivalries, and global power shifts. The energy and raw materials sectors are particularly significant in this regard. Russia's war against Ukraine has once again exposed Europe's dependence on external energy suppliers and has elevated the Maghreb as an alternative and complementary energy space. Algeria

DOI: 10.4324/9781003730750-2

plays a pivotal role as a gas supplier to Europe, while Morocco and Tunisia are increasingly important emerging actors in the field of renewable energy.

The global energy transition adds a new dimension to this strategic role. Europe's dependencies are not disappearing but rather shifting—from fossil fuels toward critical raw materials, renewable energy sources, and green electricity. Within this context, the Maghreb has become a key component of Europe's decarbonization strategy. In addition to energy, mineral resources have moved to the forefront of geopolitical interest. The region's substantial reserves of phosphates, natural gas, and other critical materials—including those located in Western Sahara—confer growing geo-economic significance on the Maghreb.

Within this evolving landscape, Maghreb states occupy differentiated positions. Morocco is of central importance due to its vast phosphate reserves and its ambitious solar and wind energy projects. Algeria remains a crucial supplier of fossil energy while increasingly positioning itself in the fields of solar power and green hydrogen. Tunisia, owing to its geographical location, holds significant potential as a transit and production hub for green energy and as a hub for cross-Mediterranean electricity connections. This differentiation highlights the emergence of a new geo-economic order in the Maghreb, in which energy, climate, and security concerns are deeply interconnected.

The future geopolitical significance of the Maghreb will largely depend on its economic and energy-policy orientation. Renewable energy offers the region's states an opportunity to move beyond the role of mere raw material suppliers and to address long-standing structural development challenges. Investments in solar energy, wind power, and green hydrogen have the potential to foster industrial diversification, generate employment, and strengthen state capacity.

At the same time, this new salience reproduces an older logic: the region's international relevance is still defined by external demand and unequal specialization, now reconfigured around green technologies rather than fossil fuels. The challenge and the central question of this chapter are whether these new forms of dependence can be transformed into the basis of a more autonomous and inclusive development model. The Maghreb matters to Europe not only for what it supplies but also because its internal political economy will fundamentally shape the future of Euro-Mediterranean relations in the age of green transformation.

The global race for decarbonization has thrust the Maghreb into an unexpected position of strategic prominence. Across North Africa, governments have announced projects to produce solar and wind power at unprecedented scale, to develop export-oriented green hydrogen, and to consolidate their control over phosphate and other critical minerals central to the global energy transition. Yet these initiatives unfold in political economies historically shaped by unequal specialization, state–class formation, and rents in old and new forms.

The key argument of this chapter is that the global energy transition does not eliminate those rents. Instead, it transforms them. As hydrocarbon rents erode, new "green rents" emerge linked to solar radiation, wind corridors, desert land, cross-Mediterranean interconnectors, hydrogen-export hubs, and phosphate reserves. These new rents simultaneously open opportunities for economic diversification and threaten to deepen older patterns of dependence and extractivism. Nowhere is this tension more visible than in the Maghreb. While Algeria, Morocco, and Tunisia differ significantly in state structures, class configurations, and economic trajectories, they share a fundamental characteristic: they are rent societies whose development has long been shaped by the appropriation and redistribution of rent-based surplus. The question today is whether the green transition will reinforce these structures or destabilize them in favor of new coalitions and new development pathways.

Understanding the contemporary moment requires historical depth. The origins of extractivism in the Maghreb lie not only in the postcolonial era but also in the colonial importance of their economies. From the mid-19th century onward, colonial forces established patterns of agricultural and mineral extraction, export-oriented infrastructure, and the incorporation of local elites, thereby entrenching unequal specialization and preventing early industrialization (Bennoune, 1976; Halvorsen, 1978). In the case of Morocco, General Hubert Lyautey, the principal architect of French colonial penetration, drew a clear distinction between "le Maroc utile et le Maroc inutile," a "useful" Morocco and an "useless" Morocco (Puyo, 2022), and acted accordingly. Phosphates, agricultural production, and precious metals were identified as priority natural resources to be explored and exploited (Aamimri & Elfalih, 2024). After the Second World War, this configuration hardened into a structural dependence on raw material exports, oil and gas from Algeria and Libya, phosphate from Morocco, and low-value manufacturing and tourism from Tunisia.

Independence did not break these patterns. Instead, postcolonial state-building reinforced and even deepened them. Through nationalization, import substitution, and the strategic use of external rents, state classes emerged that controlled the circuits of surplus and converted resource revenues into instruments of power, patronage, loyalty, and even political containment. During the second half of the 20th century, social contracts across the Maghreb were built on this logic, even as they produced cycles of conflict, impeded middle-class advancement, and sparked periodic rebellions.

The energy transition now intersects with these deeper logics of rent-led development trajectories. Green rents, unlike fossil rents, are generated not by scarcity but by geography, security, technology, and Europe's urgent demand for decarbonized energy in a geopolitical reconfiguration of the world economy. This creates a paradox: it increases the Maghreb's global relevance while simultaneously risking a renewed form of unequal specialization in which the region supplies the primary energy inputs for Europe's green transformation while remaining marginal to technological upgrading and productive diversification.

This chapter proceeds from the premise that rents, whether fossil, green, migratory, or commercial, remain the most powerful analytical lens through which to understand the Maghreb's political economy. It offers a comparative analysis of three similar yet distinct trajectories: Algeria, where the erosion of hydrocarbon rents intersects with an entrenched state class and a fragile yet resilient regime. Algeria is particularly significant in the current transition from established fossil fuel energy systems to emerging renewable energy systems. Morocco, where phosphates, solar megaprojects, and industrial integration with Europe generate both green rentierism and aspirations for industrial upgrading, and Tunisia, where the relative absence of strong fossil rents has produced a different form of state–class rule and a more volatile political economy now seeking new external anchors. Across these cases, the chapter demonstrates that the Maghreb's future will be shaped by how these societies navigate the transition from fossil to green rents, and by whether new coalitions can use the energy transition as a lever for structural transformation rather than as a vehicle for reproducing the past.

Our analysis unfolds in four steps. First, it traces the historical emergence of rents, extractivism, and unequal specialization as the region's structural position in the world economy. Second, we focus on the formation and evolution of state–class rule, and its role in appropriating and redistributing rents. Third, we compare cycles of conflict, blocked middle classes, and rebellion, and their relation to rent dynamics. Fourth, we assess the impacts and risks of the green transition, focusing on whether green rents can break or reproduce Maghreb trajectories.

Taken together, these elements help explain why the Maghreb is once again at the center of geopolitical attention—and why its internal political economy will determine whether the region can seize the transformative possibilities of the global energy transition.

Rent, State Formation, and Unequal Specialization in the Maghreb

These contemporary dynamics do not emerge in a vacuum. They rest on a deeper, long-term configuration in which external rents, state–class formation, and unequal specialization have jointly defined the Maghreb's position in global capitalism. Before examining the political and social trajectories of Algeria, Morocco, and Tunisia, it is essential to clarify the theoretical lens through which these mechanisms become visible.

Rent, Surplus, and Unequal Specialization: A Theoretical Lens

The political economy of the Maghreb cannot be captured by a narrow reading of concepts such as the rentier state or rent-seeking alone, as the introduction to this book highlights. While the rentier paradigm has shed important light on the stabilizing function of external revenues, it tends to obscure the broader logic of unequal specialization and the role of non-capitalist surplus appropriation that shape Maghreb societies.

Following the surplus approach (Warnecke-Berger & Ickler, 2023; Warnecke-Berger, 2025; Elsenhans, 2023), rents are better understood as a structural feature of uneven development on the global scale and as an outcome of ruptures of global capitalism: a form of surplus generated by natural or political monopolies, appropriated outside competitive markets, and embedded in historically constituted relations of power.

From our perspective, rent is not merely a revenue but a mode of social reproduction and a logic of ordering society. It structures class relations, delineates political coalitions, shapes the division of labor, and mediates the Maghreb's integration into the world economy (Warnecke-Berger, 2021c). Most importantly, rent links domestic politics to the international hierarchy of production, division of labor, technology, and currency. The Maghreb's position in this hierarchy is characterized by unequal specialization, resulting in a long-standing pattern in which economies export raw materials and low-technology goods while importing sophisticated technologies and high-value manufactures (Elsenhans, 2023). This structural configuration is deeply rooted in processes of global uneven development, colonial patterns of exploitation, enclave development, and infrastructural orientation toward European markets.

Today, the global energy transition is reconfiguring the underlying global surplus structure. Hydrocarbons, still responsible for over 80% of global energy consumption, are expected to decline dramatically, while demand surges for renewable energy, strategic minerals, storage systems, and clean hydrogen (Gielen, 2021; International Energy Agency, 2021). This shift expands the domain of what we may call "green rents." By green rents, we refer to the differential advantages arising not from scarcity but from geography, climate, security, and the Global South's role in providing solar, wind, and mineral resources in the context of an emerging geopolitical reconfiguration of the world economy.

This transformation has two implications for the Maghreb: (1) externally, it amplifies the region's geopolitical importance by positioning it as a supplier of new energy sources and critical materials; and (2) internally, it reopens the question of how rents are appropriated, by whom, and for what type of development strategy, and to what extent new forms of rent are reshaping social structures.

In all three Maghreb states, old and new rents (fossil, mineral, agrarian, commercial, or migratory)—and the rentier social contracts associated with them—structure state–society relations through structural heterogeneity and the sectoral decoupling of labor productivities, through enclave sectors, and through fragmented class formations. The challenge of the energy transition is therefore not merely technological but political: can new green rents be mobilized to overcome historical blockages, or will they merely reproduce the logic of unequal specialization under a sustainable label?

The International Role of Rent: Positioning the Maghreb in the Global Hierarchy

The international dimension of rent has long defined the Maghreb's insertion into the global economy. Algeria's membership in the Organization of the Petroleum Exporting Countries (OPEC), Morocco's dominance in global phosphate markets, and Tunisia's integration into European production networks all reflect the region's structural role in supplying external markets with raw materials, energy, and low-cost labor.

Algeria is the paradigmatic case of an externally anchored rent economy (Elsenhans, 2016). Hydrocarbon exports have long provided the state with a steady flow of differential rent, enabling expansive public spending, large-scale infrastructural investment, and periodic redistributive measures that buy political stability. As Bellal (2017) notes, this model is inherently cyclical: periods of high oil prices coincide with social appeasement, while downturns expose deep structural vulnerabilities and provoke unrest, as seen in 1988 and again in the Hirak movement of 2019. Externally, Algeria mobilizes its energy endowments to secure geopolitical partnerships. Europe's dependence on Algerian gas, heightened after Russia's invasion of Ukraine, has strengthened Algiers' bargaining power, even as it reinforces the country's structural dependence on external demand. This dynamic illustrates a central theme of this chapter: rent provides leverage, but leverage does not translate into structural transformation.

Morocco and Tunisia illustrate other forms of external rent. Morocco's phosphate sector, dominated by the *Office Chérifien des Phosphates* (OCP), generates a form of green-adjacent rent linked to both fertilizer markets and emerging battery technologies (Boussaid, 2016). Meanwhile, Tunisia's integration into European value chains, its tourism sector, and its significant inflows of external assistance constitute additional channels of rent, albeit with lower magnitude and more volatility than Algerian hydrocarbons (Bellin, 1994).

In all cases, external rents anchor the Maghreb in a hierarchical world economy where the region specializes in primary commodities and low-skill manufactures, while importing high-value technologies and capital goods (Elsenhans, 2023). The green transition risks deepening this dependency: Europe's demand for renewable electricity, green hydrogen, and critical minerals may reassert the region's position as a provider of green primary goods without enabling technological upgrading.

Thus, the international role of rent is not simply material. It is entangled in deeply rooted social structures. It shapes bargaining positions, development trajectories, and the possibilities for autonomy. Understanding this dimension is crucial for analyzing how green rents might transform or reproduce existing patterns.

National Appropriation of Rent: State-Owned Enterprises and Technological Gatekeeping

The domestic dimension of rent concerns not the generation of surplus but its appropriation, redistribution, and political conversion. Across the Maghreb, rents flow primarily into the state apparatus, which is managed by political elites, bureaucratic networks, and state-owned enterprises (SOEs). These organizations serve dual functions: first, they channel rents into development projects, subsidies, and social spending; and second, they allocate access to rent and technology in ways that consolidate state–class power.

In Algeria, SOEs have historically been the main vehicles for rent appropriation. Despite repeated attempts at industrialization, most notably the "industries industrialisantes" strategy of the 1970s, technological transfer remained confined to segments controlled by the state class (Ahmed, 1989). The result was a dual economy: internationally competitive energy and petrochemical sectors coexisting with stagnant domestic industries generating little employment or spillover effects (Aghrout & Bougherira, 2004; Andreff, 2009). In this context, technology becomes a political resource. Access to foreign partners, industrial contracts, and state licenses is mediated by political networks, reinforcing economic elites' dependence on the state rather than fostering an autonomous capitalist class.

Morocco and Tunisia exhibit similar patterns in different forms. Morocco's OCP combines technocratic efficiency with political embeddedness, making it a central pillar of the Makhzen's economic and political power. The firm's international expansion has brought technological upgrading, yet its benefits remain unevenly distributed (Boussaid, 2016). Tunisian business elites, particularly under Ben Ali, accumulated wealth not through innovation but through privileged access to licenses, protection, and state contracts (Bellin, 1994), reinforcing a patrimonial structure that inhibited independent capitalist development.

In all three countries, the national appropriation of rent produces structural heterogeneity: enclave sectors with high productivity and rent flows versus broad segments of the economy characterized by low technology, low wages, and limited mobility. This is not a deviation from capitalism but a specific form of rent capitalism, where political access to surplus matters more than market competition.

Across the Maghreb, the literature consistently shows that there is no autonomous market sphere detached from political power. Economic actors are structurally embedded in dense networks linking them to political and, in some cases, military elites. Classic studies of Morocco already demonstrated how economic accumulation was mediated through proximity to the monarchy and the state apparatus rather than through competitive markets (Waterbury, 1970; Leveau, 1976). More recent work has extended this insight, showing how liberalization and privatization have not reduced state power but instead reconfigured it, reinforcing patterns of elite capture and politically mediated accumulation (Hibou, 2006; Catusse, 2008). In this context, business elites, large landowners, and strategic investors derive their market positions from political access, regulatory privilege, and control over rents, rather than from productivity or innovation. The state thus remains the central broker between economic resources and social actors, blurring the boundary between political authority and market activity and limiting the emergence of independent capitalist classes.

The Dynamics of State–Class Formation

The concept of the state class provides the analytical bridge between international rents and domestic social reproduction (Elsenhans, 1996; Ouaissa, 2005). In rent societies, political power rests not on net investment, labor productivity, or the capitalist production-for-profit mechanism described by Kalecki (1971) but on the control and allocation of surplus. The state class comprises bureaucratic, military, administrative, and business elites whose cohesion derives less from ideology than from privileged access to rent channels.

Crucially, rents in the Maghreb have never been large enough to provide broad-based prosperity for the entire population. This structural constraint forces the state class to develop selection mechanisms that determine how rents are distributed and to whom. Consequently, two logics are closely linked: one focused on productive rent investment, and the other on political strategies that secure loyalty, stabilize coalitions, and preserve elite cohesion. In practice, these logics reinforce one another. State classes oscillate over time between mass-oriented development strategies and elite-oriented strategies of self-enrichment, depending on fiscal cycles, geopolitical pressures, and social unrest. Rent, therefore, serves simultaneously as an economic instrument and a political technology, as observed in other world regions, such as Latin America (Warnecke-Berger et al., 2023).

Yet the dominance of state–class power is accompanied by a persistent structural counterpart: a large and enduring labor surplus, which has become particularly entrenched in the Maghreb. Youth unemployment is especially pronounced (Adair & Gherbi, 2023; Frontenaud, 2023; Hadibi & Musette, 2023). Youth unemployment underscores the Maghreb's entrenched labor surplus: in 2024, it stood at roughly 29.8% in Algeria, 40.1% in Tunisia, and 22.1% in Morocco (World Bank, 2025). For many young people, this structural blockage narrows viable mobility strategies to emigration or entry into the state apparatus, with the latter largely mediated through educational and professional channels controlled by the state class.

This is where migration and remittances enter the picture as a distinct political–economic mechanism. When domestic absorption fails, migration functions as a social safety valve (Warnecke-Berger, 2021a). Highly educated, multilingual, and mobile young people migrate to Europe and the Gulf, generating significant remittances, effectively a "second rent" that stabilizes households and eases fiscal pressures on the state (Warnecke-Berger, 2022). These inflows reduce domestic labor supply, help sustain consumption, and mitigate immediate social grievances. Yet they also erode workers' bargaining power, as outward mobility replaces domestic contestation.

Remittances diversify the region's sources of surplus but reproduce dependency in a new form: they stabilize internal markets and uphold fragile social contracts, yet they do not induce structural transformation. Instead, they consolidate a dual economy in which external money sustains internal demand while domestic production remains stagnant. The strongest irony of the region's political economy is that migration contributes to the reproduction of regimes whose lack of development helped trigger migration in the first place.

In Algeria, the state class has historically been centralized and cohesive, drawing legitimacy from anti-colonial nationalism and hydrocarbon rents (Ouaissa, 2009). Periods of crisis, such as the oil shocks, the civil war of the 1990s, and Hirak, illustrate how the state class uses rent to absorb pressure, selectively redistribute, and maintain stability (Ouaissa, 2018). In Morocco, the monarchy plays the integrative role that the state apparatus fulfils in Algeria. Rents from phosphates, land, and foreign investment reinforce the Makhzen's capacity to co-opt social groups, particularly segments of the middle classes. Despite a more diversified economy, the structure of power remains deeply rent-bound, with modernization efforts tied to political centralization (Akesbi, 2009; El Mabrouki & Znagui, 2015). Tunisia followed a distinct path, combining early state-led industrialization and human capital investment with neo-patrimonial stagnation under Ben Ali. The absence of strong fossil rents did not prevent the formation of a state class; rather, it produced a more fragile, externally dependent variant that relied heavily on foreign aid, tourism, and remittances (Krichen, 2021; Hibou, 2011).

Across the region, the state class is the primary agent of rent conversion, transforming external revenues into political order and loyalty. This function explains the Maghreb's paradoxical combination of micro-instability and macro-resilience, a theme explored in the next section.

Cycles of Conflict, Blocked Middle Classes, and Rebellion

The post-independence political economies of the Maghreb have been characterized by recurring cycles of economic volatility, social unrest, and political crisis (Ouaissa, 2014). These cycles are not anomalies but the predictable outcome of rent-based accumulation, structural heterogeneity, and the region's long-standing pattern of unequal specialization. Across Algeria, Morocco, and Tunisia, regimes have repeatedly absorbed social pressures, most visibly those emerging from marginalized youth and frustrated middle classes, through redistribution, public-sector hiring, and expansion of low-productivity services. This strategy has generated macro-level political stability while entrenching micro-level instability and periodic waves of rebellion.

Exclusive Growth and the Geography of Discontent

Economic growth in the Maghreb has been exclusive rather than inclusive. Urban elites, coastal regions, and enclave sectors have captured the lion's share of rent-induced development, whereas rural areas, interior regions, and informal workers remain structurally marginalized.

Figure 2.1 illustrates the evolution of sectoral productivity shares in Morocco and Tunisia over three decades. In both countries, productivity gains are overwhelmingly concentrated in extractive and enclave-oriented sectors, while agriculture and large parts of industry remain persistently low productivity. This pattern points to a structural decoupling between growth and employment: sectors that generate rents and productivity gains absorb little labor, whereas labor-intensive sectors remain stagnant. The result is a geography of exclusive growth that reinforces regional and social inequalities and helps explain why periods of rent contraction repeatedly translate into social unrest rather than broad-based adjustment.

This configuration can be summarized as structural heterogeneity, a development pattern in which high-productivity enclaves coexist with low-productivity mass sectors, producing a growth model that is socially and spatially exclusive and relies on rent (Amin, 1973; Elsenhans, 2022).

Figure 2.2 complements this picture by tracing the long-term evolution of cereal production balances in Algeria, Morocco, and Tunisia. Across all three countries,

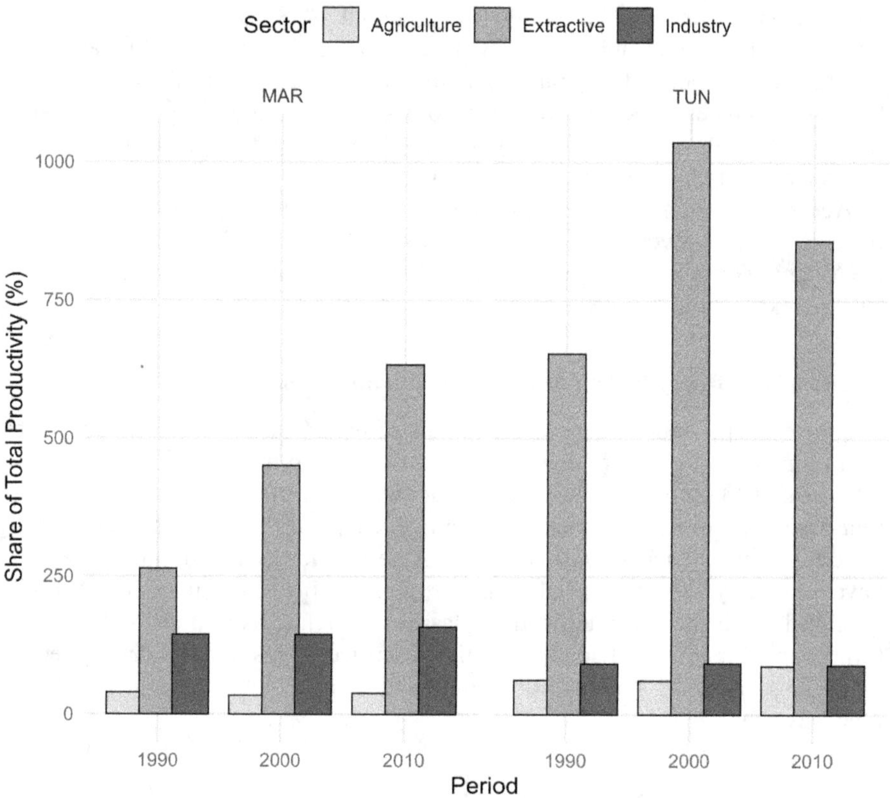

Figure 2.1 Sectoral productivity shares, Tunisia and Morocco (ten-year averages).

Source: own elaboration based on data from the Economic Transformation Database, GGDC/UNU-WIDER, release February 2021 (see Kruse et al., 2022).

the figure reveals a persistent and deepening structural weakness of domestic agriculture. Since the 1970s, cereal production has systematically fallen short of domestic consumption, turning all three Maghreb economies into chronic net importers of basic foodstuffs.

This agricultural underperformance is not cyclical but structural. It reflects decades of neglect of smallholder agriculture, limited productivity gains in rain-fed farming, and a development strategy that prioritized rent-generating enclave sectors over food security. As a result, food imports have become a macroeconomic necessity rather than a policy choice.

This dependence has far-reaching macroeconomic consequences. Reliance on cereal imports constrains exchange-rate policy and raises the political cost of devaluation and narrows the effective policy space for exchange-rate adjustment. Any significant depreciation immediately translates into higher food prices, social unrest, and political instability. Food dependency thus acts as a powerful disciplinary

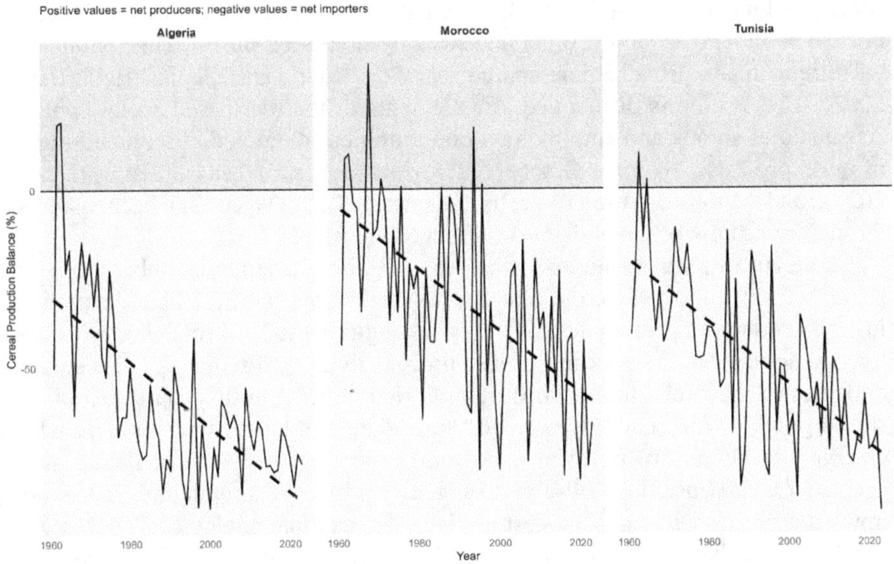

Figure 2.2 Food sovereignty in the Maghreb.

Note: Own elaboration based on FAO (2026) Food Balance Sheets (Historic and current normalized datasets). The cereal production balance is calculated as (production − domestic supply)/domestic supply × 100, using Item Code 2905 (cereals) and the respective FAO element codes for production and domestic supply.

mechanism, tying macroeconomic management to external markets and reinforcing the region's vulnerability to global price shocks.

In this sense, weak agricultural performance deepens structural heterogeneity: while rent-based sectors generate foreign exchange, large segments of the population remain dependent on imported basic goods. The resulting combination of external vulnerability, blocked rural development, and limited macroeconomic policy space amplifies the geography of discontent and helps explain why economic crises in the Maghreb so often take the form of food riots, subsidy protests, and regime-threatening uprisings rather than gradual adjustment.

This spatial and social inequality has repeatedly translated into political unrest, producing well-known episodes of contention such as Morocco's bread riots (1981, 1984), Tunisia's phosphate-belt uprisings Gafsa (2008), the Arab Spring, and Algeria's October 1988 protests and the Hirak (2019–2020). These episodes reveal a shared pattern: when rents tighten and states lose their capacity to reproduce political order through selective redistribution, social discontent moves from latent tension to open confrontation.

Structural Adjustment and the Erosion of Social Contract

The 1980s marked a decisive rupture. Falling oil prices and rising external debt triggered widespread structural adjustment. Under pressure from the International

Monetary Fund (IMF) and World Bank, Maghreb governments opened their economies to neoliberal economic order and strongly supported subsidy cuts, public-sector retrenchment, privatization, and currency devaluations (Dillman, 1998; Bayat, 2002). These reforms dismantled key elements of the rent-based social contract. As subsidies shrank and employment opportunities contracted, discontent erupted in mass protests: Algeria's October 1988 riots, Tunisia's 1984 uprising (Dakhli, 2021), and Morocco's urban revolts (Bogaert, 2015). What had been managed through rents now became visible as structural tension.

The crisis of rentier regimes in the Maghreb, intensified by neoliberal opening processes since the 1980s, did not lead to sustainable political liberalization but instead produced a profound crisis of regime legitimacy. The erosion of redistributive capacities, the dismantling of social protections, and rising social inequality undermined the social foundations of authoritarian rule. In this context, declining state legitimacy facilitated the rise and consolidation of Islamist movements, which emerged as alternative political and moral orders capable of articulating social grievances. As Losurdo (2004) argues, socially blocked middle classes– whose upward mobility was curtailed despite rising educational attainment—became the primary social base of Islamist movements.

Across the Maghreb, regimes adopted divergent strategies toward Islamist actors, ranging from controlled co-optation to outright prohibition (Werenfels, 2005). In all three states, competition between ruling elites and increasingly influential Islamist movements intensified around the mobilization of these blocked middle strata, whose economic exclusion and political marginalization made them particularly receptive to oppositional projects.

In Morocco, the regime pursued a strategy of controlled co-optation. The *Makhzen* incorporated the Islamist *Parti de la Justice et du Développement* (PJD) into the institutional framework in order to channel social protest and regulate political competition. In Tunisia, by contrast, Islamist parties were entirely banned and excluded from formal political life, reinforcing a strategy of repression rather than incorporation.

Algeria represents the most dramatic case of rent-driven escalation of political crisis. The collapse of oil revenues in the late 1980s deprived the regime of its central redistributive foundation, weakened patronage networks, and generated widespread socioeconomic frustration. Under these conditions, the *Front Islamique du Salut* (FIS) rapidly gained political relevance by combining social and moral claims and serving as a vehicle for protest against social marginalization, corruption, and political exclusion.

The FIS's electoral victory in 1991 and the subsequent civil war (1991–2000) reveal the close entanglement of rent-based political economy, authoritarian governance, and religious mobilization. Islamism functioned less as a purely religious project than as a discursive framework through which social exclusion and blocked upward mobility—particularly among urban and peri-urban middle classes—were articulated. The state elite responded through a combination of large-scale repression and selective co-optation. When rent flows recovered in the late 1990s, the regime rebuilt patronage structures and reintegrated segments of Islamist actors into the political field.

The Algerian civil war, therefore, cannot be understood without reference to the political economy of rent. When rents contracted, the symbolic and institutional glue holding the regime together dissolved; when rent flows resumed, the state re-absorbed conflict through repression and redistribution, thereby partially siphoning off accumulated social pressures.

In this regard, one of the region's most persistent contradictions is the emergence of blocked middle classes, segments educated enough to aspire to mobility but excluded from political participation and meaningful economic opportunities. As Ouaissa (Ouaissa, 2018, 2023; Ouaissa & Sold, 2017) shows, these middle classes oscillate between protest and co-optation. They mobilize during crises (1988 Algeria, 2011 Tunisia, 2019 Algeria), are partially reintegrated through public-sector hiring, credit programs, or professional licenses, yet their structural position remains precarious because their income and status depend on the state's distributive logic. This produces a form of paradoxical stability. The middle classes tend to be frustrated, which eventually leads to continuous politics and even rebellion; at the same time, they are sufficiently dependent on rent-based redistribution to be neutralized.

A key strategy for maintaining the state–class rule in the Maghreb is the state's capacity to absorb labor surpluses by providing unproductive or low-productivity jobs, as elsewhere in the world (Bhattacharya et al., 2023; Warnecke-Berger, 2021b). Throughout the region, governments have relied on large public administrations, para-statal agencies that generate excessive but unproductive employment, inefficient service roles, municipal hiring booms, and public works programs. This strategy allows regimes to convert rents into political support by distributing positions that generate income but are not productive.

From the perspective of the surplus approach, this is rational: rent societies need not maximize productivity but only preserve political order. If hydrocarbon or phosphate rents were abundant, the strategy would have been easy to finance. But in the context of the green transition, this mechanism acquires new meaning.

Taken together, these dynamics produce a distinct and remarkably persistent pattern across the Maghreb. Localized uprisings erupt with regularity, often sparked by price hikes, service shortages, or police abuses. Periodic national crises, whether fiscal ruptures, political breakdowns, or legitimacy shocks, puncture the veneer of stability. Layered on top is a deep generational frustration, especially among young people who face blocked mobility, chronic unemployment, and a political order that has little space for their aspirations.

Despite the presence of this volatile mixture, Maghreb regimes have demonstrated exceptional resilience. This resilience does not derive from legitimacy rooted in democratic or developmental principles. Rather, it is based on a repertoire of rent-based stabilization mechanisms that transform external revenues into instruments of political control. Unproductive employment within a bloated public sector absorbs labor surpluses and alleviates pressure. Selective redistribution fosters loyalty in specific groups while avoiding broad entitlement frameworks. Migration acts as a safety valve: those unable to be absorbed domestically depart, and their remittances support household consumption. The middle classes, hindered in their political participation, are effectively neutralized through co-optation, credentialism, and restricted access to state-affiliated professions. Cultural and religious co-optation, particularly evident in Algeria's post–civil war trajectory and Morocco's monarchical strategies, further consolidates the state's position within the societal symbolic order.

These stabilizing mechanisms have enabled regimes to endure crises for decades; however, they now face novel pressures stemming from the global energy transition. As revenues from fossil fuels diminish and green rents arise, the fundamental underpinnings of political stability are being reconsidered. The subsequent pivotal inquiry, serving as the foundation for the ensuing section, is thus unavoidable: can green rents be harnessed to dismantle this cycle of rent-dependent stability and structural exclusion, or will they merely perpetuate it under the guise of sustainability associated with the green transition?

Greening the Maghreb: Green Rent, and the Political Economy of the Energy Transition

The global energy transition places the Maghreb at the center of a new global geo-economic and geopolitical configuration. While fossil rents are declining in strategic relevance, a new generation of green rents, hence solar, wind, hydrogen, and phosphates, emerges. These rents, however, do not automatically lead to structural transformation; rather, they intersect with long-standing patterns of rent-based accumulation, state–class power, and unequal specialization. Whether they will generate development or reproduce extractivism depends on the political coalitions that mobilize them and the institutional frameworks that govern their distribution.

The Maghreb's Green Endowments: Abundance and Ambivalence

In purely physical terms, the Maghreb possesses one of the world's most impressive concentrations of renewable energy potential. The region receives exceptionally high levels of solar irradiation—over 2,000–3,500 kWh/m²/year in large parts of Algeria and southern Morocco, placing North Africa among the most attractive solar geographies globally (Gairaa & Bakelli, 2013). Wind conditions are equally favorable: Morocco's Atlantic coastline and Tunisia's Cap Bon register some of the highest and most stable wind speeds in the wider Mediterranean, making them prime zones for onshore and offshore wind development. Algeria alone could, in principle, install several hundred gigawatts of solar power on unused desert land. Beyond energy flows, the region hosts strategic mineral endowments central to the global energy transition. Morocco controls around 70% of the world's known phosphate reserves, a resource indispensable not only for global food security but also increasingly for emerging battery chemistries, green ammonia production, and other low-carbon technologies (United States Geological Survey, 2022). In a world where critical minerals increasingly shape geo-economic power, phosphate constitutes the Maghreb's most significant "green-adjacent" rent.

Figure 2.3 situates these green endowments within the Maghreb's existing rent structure by comparing the region's share of global production in green-adjacent

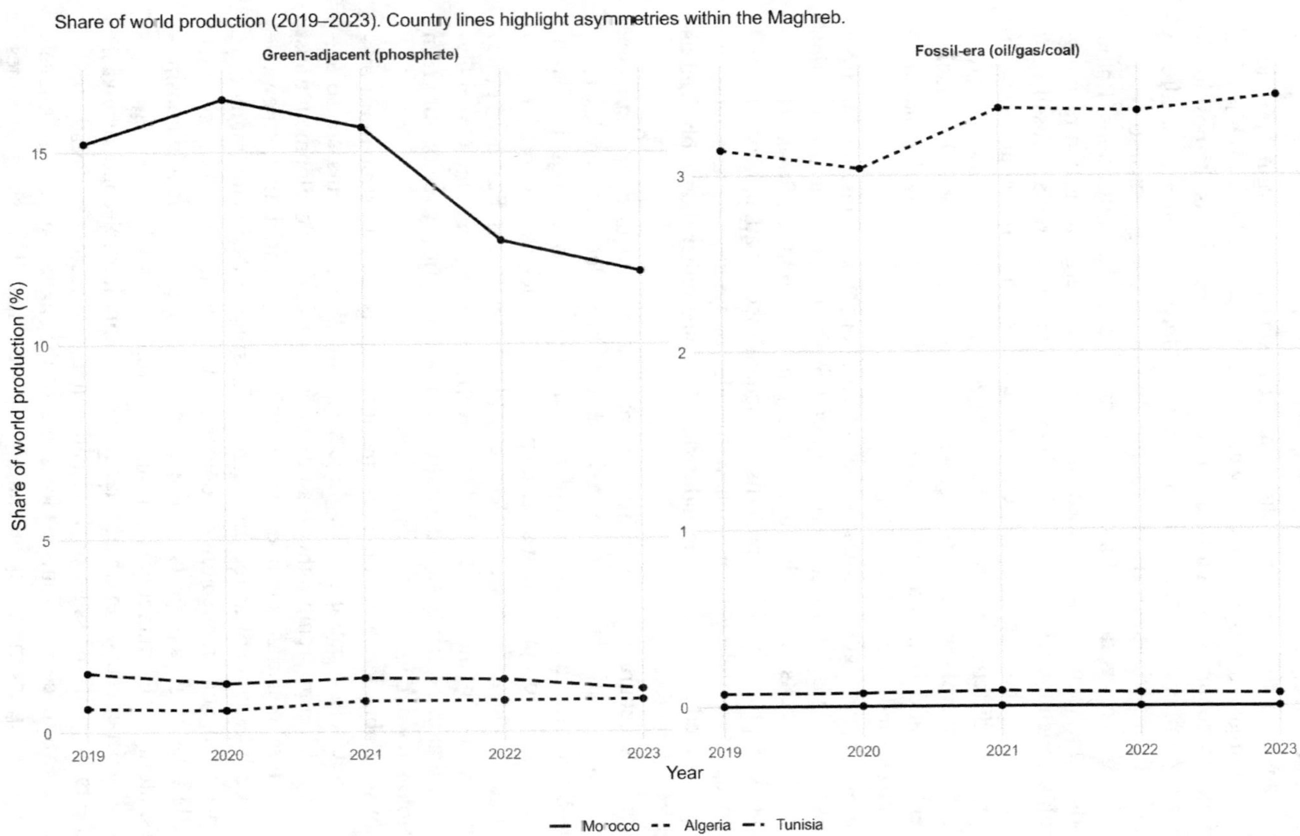

Figure 2.3 Raw material production in the Maghreb (2019–2023).

Note: Own elaboration based on Austrian Federal Ministry of Finance (2025), World Mining Data 2025. World production totals are calculated by commodity and year, and each country's share is computed.

minerals (phosphate) and fossil-era outputs (oil, gas, and coal) between 2019 and 2023. The figure reveals two crucial dynamics. First, it underscores the extreme concentration of green-adjacent rents: Morocco dominates global phosphate production by a wide margin, whereas Algeria and Tunisia occupy marginal positions. Second, it highlights the asymmetry between old and new rent bases. While Algeria continues to command a significant share of fossil-era outputs, its position in green-adjacent minerals remains limited, whereas Morocco's rent base is already structurally aligned with the material requirements of the energy transition.

This divergence has far-reaching political and economic implications. Rather than producing a homogeneous "green Maghreb," the energy transition reconfigures surplus structures within the region. Green rents do not replace fossil rents evenly; they redistribute geopolitical relevance and bargaining power across countries, reinforcing differentiated development trajectories. Morocco enters the green transition as a mineral rent powerhouse, Algeria as a fossil rent incumbent facing gradual erosion, and Tunisia as a marginal rent holder increasingly dependent on external finance and energy partnerships.

In this sense, the figure illustrates that green abundance is inseparable from ambivalence. The Maghreb's strategic importance for Europe's decarbonization is growing, but it rests on a highly uneven geography of rent-led flows. This unevenness risks reproducing older patterns of unequal specialization, now reframed around phosphates, hydrogen, and renewable electricity, unless green rents are deliberately embedded in domestic industrial strategies rather than mobilized as export-oriented enclaves.

The region's geographic proximity to Europe further enhances this strategic relevance. Short maritime distances, existing undersea electricity cables (e.g., Morocco–Spain interconnectors), and planned hydrogen corridors position North Africa as the EU's most promising external partner for large-scale imports of green hydrogen, ammonia, and renewable electricity (Tanchum, 2024). European policy documents, especially the EU's 2022 "REPowerEU" strategy and the Green Hydrogen Accelerator, explicitly single out the Maghreb as a priority region for green energy diplomacy and long-term energy security.

Yet physical abundance does not automatically translate into structural transformation. Precisely because the Maghreb's renewable endowments are so significant, they risk reinforcing rather than overcoming existing development traps. Several structural constraints temper the region's green potential: first, renewable abundance collides with infrastructural scarcity. Existing grids remain fragmented, under-capacitated, and oriented toward domestic fossil-dominated energy systems. Large-scale solar or wind projects require massive upfront investment in transmission lines, storage, and interconnection infrastructure, areas where the region remains heavily dependent on external financing and technology. Second, renewable megaprojects intensify pressure on land and water, two resources already under severe stress. Morocco and Tunisia face some of the highest water stress levels globally. Producing green hydrogen, extremely water-intensive, exacerbates these vulnerabilities. Algeria's desert regions offer ample land but limited water availability, creating tensions between energy ambitions and socioecological constraints. Third, the industrial basis for capturing value remains thin.

The Maghreb imports nearly all high-tech inputs for renewable installations, turbines, photovoltaic modules, inverters, and electrolyzers, locking the region into low-value segments of the green supply chain. Without deliberate industrial policy, solar farms may simply replicate the logic of extractive enclaves: land is used locally, and value is extracted externally. Fourth, the region's green potential is deeply entangled with political economies marked by rent logics. Megaprojects risk reinforcing state–class control rather than enabling productive coalitions. In Morocco, OCP already uses its phosphate rent to anchor hydrogen and ammonia strategies, raising concerns about oligopolistic control over future green rents. In Algeria, the solar agenda remains subject to bureaucratic fragmentation, overlapping mandates, and competition among state factions. Tunisia, facing a fiscal crisis, increasingly relies on foreign capital to develop renewable projects, thereby exposing itself to new forms of external dependence.

Hence, proximity to Europe creates both opportunity and vulnerability. While Europe's demand promises stable markets, it also risks structuring North Africa's transition around European priorities rather than domestic development strategies. A hydrogen-export model that produces green molecules for Europe but leaves little electricity for domestic industry could reproduce a familiar pattern: a region that exports primary energy while importing high-value manufacturing and technology.

Three Different Trajectories Ahead?

These dynamics create a fundamental ambivalence. The Maghreb is simultaneously one of the world's most promising green energy regions and one of the regions where green abundance could most easily reinforce unequal specialization. The decisive question, therefore, is not whether the Maghreb has the resources to become a renewable powerhouse, but whether those resources can be harnessed to strengthen domestic productive capacities rather than deepen the extractive logic that has shaped the region since the colonial era.

Morocco has positioned itself as the Maghreb's green frontrunner (Sabry, 2025). The Noor Ouarzazate complex, one of the largest solar installations in the world, along with rapid wind expansion and an ambitious green hydrogen roadmap, signals a clear attempt to anchor industrialization within the global energy transition. The country's strategic narrative is explicit: to become a "green gateway" connecting European markets with African energy systems (El Hafdaoui et al., 2025).

Yet beneath the dynamism lies a deeper structural ambivalence. Rather than breaking with the rentier logic, Morocco's green transition risks consolidating it in new forms. First, phosphate rent remains central to state–business alliances. The OCP underpins much of the financial and political architecture behind Morocco's green ambitions. Its revenues continue to structure economic power and shape state-led investment priorities. Second, OCP-led hydrogen initiatives may strengthen oligopolistic control. By dominating early investments in hydrogen and green ammonia, OCP could lock emerging technologies within a narrow corporate–state nexus, limiting spillovers to smaller firms and regional economies. Third, green megaprojects serve political as much as economic objectives. Large renewable projects consolidate monarchical legitimacy, attract foreign finance, and reinforce Morocco's external positioning as a stable, technologically ambitious partner. Internally, they preserve highly centralized decision-making structures. Fourth, domestic value chains remain shallow. Despite industrial-policy efforts, Morocco relies heavily on imported turbines, photovoltaic modules, electrolyzers, and other high-tech components. Local manufacturing capacity remains limited, raising the risk that the country remains confined to low-value segments of green supply chains. Finally, renewable expansion intensifies existing socioecological pressures. Water scarcity, land competition, and regional inequalities intersect with large-scale solar and wind projects, creating tensions between national ambitions and local realities.

Morocco, therefore, exemplifies a model of green rentier modernization: genuine technological upgrading accompanied by persistent concentration of economic and political power. Whether this trajectory becomes a driver of broad-based development or reinforces existing hierarchies will depend on the extent to which green rents can be linked to diversified value chains, regional inclusion, and institutional reform.

Algeria's green transition unfolds under the heavy shadow of its hydrocarbon economy. The country remains one of Africa's major energy producers, supplying roughly 11–13% of the EU's natural gas imports in recent years, depending on fluctuations in Russian supply. Hydrocarbons account for about 95% of Algeria's export revenues and between 35% and 45% of government income, depending on global price cycles. This structural weight makes the shift toward renewables both urgent and exceptionally difficult: Algeria has some of the highest solar potential in the Mediterranean region—an estimated 2,500–3,500 kWh/m²/year of direct sunlight across much of its territory—yet its renewable energy deployment has remained slow and uneven.

For more than a decade, Algeria has announced ambitious renewable energy programs but has not achieved proportional implementation. The 2011 national target of installing 22,000 MW of renewable capacity by 2030 resulted in less than 500 MW of actual installations by the early 2020s, most of its small-scale solar PV. The more recent 15,000 MW solar program, launched with significant political visibility, marks a renewed effort, but it still faces structural constraints: regulatory instability stemming from frequently revised procurement rules; institutional fragmentation between Sonelgaz, the Ministry of Energy Transition, the Ministry of Energy and Mines, and various state agencies; and a persistent preference for turnkey imports of high-tech systems rather than local manufacturing or technology transfer.

These institutional bottlenecks are reinforced by the logic of the rentier social contract. As long as oil and gas rents ensure fiscal stability, the state class has little incentive to restructure the economy. Renewable investments thus function primarily as geopolitical signaling—affirming Algeria's desire to remain a key energy partner for Europe in the post-hydrocarbon era—rather than as drivers of domestic economic transformation. This is evident in Algeria's continued prioritization of upstream gas investment, pipeline diplomacy, and LNG capacity expansions, even as it rhetorically commits to decarbonization.

Yet Algeria's renewable potential is undeniable. The country possesses vast expanses of flat, uninhabited desert land suitable for utility-scale solar farms, and renewable electricity could support new green industrial segments such as desalination, green hydrogen, and solar-powered mineral processing. Moreover, Algeria faces a growing internal energy challenge: domestic electricity demand increases by roughly 5–7% per year, placing a strain on natural gas supplies that are simultaneously needed for export revenues. Expanding solar capacity would free up gas for export, easing both fiscal pressures and external balances.

The political economy question is whether Algeria can convert this potential into a productive green transition. Doing so would require redirecting rent flows toward labor-intensive renewable infrastructure, local value chains, and vocational skill development. It would also require restructuring the state-controlled energy sector to enable technological learning rather than relying on imported turnkey solutions. It would require breaking with the political logic that links hydrocarbon rents to patronage, fiscal cushioning, and political quietism.

At present, Algeria stands at a crossroads. On one side is a cautious, rent-preserving green diversification strategy, in which solar projects supplement the hydrocarbon economy without altering its foundations. On the other side lies the possibility of a more significant reorientation that uses renewable investments to absorb surplus labor, diversify the productive base, and gradually reduce the country's exposure to volatile global oil and gas markets. Whether Algeria can move beyond symbolic announcements toward a substantive energy transition depends on its capacity to renegotiate the role of hydrocarbons within the rentier state, reshape the incentives of the state class, and link the expansion of renewables to broader developmental goals.

Tunisia enters the global energy transition with considerable renewable potential but under exceptionally adverse structural conditions. The country possesses some of the most favorable solar irradiation levels in the central Mediterranean, averaging between 1,800 and 2,200 kWh/m²/year across large parts of its interior regions, and significant onshore wind potential in areas such as Sidi Daoud, where some of North Africa's earliest wind installations were built. In principle, this resource base could support substantial expansion of renewable electricity, green hydrogen production, and regional energy integration.

In practice, however, Tunisia's green transition is severely constrained by its deteriorating political and economic landscape. A protracted fiscal crisis—exacerbated by slow growth, high public-sector wage bills, energy subsidies, and rising debt—limits the state's capacity to finance long-term infrastructure. Public debt has hovered around 80–90% of gross domestic product (GDP) in recent years, and servicing obligations leave little fiscal space for strategic investment in renewables or grid modernization. The national utility, *Société Tunisienne de l'Electricité et du Gaz* (STEG), itself faces mounting financial pressures from tariff subsidies and high gas import costs, thereby reducing its capacity to co-finance or manage new renewable projects.

Political volatility further compounds these constraints. Since President Kais Saied's consolidation of power in 2021, institutional checks and balances have weakened, investor confidence has declined, and administrative decision-making has become slower and less predictable. Regulatory uncertainty, especially around power purchase agreements, land allocation, grid access, and the role of private producers, has discouraged both domestic and foreign investors. Despite a pipeline of proposed solar and wind projects, many remain stalled at the feasibility or negotiation stage.

As a result, Tunisia's ability to pursue an autonomous green transition increasingly depends on external anchor points, particularly the EU, Germany, and international financial institutions such as the EIB, EBRD, and the World Bank. European climate diplomacy frames Tunisia as a potential platform for future green hydrogen exports, tied to the EU's broader REPowerEU agenda. Several feasibility studies, funded by European partners, examine the feasibility of producing green hydrogen or ammonia in southern Tunisia for export via Mediterranean shipping routes or future interconnectors.

While such partnerships offer much-needed capital and technical expertise, they also pose a strategic risk. If structured primarily around European decarbonization needs, Tunisia could become an energy export platform without achieving domestic industrial upgrading. Large-scale hydrogen projects require substantial land and water resources, yet may create limited local employment and few linkages to Tunisian manufacturing. Moreover, reliance on donor-financed renewable infrastructure risks reproducing an aid-dependent development trajectory, rather than building the institutional and productive capabilities necessary for long-term transformation.

Tunisia's green ambitions thus unfold within a fragile political economy: one characterized by fiscal stress, social discontent, declining investment, and renewed authoritarian drift. The country's renewable potential is unquestionably significant, but the wider political economy raises the possibility of what might be termed green dependency—a situation in which Tunisia contributes to the energy transition of external actors without generating meaningful domestic upgrading, technological learning, or employment. Whether Tunisia can convert its renewable endowment into a lever for inclusive development will depend on its capacity to stabilize governance, reform state enterprises, negotiate balanced partnerships with Europe, and link green investment to domestic productive strategies.

Conclusion: An Open Political Question

The Maghreb's future can be sketched in stylized terms along three possible trajectories. In a scenario of green rentier stability, rents shift from hydrocarbons to hydrogen and solar, allowing regimes to maintain existing patterns of patronage, selective redistribution, and unproductive employment. Macro-stability persists, micro-instability remains, and unequal specialization hardens around green exports. In a more adverse scenario of green extractivism, megaprojects proliferate without domestic upgrading, land and water conflicts intensify, and value creation is externalized, deepening dependency under a sustainable label. In a more hopeful scenario of inclusive green transformation, rents are mobilized to support industrialization, labor absorption, domestic value chains, and technological learning, underpinning new coalitions that gradually loosen the grip of rentier logics.

However, the key issue is not the mere emergence of green rents, but how rent-mediated systems of clientelism are reconstituted internally and externally. Central questions concern which social classes and economic actors gain access to and benefit from the green transformation, and which forms of geopolitical clientelism emerge vis-à-vis external partners, such as the EU or China. These processes will shape the redistribution of green rents, the reconfiguration of state–class relations, and the reproduction or transformation of external dependencies.

This chapter has not attempted to predict which of these trajectories will prevail. Instead, it has sought to show that their likelihood hinges on three interrelated dimensions: the strategic use of rent, the reconfiguration of state–class power, and the way geopolitics is woven into domestic conflicts and alliances. Green rents will not automatically democratize or develop the Maghreb; nor will they inevitably entrench authoritarian rule and dependency. They will become the object of struggle.

What emerges, then, is an open political question rather than a deterministic forecast. As fossil rents decline and green rents rise, the Maghreb can either reinvent or reproduce its development model. The outcome will depend on how state classes, domestic economic actors, social movements, and external partners negotiate the intersection of energy, migration, security, and industrial transformation. It is in these negotiations—where geopolitical projects meet the everyday realities of surplus labor, blocked middle classes, and contested land—that the future of Euro-Mediterranean relations will be decided.

The crossroads are clear. Whether the Maghreb moves toward green growth or green rentierism, toward new productive coalitions or renewed extractive equilibria, remains undecided. What is certain is that the geopolitics of the green transition will not remain external to domestic struggles; it will become one of their central cleavages.

References

Aamimri, M., & Elfalih, T. (2024). Colonialism and local elites: Lyautey's colonial experience in Morocco as a case study. *British Journal of Philosophy, Sociology and History, 4*(2), 35–41. https://doi.org/10.32996/bjpsh.2024.4.2.4

Adair, P., & Gherbi, H. (2023). Inégalités de genre entre les jeunes en Afrique du Nord: Écarts de revenu et emploi informel. *Maghreb–Machrek, 250–251*(1), 167–182. https://doi.org/10.3917/machr.250.0167

Aghrout, A., & Bougherira, M. R. (Eds.). (2004). *Algeria in transition: Reforms and development prospects*. Routledge.

Ahmed, A. S. (1989). *Economie de l'industrialisation à partir des ressources naturelles: Tome 1: Faits, pratique et théories*. Publisud.

Akesbi, A. (2009). La corruption endémique au Maroc béquille de l'économie de la rente, (24), 113–132. https://doi.org/10.48409/IMIST.PRSM/ce-n24.1584

Amin, S. (1973). *Le développement inégal: Essai sur les formations sociales du capitalisme périphérique*. Les Éditions de Minuit.

Andreff, W. (2009). Réformes, libéralisation, privatisation en Algérie. *Confluences Méditerranée, 71*(4), 41–62. https://doi.org/10.3917/come.071.0041

Austrian Federal Ministry of Finance. (2025). *World mining data 2025*. Federal Ministry of Finance.

Bayat, Asef. (2002). Activism and social development in the Middle East. *International Journal of Middle East Studies*, *34*(1), 1–28.

Bellal, S. (2017). *La crise du régime rentier: Essai sur une Algérie qui stagne*. Editions Frantz Fanon.

Bellin, E. (1994). The politics of profit in Tunisia: Utility of the rentier paradigm? *World Development*, *22*(3), 427–436. https://doi.org/10.1016/0305-750X(94)90133-3

Bennoune, M. (1976). The origin of the Algerian proletariat. *Dialectical Anthropology*, *1*(3), 201–222.

Bhattacharya, S., Kesar, S., & Mehra, S. (2023). Exclusion, surplus population, and the labour question in postcolonial capitalism: Future directions in political economy of development. *Review of Political Economy*, *35*(1), 145–173. https://doi.org/10.1080/09538259.2022.2134650

Bogaert, K. (2015). The revolt of small towns: The meaning of Morocco's history and the geography of social protests. *Review of African Political Economy*, *42*(143), 124–140. http://www.jstor.org/stable/24858330

Boussaid, F. (2016). *The political economy of state-business relations in Morocco* (Doctoral dissertation, University of Oxford).

Catusse, M. (2008). *Le temps des entrepreneurs?* Institut de recherche sur le Maghreb contemporain.

Dakhli, L. (2021). The fair value of bread: Tunisia, 28 December 1983–6 January 1984. *International Review of Social History*, *66*(S29), 41–68. https://doi.org/10.1017/S0020859021000110

Dillman, B. (1998). The political economy of structural adjustment in Tunisia and Algeria. *The Journal of North African Studies*, *3*(3), 1–24. https://doi.org/10.1080/13629389808718335

Dirèche, K., Znaien, N., & Dusserre, A. (2023). *Histoire du Maghreb depuis les indépendances: États, sociétés, cultures*. Armand Colin.

El Hafdaoui, H., Khallaayoun, A., & Al-Majeed, S. (2025). Renewable energies in Morocco: A comprehensive review and analysis of current status, policy framework, and prospective potential. *Energy Conversion and Management: X*, *26*, 100967. https://doi.org/10.1016/j.ecmx.2025.100967

El Mabrouki, N., & Znagui, B. (Eds.). (2015). *Les diverses ficelles de l'économie de rente au Maroc*. Economia HEM.

Elsenhans, H. (1996). *State, class and development*. Radiant Publishers.

Elsenhans, H. (2016). Les tribulations rentières: Pourquoi l'Algérie souffre de la rente, pourquoi les critiques officielles et officieuses ne comprennent pas comment. *The Maghreb Review*, *41*(3), 395–419.

Elsenhans, H. (2022). *Capitalism, development and empowerment of labour: A heterodox political economy*. Routledge.

Elsenhans, H. (2023). *Capitalism and rent: A destructive relationship: Why the Maghreb does not join the newly industrialising countries*. Editions Arabesque.

Food and Agriculture Organization of the United Nations. (2025). *Food balance sheets*. FAOSTAT. Retrieved February 23, 2026, from https://www.fao.org/faostat/en/

Frontenaud, A. (2023). The quality of employment in MENA countries: A deteriorating dynamics for middle-class wage employees. *Maghreb–Machrek*, *254*(2–3), 17–35. https://doi.org/10.3917/e.machr.254.0017

Gairaa, K., & Bakelli, Y. (2013). Solar energy potential assessment in the Algerian south area: Case of Ghardaïa region. *Journal of Renewable Energy*, *2013*, 1–11. https://doi.org/10.1155/2013/496348

Gielen, D. (2021). *Critical materials for the energy transition* (Technical Paper No. 5/2021). International Renewable Energy Agency.

Hadibi, Z., & Musette, M. S. (2023). Does brain drain weaken or strengthen the middle classes in the Maghreb countries? *Maghreb–Machrek, 254*(2–3), 65–79. https://doi.org/10.3917/e.machr.254.0065

Halvorsen, K. H. (1978). Colonial transformation of agrarian society in Algeria. *Journal of Peace Research, 15*(4), 323–343.

Herbert, M. (2022). *The challenge of coordinating border management assistance between Europe and the Maghreb*. Migration Policy Institute.

Hibou, B. (2006). *La force de l'obéissance: Économie politique de la répression en Tunisie*. La Découverte.

Hibou, B. (2011). *Anatomie politique de la domination*. La Découverte.

International Energy Agency. (2021). *The role of critical minerals in clean energy transitions: World energy outlook special report*. IEA.

Kalecki, M. (1971). *Selected essays on the dynamics of the capitalist economy 1933–1970*. Cambridge University Press.

Krichen, A. (2021). *La gauche et son grand récit: Comprendre l'économie rentière*. Mots Passants.

Kruse, H., Mensah, E., Sen, K., & de Vries, G. (2022). A manufacturing (re)naissance? Industrialization in the developing world. *IMF Economic Review*. Advance online publication. https://doi.org/10.1057/s41308-022-00183-7

Leveau, R. (1976). *Le fellah marocain defenseur du trone*. Presses de la Fondation Nationale des Sciences Politiques.

Losurdo, D. (2004). What is fundamentalism. *Nature, Society, and Thought, 17*(1), 5–46.

Ouaissa, R. (2005). *Staatsklasse als Entscheidungsakteur in den Ländern der Dritten Welt*. LIT.

Ouaissa, R. (2009). Dynamik der Staatsklasse zwischen Konsolidierung und Segmentierung am Beispiel Algerien. In M. Beck, C. Harders, A. Jünemann, & S. Stetter (Eds.), *Der Nahe Osten im Umbruch* (pp. 78–99). VS Verlag für Sozialwissenschaften.

Ouaissa, R. (2014). *Die Rolle der Mittelschichten im Arabischen Frühling: Ein Überblick*. Springer VS. http://gbv.eblib.com/patron/FullRecord.aspx?p=1783446

Ouaissa, R. (2018). Classes moyennes algériennes, rente et stagnation politique. *Naqd: Revue d'études et de critique sociale, 36*(1), 121–145.

Ouaissa, R. (2023). Rents hinder capitalism: The rentier middle classes in the Middle East. In H. Warnecke-Berger & J. Ickler (Eds.), *The political economy of extractivism: Global perspectives on the seduction of rent* (pp. 199–214). Routledge.

Ouaissa, R., & Sold, K. (2017). Mittelschichten im politischen Transformationsprozess der Maghreb-Staaten. In T. Demmelhuber, A. T. Paul, & M. Reinkowski (Eds.), *Arabellion: Vom Aufbruch zum Zerfall einer Region?* (pp. 66–92). Nomos (Leviathan Sonderheft, 31).

Puyo, J.-Y. (2022). La mise en récit colonial du "Maroc utile". In M. Lakhdar & J. Ourya (Eds.), *Le récit de voyage à l'épreuve du fait historique* (pp. 5–36). Le Printer.

Sabry, M. I. (2025). The green transition in Morocco: Extractivity, inclusivity, and the stability of the social contract. *The Extractive Industries and Society, 22*, 101614. https://doi.org/10.1016/j.exis.2025.101614

Tanchum, M. (Ed.). (2024). *Renewable energy and electricity interconnection megaprojects in North Africa: Prospects for Euro-North Africa cooperation*. European Institute of the Mediterranean. https://www.euromesco.net/wp-content/uploads/2024/07/Policy-Study34-Megaprojects.pdf

United States Geological Survey. (2022). *Mineral commodity summaries 2022*. U.S. Geological Survey.

Warnecke-Berger, H. (2021a). Dynamics of global asymmetries: How migrant remittances (re-)shape North–South relations. *Third World Quarterly, 42*(11), 2767–2784. https://doi.org/10.1080/01436597.2021.1954501

Warnecke-Berger, H. (2021b). Fixing the labour surplus in existing economic structures. In N. Wilcock & E. Federzoni dos Santos (Eds.), *Not paying the rent: Imagining a fairer capitalism* (pp. 157–166). Palgrave Macmillan.

Warnecke-Berger, H. (2021c). Rent, capitalism and the challenges of global uneven development. In H. Warnecke-Berger (Ed.), *Development, capitalism, and rent: The political economy of Hartmut Elsenhans* (pp. 1–16). Palgrave Macmillan.

Warnecke-Berger, H. (2022). Rents, the moral economy of remittances, and the rise of a new transnational development model. *Revue de la régulation, 31*(2). https://doi.org/10.4000/regulation.20809

Warnecke-Berger, H. (2025). Surplus, rent and unequal development: Raw materials and remittances as the motor of rent societies in the Global South? In B. Sanghera (Ed.), *Global rentier capitalism: Theory and development* (pp. 210–224). Routledge.

Warnecke-Berger, H., Burchardt, H.-J., & Dietz, K. (2023). The failure of (neo-) extractivism in Latin America: Explanations and future challenges. *Third World Quarterly, 44*(8), 1825–1843. https://doi.org/10.1080/01436597.2023.2203380

Warnecke-Berger, H., & Ickler, J. (Eds.). (2023). *The political economy of extractivism: Global perspectives on the seduction of rent*. Routledge.

Waterbury, J. (1970). *The commander of the faithful: The Moroccan political elite: A study in segmented politics*. Weidenfeld & Nicolson.

Werenfels, I. (2005). *Vom Umgang mit Islamisten im Maghreb: Zwischen Einbindung und Unterdrückung* (SWP-Studie). Stiftung Wissenschaft und Politik.

World Bank. (2025). *World development indicators database*. https://databank.worldbank.org/source/world-development-indicators

3 Economy and Society in 21st-Century Algeria

Outline of an Applied Political Economy of Rents

Ahcène Amarouche

Introduction

Algeria celebrated 60 years of independence in 2022 in a climate of latent crisis. The immense hopes born of this event have long since dissipated: despite numerous achievements, the country is struggling to find its way to development. The political strife that clouded the country's prospects both before[1] and immediately after its accession to its new status has faded only superficially. The ensuing crisis in the summer of 1962 resulted in the physical liquidation of some of the players (both civilian and military) who had led the war, their placement under house arrest in the south, or their exile (where several of them ended up being murdered). The settling of scores between the players continued after the coup d'état of 19 June 1965, which ushered in a policy of accelerated industrialization to pull the country out of underdevelopment. It was not possible to bring this policy to fruition for reasons that had as much to do with its internal coherence (technical, institutional, and sociopolitical) as with the nature of the resources intended to finance it.

On the technical side, there have been serious shortcomings in the sequencing of industrial processes at the level of each sector of activity on the one hand, and in the articulation of these processes between sectors on the other. As far as the institutional order is concerned, it is the mode of regulation of the economy which has been found to be at fault in terms of industrial performance, but this is also due, and probably even more so, to the sociopolitical practices involved in the adjustments to the institutional order in question, which will be discussed in detail later in this study. For all the lack of coherence that we are going to discuss, the nature of the resources is considered under the concept of rent as their junction point and as their mode of articulation. In this sense, the country's economy is very much part of the development model based on the extraction of mineral and non-mineral materials that provide income, a model shared, despite their differences, by many countries in Latin America, Africa, and Asia, and more particularly by the countries of the MENA region[2] as far as oil and gas are concerned.

The purpose of the study is to outline an analysis of Algeria's economic and sociopolitical situation at the beginning of the 21st century from a historical perspective. The facts relating to the country's contemporary history will serve as a basis for the study, the content of which, as indicated in the subtitle, revolves around the

DOI: 10.4324/9781003730750-3

concept of rents. The hypotheses underlying the research mobilize the concepts of the centrality of resources and of the state, on the one hand, and of the exteriority of state power in independent Algeria, on the other, in a sense we will define in the body of Section 2 of this study.

It is divided into three sections. In the first section, titled "Algeria's Industrial Project and Its Financing: The Beginnings of a Crisis in Rent-Based Financing," we briefly present Algeria's development strategy in the 1970s, highlighting its strengths and weaknesses. While the technical, institutional, and sociopolitical aspects played a significant role in the success of this strategy (during the 1970s) and its subsequent failure (during the 1980s), it was rents as the sole source of foreign currency financing for investment that played a decisive role in the intermittent but chronic crisis that the country is experiencing. As we shall see, it is not so much a lack of resources as an excess of them that constitutes a constraint during the first period. This constraint is defined later under the concept of the economy's capacity to absorb investment, or under the more general concept of the economy's capacity to absorb projected investment and consumption expenditure—in other words, effective demand in Keynes's sense. In the second section, titled "Centrality of Resources, Centrality of the State, and Exteriority of State Power in Independent Algeria," we attempt an economic-institutional approach to the evolution of Algeria's post-independence situation in relation to the centrality of resources and the state on the one hand, and the exteriority of state power on the other. With reference to the work on the subject by Douglass C. North et al. (2010), which we believe provides a relevant framework for analyzing the various situations of mineral resource-producing countries (and Algeria in particular), this section examines the concept of rents in order to provide a definition that is congruent with the context. In the third section, titled "Net Rent and Crises of Governance in Algeria," we supplement the economic analysis developed in Sections 1 and 2 with a sociopolitical analysis in which we attempt to show the existence of an organic link between rent, governance, and sociopolitical culture. The issue of rents is examined first from an economic point of view, to show their constraining effects on accumulation, and then from a sociopolitical point of view, to characterize the clientelist practices based on rents, with the aim of personal enrichment rather than productive accumulation. The presentation focuses on the concept of net rent, which we have coined to reflect the realities arising from the external nature of state power in relation to society.

In addition to analyzing the role of rents in the economy, the study also aims to understand the processes by which rents act as a moral dissolver on institutions, social groups, and individuals.

Algeria's Industrial Project and Its Financing: The Beginnings of a Crisis in Rent-Based Financing

The industrial project had a theoretical dimension, the foundations of which had been laid by Gérard de Bernis (De Bernis, 1971), its designer, in an article that has remained famous in Algerian annals. Without mentioning the initial economic and sociopolitical conditions, or those which the project itself would bring about, he nonetheless outlined the general outline in quasi-mathematical terms: the aim was to develop a "blackened inter-industrial matrix, that is, one in which the various sectors are interconnected by their inputs and outputs, which implies the presence of sectors producing capital goods and intermediate products intended for internal productive consumption" (De Bernis, 1971, p. 547). The implementation of this project during the 1970s led to the creation of a fairly extensive industrial fabric, spearheaded by state-owned enterprises in cooperation with numerous foreign companies of international stature. Although the oil and gas sector was not explicitly mentioned in the original plan as the main source of foreign currency financing[3] for investments in all branches of industry, it did play this role. In addition to oil revenues, supplier credits for companies and State loans abroad, facilitated by the plethora of petrodollars induced by the sudden rise in hydrocarbon prices on international markets, helped to ease the resource constraints on the economy as a whole for a time, creating a veritable paradox: as the easing of the resource constraint led to a constraint on the economy's capacity to absorb investment (see definition later), the country emerged from one crisis only to enter another from 1978 onward.

Financial Strength Versus Limited Economic Absorption Capacity

While the total investment planned for the first four-year plan (1970–1973), which was already high in relation to these capacities, amounted to more than 27 billion dinars, the budget allocated to the second four-year plan (1974–1977) was increased to 110 billion dinars (MPAT, 1980). It is hardly surprising, therefore, that from 1978 onward, outstanding commitments (RAR in the technical language of decision-makers) began to appear. These outstanding commitments are the very expression of what we call the economy's limited capacity to absorb investment. By absorption capacity, we mean the existence of the right conditions for productive activity to enable new investments to be developed to the performance standards defined.[4]

In practice, although there was a sustained drive to create factories in all non-hydrocarbon industrial sectors throughout the so-called development decade (1967–1978), the share of value added in these sectors in GDP fell sharply from 20% to 12% between the first four-year plan and the second, as shown in Table 3.1.

Table 3.1 Share of Sectoral Value Added in GDP (Rounded Figures)

Sectors of activity	*1970–73*	*1974–77*	*1978–79*	*1980–84*	*1985–89*
Agriculture	12	11	10	10	13
Hydrocarbons	17	35	32	35	22
Non-hydrocarbon industries	20	12	13	13	17
Building/Public works	13	16	18	17	19
Services	38	26	27	25	29
Total	100	100	100	100	100

Source: Compiled by us from the statistical bulletins of the Office National des Statistiques (ONS)

In contrast, the share of value added of the hydrocarbons sector in GDP more than doubled over the same period, while for the years 1978–1989, the evolution of this indicator for hydrocarbons was erratic but on a downward trend, so that non-hydrocarbons industries regained some strength in relative terms. But the physical limits of the productive system seemed to have been reached: between 1984 and 1989, material production (in physical units) of the main goods of public industry excluding hydrocarbons was characterized by stagnation, as the figures in Table 3.2 attest.

In 1946, the Algerian rail network had 5,014 km of track, according to an SNTF document[5] (2012), whereas today it has only 4,498 km, due to the decommissioning of some tracks and the transformation of others into roads. This weakness can obviously be attributed to the technical inconsistencies of Algeria's industrial project, the importance of which to the development process was not appreciated by its designers, although, as Eric J. Hobsbawm reminds us, the railways were the spearhead of the industrial revolution.[6] The fact that the railways were not taken into account in the industrial project is all the more damaging given that, out of concern for regional balance and social equity, the industrial production units of the various public companies were scattered throughout the country's North-Saharan territory. As the main complex supplying them with ferrous inputs was located in the far northeast (Annaba), they could only be supplied by road, which meant disproportionately high transport costs, while the economy found itself increasingly dependent on foreign countries for the acquisition of rolling stock and the parts needed to maintain it. Need we add that today most railways are single-track, with diesel locomotives running at reduced speed (apart from a few short-electrified lines)? You can imagine the delay in economic development caused by this technical weakness, which also prevented the mixing of populations in a social dynamic driven by industrialization and feeding it in return.

Other technical weaknesses could be pointed out if the format of this study allowed. The fact remains that the combination of a number of factors has had the opposite effect to that expected, due both to the economy's low capacity to absorb investment and to the nature of the resources mobilized, which Benabdellah (1999)[7] described as debt -rent and which many analysts debate as to whether they are a blessing or a curse for the recipient countries.[8] While the oil sector plays the role of a provider of foreign currency income to finance investment and certain durable consumer goods, borrowing in foreign currencies (which by its very nature is an anticipated use of the country's future income in these currencies) becomes too heavy a burden for the economy when oil prices fall drastically. This is what happened with the so-called oil counter-shock in mid-1986, which happened again in August 2014 after more than a decade of recovery.

High Additional Costs When Resources Are Limited

However, as mentioned earlier, the economy was running out of steam as early as 1978: not only were there shortcomings in the industrial processes that were

Table 3.2 Physical Production of Certain Industrial Goods (Unit: Thousands of Tons Unless Otherwise Indicated)

Types of products	*1984*	*1985*	*1986*	*1987*	*1988*
Steel products					
Rough casting	1.176	1.462	1.246	1.716	1.575
Steel	1.143	1.390	1.218	1.674	1.671
Sheet metal	744	683	826	904	935
Bars and strips	456	331	355	380	360
Tubes	268	233	227	273	156
Mechanical products and vehicles					
Diesel engines	10.976	12.035	11.561	7.788	9.600
Wagons	895	857	708	503	488
Trucks	6.619	5.722	6.671	5.787	5.290
Tractors	5.927	6.250	6.323	3.513	5.500
Motorbikes	47.000	47.434	48.340	43.636	47.000
Bicycles	43.097	47.213	53.000	45.567	50.000
Electrical equipment					
Cables and wires	20	36	35	38	...
Televisions (units)	291.900	324.900	381.700	315.000	386.000
Batteries (thousands of units)	64.864	67.584	76.900	70.776	...
Electric cookers (units)	73.700	79.200	79.600	78.000	130.000
Refrigerators (units)	100.000	102.000	104.000	225.000	468.000
Radio receivers (units)	219.900	247.300	308.800	464.000	...
Food, beverages and tobacco					
Wheat flour and semolina	2.162	2.252	2.334	2.500	2.580
Edible oils	272	270	295	303	320
Sugar	214	197	220	205	220
Mineral water (10^3 hl)	1.129	1.118	1.220	1.157	1.050
Non-alcoholic beverages (10^3 hl)	1.232	1.553	1.760	1.706	1.330
Beer (10^3 hl)	520	526	505	491	450
Soap	77	76	78	81	85
Tobacco	28	28	28	27	25
Textiles and leather products					
Spun yarns (excluding jute)	31	30	36	33	39
Fabrics (10^6 meters)	106	100	98	100	99
Manufacturing (10^3 units)	24.268	21.699	21.000	17.900	18.000
Animal skins (10^6 square feet)	52	47	47	41	29
Shoes (10^3 pairs)	18.138	17.900	18.400	18.100	15.000
Wood and paper products					
Planks (10^3 cubic meters)	96	118	120	129	139
Paper	111	105	110	160	160
Matches (10^6 units)	844	849	863	1.040	800
Building materials					
Cement	5.539	6.096	6.450	7.600	7.250
Plaster	143	120	145	168	170
Bricks and tiles	1.661	1.617	1.660	1.700	1.660
Tiles (10^3 square meters)	2.299	2.315	2.200	2.200	2.220

Source: IMF, Report on Algeria 1985

restricting its activity in terms of volume, but also production costs (the foreign currency content of which was substantial) were rising well beyond forecasts. There were even cost overruns, mainly due to overpricing by foreign suppliers and demurrage on imported products and equipment, paid because delivery ships were waiting in port. The financial situation of companies suffered all the more as a lack of qualified local labour forced them to resort to costly foreign cooperation.

But the proven sources of additional costs did not exhaust the list of causes of constraints on resources that weighed on companies: hidden or public but effective, institutional, legal, political, administrative, and security interferences were the daily lot of company directors and managers at all levels who, incidentally, were themselves part of the machinery of the centralized administrative regulation of the economy that had been put in place.[9] This was the result of an original combination of the centrality of resources and of the State on the one hand, and the externality of State power on the other, both of which had to do with the country's recent political history and with the nature of these resources, which (conveniently for authorities in need of legitimacy) turned out to be the debt rent mentioned earlier insofar as it relieved them of the need to exert excessive fiscal pressure on the population.[10] As for the nature of the resources, it was later, following the oil crisis of 1986 and the liberalization of the economy with which the new authorities thought they could curb it, that they produced their most perverse effects: by perpetuating the mode of administrative regulation in the conduct of reforms, the regime in place brought together all the ingredients for their failure, as Smaïl Goumeziane (1994) describes in detail, although we will criticize his approach and arguments later. In particular, we shall see how, against all logic, the reforming government undermined its own reform project in the way it dealt with the nagging problem of inter-company claims and debts, which developed as a result of the scarcity of bank credit during the oil crisis. At the same time, by co-opting the appointment of new managers in charge of companies and other public entities, it introduced a form of allegiance to them that was akin to clientelism and contrary to the very spirit of the reform. We must therefore ask ourselves what caused the failure of the Algerian development strategy of the 1970s and the reforms of the 1980s, not only from an economic point of view but also from a sociopolitical one.

A system of administrative governance, political control of the economy, security control of society, and management of companies by co-optation and allegiance formed a sociological matrix for the successive failures of the economic policies initiated by the authorities, including the attempt at reform led by the government of Mouloud Hamrouche, who said of himself and his government that they broke into office.[11]

Centrality of Resources, Centrality of the State, and Exteriority of State Power in Independent Algeria

Today, the concept of centrality is used by geographers, urban planners, and economists to describe the attraction that certain cities exert on their environment through the density of the network of physical and economic relationships of which they are the center. Paul Claval (2000) points out, however, that a symbolic dimension of centrality is associated with the possession of religious power, and then with political sovereignty. By analogy, we will speak of the centrality of resources to signify the holding of the power to allocate resources by the central state. It goes without saying that the centrality of resources is dictated by the nature of these resources as rents in the case of countries that produce and export raw materials. On the other hand, the externality of state power is used to signify the state's autonomy in terms of resources in relation to the society it governs, by virtue of the very centrality of resources.

Most oil- and gas-producing countries (to say nothing of those producing other raw materials) therefore benefit from a mining rent, the size of which depends on their production potential, export capacity, and market price trends. But although the classic definition of the notion of rent, associating it with private property,[12] is the one most commonly accepted by economists, the concept remains ambiguous. It is questionable whether this definition applies to rents received by the state when it has a monopoly on subsoil ownership. Unless we consider that the sectors that generate rents are part of the State's private domain, such a definition contains a major ambiguity. Another ambiguity in the classic literature is whether, as income, rent can be used for accumulation in the same way as profit, which would mean postulating the possibility of its transformation into capital. This section will therefore attempt to supplement the classical definition of rent with the definition given by Douglass C. North et al. (2010) before proposing a situational analysis on the basis of an adapted definition.

On Rent and Its Ambiguous Definitions

The countries that produce oil and other raw materials belong to what the aforementioned authors call "limited-access social orders," in which "natural states" of varying degrees of maturity assert themselves; social orders that they characterize by the existence of strong personal relationships in place of strong institutions, and by clientelist networks as a means of organizing community life. Although these authors state quite bluntly that natural states "manipulate the economy in order to produce rents which, in turn, guarantee the maintenance of the political order" (North et al., 2010, p. 42), in the same paragraph they provide a definition of rent that does not apply to their characterization of limited-access social orders but to what they call open-access social orders, which correspond to the various configurations of the modern liberal state where the economy obeys the laws of the market. According to these authors, rent is "a return on an asset that exceeds the return that could be generated by a better investment of the same asset" (North et al., 2010, p. 43). The advantage of this definition for our study is that it removes the first ambiguity noted earlier, in that it does not refer specifically to private property; in this case, rent-bearing assets may be owned by the state. Although implicit, the deeper meaning of this definition is that rent differs from profit only in that it consists of the excess of return over average return (in other words, an excess of profit over average profit), which is why the aforementioned authors agree with Marx that rent originates in excess profit.[13] Thus, within the framework of the laws and institutions of the market, which presuppose competition between assets, it can be converted into additional capital and thus serve accumulation. The same is not true of rents in modern natural states. Here, rents are the main return on productive assets whose use only apparently conforms to the laws of the market, as they are dedicated assets—that is, univocally allocated to the sectors that generate rents.[14] In this case, rents do not necessarily imply a process of accumulation but are the very focus of struggles to monopolize them, for the purposes of enrichment and power.

The definition of rent that we will use for social orders with limited access (and therefore for natural states) will therefore be different, although it will be based on the same model, so as to include in the reasoning the rent received by the state. The point is to take account of realities that are only weakly reflected by the laws of the market, even if these laws overdetermine the processes of rent constitution on a global scale. We therefore propose to use the following three elements to characterize, from an economic point of view, social orders with limited access where the law of rents operates in place of the law of profit within the formal framework of the market economy.

1) Weakness of national production systems outside rent-producing sectors[15] (first characteristic);
2) Relative availability of resources in producer countries and relative scarcity of resources in consumer countries as sources of rent (second characteristic);
3) Centrality of resources and struggles for power in order to gain control of the central state and, consequently, access to rents, so that they can be used for discretionary and clientelist purposes (third characteristic).

On this basis, we will correct the definition of rent in the case of countries belonging to contemporary limited-access social orders as follows:[16] a profit on dedicated non-competitive assets that exceeds the ordinary remuneration of non-dedicated assets in the country. While there is no other "better investment" for these assets outside the rent-producing sector, due to the first characteristic of limited-access social orders, the relative availability of resources in producer countries and their relative scarcity in consumer countries (second characteristic) help to create rents and make them the main power issue in situations of resource centrality (third characteristic). Their control over the administrative machinery and institutions of the state enables the social forces holding state power, if not to legitimize, at least to legalize their appropriation of rents in all possible forms, the effects of which are not solely economic: while some authors, following the example of Lise Garon (1994) in the case of Algeria, emphasize the systemic nature of this mode of rent-based regulation of the economy, which stems from the centrality of resources, others, following the example of Raouf Boucekkine and Rafik Bouklia-Hassane (Boucekkine & Boukila-Hassane, 2011), associate the characteristics of regularity of this mode of regulation with a moral component under the terms of corruption, crime, and theft.

It is from this perspective that we shall attempt to analyze the situation in Algeria and conclude with an unprecedented delineation of it, that we can summarize here as the predominance of the logic of distribution over the logic of accumulation as far as the economy is concerned, and the predominance of the logic of moral disempowerment over the logic of empowerment of the political forces and social actors, caught up in the race for access to the rent, as far as civil and political society is concerned; all this amounts to postulating the prevalence of the law of rents over the law of profit within the very framework of the market economy.

Industrial Inefficiency, Reforms, and the Balance of Power

Let us take the three elements set out earlier to describe the situation:

- The weakness of the Algerian production system means that a greater volume of hydrocarbons can be exported, thereby also increasing the volume of rent. However, this circumstance is countered by the rise in domestic needs linked to demographic growth (household consumption) and the current and future number of factories (all sectors combined) with low technological added value but high energy consumption.
- The relative availability of resources improves Algeria's supply of hydrocarbons on foreign markets by exploiting new deposits.[17] Their relative scarcity in consumer countries increases demand for these products and improves Algeria's position in negotiations on quantities and prices,[18] which in theory translates into a greater volume of rent.
- As indicated in the introduction, the centrality of resources is linked to two sets of historical circumstances: the colonization of the country and its independence. The first led to the creation of a unitary Algerian state modeled on the French central state, while the second, even before independence, led to merciless battles between rival armed forces, with the best equipped and least involved in the war because of its position outside the country (the border army). The first relate to the State as an abstract entity and as the collective Being of the national community (political centrality); the second relate to the exercise of State power and to forms of governance that we will describe as externalized authoritarian governance; the ultimate expression of this externalization lies in the fact that for 30 years almost all of Algeria's political personnel and their families have been grouped together in the seaside resort known as "Club des Pins" on the west coast of Algiers.

What follows is an application of this grid to a brief analysis of the Algerian economy since the Algerian development strategy came into force.

On the economic front, as early as 1980, the country's new authorities summarized the problems faced by public enterprises (which, it should be remembered, formed the backbone of Algeria's development strategy). The idea was to redirect the country's foreign currency earnings toward imports of consumer goods[19] in order to reduce the risk of social protest against the new authorities by the population as a result of this dual crisis. In a lengthy report published in May of that year by the Ministry of Territorial Planning and Development (MPAT in the rest of this study), the authors wrote, "none of them [public enterprises] has generated sufficient resources to provide for its [investment] replacement" (MPAT, 1980, p. 294).

Although factual, this observation is no less part of a questioning of the balance of power in the State as inherited from the Boumediene regime which, while being security-oriented, gave pride of place to a group of technocrats trained in the great foreign schools, responsible for leading the industrialization of the country[20] From the same factual point of view, public companies did indeed experience financial difficulties in relation to their investments, but the underlying causes of the situation had as much to do with the industrial inefficiency of the latter as with the centralized administrative mode of regulation adopted, which corresponded to the authoritarian mode of governance of the economy introduced by the Boumediene regime. However, although a form of clientelism did exist under this regime, which was essentially made up of former members of the pre-independence Ministry of Armaments and General Liaison (MALG),[21] it had not yet taken on the character of a mode of regulation which the Chadli Bendjedid regime was to confer on it under the guise of a gradual liberalization of the economy. This liberalization immediately benefited the members of the President's family, in-laws and entourage, made up of concentric circles (from the closest to the most distant associates), thus completing the process of institutional enregimentation.

Nevertheless, let us mention a few key facts from the period of authoritarian governance under the Boumediene regime which worked against the efficiency of the public companies that served as a pretext for the economic reforms of 1988. Under the regulations in force at the time, public companies were obliged to make annual payments to the Treasury in respect of their depreciation allowances in order to finance budget expenditure that was not fully covered by ordinary taxation.[22] This centralization of part of the companies' own resources further reduced their financial strength as their investments had not yet reached full maturity. The equivalent in national currency of their foreign currency costs weighed heavily on companies' operating expenses, without allowing them to use the sums entered in the depreciation accounts to improve their cash flow. In the end, they were effectively unable to maintain and renew their production equipment, a decision that required the formal agreement of the central regulatory authority represented by the Secretariat of State for Planning (which later became MPAT). On the other hand, at a time when the need for skilled labour was cruelly felt, the authorities were exerting strong pressure on companies to recruit an unskilled workforce that was in excess of the standards defined by the technological content of the machine complexes that made up their production facilities. Intended to reduce unemployment, which was exacerbated in urban areas by an irrepressible rural exodus, this measure resulted in a substantial increase in the wage bill in companies' operating costs despite the low general level of wages, dictated by the government's austerity policy. Added to this was the fact that, because of the lack of basic infrastructure in certain regions where their production units were located, these same companies were often obliged by the ministries responsible[23] to build roads and other public works at no cost to local authorities and public institutions.

There is no shortage of examples to support the observations made by MPAT on behalf of the new authorities, who were in need of political legitimacy,[24] which the sudden death of President Boumediene had brought to light. The role played by the Gestion Socialiste des Entreprises (GSE) introduced in 1971, which was supposed to give workers a stake in the ownership of their companies (Belghenou, 1992), and the Statut Général des Travailleurs (SGT) enacted in 1978, which was supposed to eliminate inequalities in treatment and working conditions in society, was undoubtedly decisive in blocking the industrialization process, which Christian Palloix had wrongly seen as "an over-Fordist endowment configuration" (Palloix, 1980): while the GSE was of a purely formal nature, allowing company managers to exploit the Management Board on which sat the workers' representatives, who henceforth formed a country-wide workers' caste, the SGT had proceeded to artificially level down pay by classifying all trades across all sectors on a rigid scale which nipped in the bud the spirit of initiative and innovation.

However, all this does not detract from the fact that the so-called development decade (1967–1978) laid the foundations for a diversified economy based on accelerated sectoral industrialization, with one or more large-scale public enterprises springing up virtually ex nihilo in each sector to cover part of the country's needs in goods of various kinds. But the general state of the companies and of the economy as a whole deteriorated and ended up in open crisis as soon as the oil counter-shock of 1986 hit. The country's foreign exchange earnings plummeted at a time when outstanding foreign debt and the servicing of that debt were at their highest.

A Technically Inadequate and Politically Inappropriate Reform

The new authorities believed that the two main causes of the inefficiency of public companies were their "gigantic size" and the way they were run. As a result, they decided against all logic:

1) To dismantle them into as many small companies (on a human scale) by separating the functions of production, marketing, and engineering into as many companies, thus breaking the organic cycle of capital in favor of its functional cycles which block its accumulation instead of liberating it. By creating pockets of rent in the substantial differentials that emerged between the prices charged by production companies and those charged by marketing companies, it was all public capital that found itself subsumed under rent, as Djilali Liabès (Liabès, 1986) pointed out even before the reform (1986), even though it was supposed to put an end to the informal but effective subsumption of capital under rent that had taken place during the development decade. However, there was no shortage of people warning against this approach, which the *Front de Libération Nationale*'s (FLN's) Economic Commission chaired by Abdellatif Benachenhou

(Benachenhou, 1980)[25] had finally adopted: in his doctoral thesis defended in 1984, Ahmed Bouyacoub had already warned against experimenting with it in one of the public companies in the textiles sector . . . to no avail!

2) To set up the new economic entities as autonomous companies with capital[26] denominated in shares on the model of foreign companies, but whose management was entrusted administratively to "Participation Funds" which were themselves nothing more than dismemberments of the "old regime" supervisory ministries, thus multiplying the procedural pitfalls in the face of initiatives to emerge from the prevailing slump.
3) Automatically and by accounting reflex, provide these new companies with an opening balance sheet weighed down with virtually irrecoverable inter-company debts, inherited from the parent companies and calculated in proportion to their capital. While it would have been sufficient to clear this double burden by simply offsetting, even partially, these receivables and debts within each company, the financial authorities followed an accounting rule that was totally unsuited to the situation. Since the balance could then be treated macroeconomically, it would have been possible to make the new entities financially viable.[27] The result of this procedure was that many companies, whose "debts" represented the bulk of their balance sheet liabilities, started out with negative net assets[28] which immediately mortgaged their business, if not their very existence. In vain did the reforming government and its successors carry out iterative financial clean-ups of companies which, according to various sources, swallowed up more than 1,000 billion dinars:[29] the public industrial sector never recovered from the reform, while the private industrial sector only developed in the rent-seeking sectors.
4) To co-opt new managers in charge of companies and participation funds on the basis of the degree of allegiance they showed to the reforming government rather than their skills or technical expertise, while at the same time putting many young public-sector managers on early retirement because of their attachment to old practices.

All these facts and many more have jeopardized the success of the reforms undertaken, even if the government had been moved by good intentions. So it is hardly surprising that the crisis has worsened, leading the authorities to call on the IMF (in return for accepting its conditionalities) to assist them in their application to the Paris and London Clubs to reschedule the country's foreign debt. The consequences of this policy were massive lay-offs of workers, cut-price privatizations of state-owned companies, rampant inflation, and budget cuts in the social welfare chapters of public finances. What followed, as we all know, was a decade of unprecedented violence in the country, with disastrous consequences for the economy and society. In the end, it was as if economic governance had been reversed in the light of Algeria's development strategy, which presaged a way out of underdevelopment through accelerated industrialization. So it is hardly surprising that, to this day, the country remains heavily dependent on oil and gas exports, while non-hydrocarbon industries are struggling to find their feet, despite numerous stimulus plans and a "new industrial strategy" that the authorities have been talking about constantly since the mid-2000s, without ever defining or—a fortiori—implementing it.

An Undiversified Economy Doubly Dependent on Exports and Imports

From 18% to 20% of GDP in the mid-1970s, non-hydrocarbon public industry now accounts for less than 5%. Despite a relative boom in private industry, overall industrial value added in GDP is struggling to return to its 1970s level, which is the very sign of poor diversification and low sophistication of the economy, as noted in the report by the United Nations Economic Commission for Africa (2019, p. 2). This observation is further corroborated by the structure of GDP growth, which we reproduce later from 2016 to 2019 as indicated in Table 3.3.

There has been a steady decline in total GDP growth over the period 2016–2019 as a result of the oil crisis that began in August 2014, while non-hydrocarbon GDP growth has been erratic, reflecting weaknesses in the overall economic structure, even though non-hydrocarbon activities in the private sector were being offered growth opportunities as a result of the many stimulus plans launched by the authorities since the early 2000s. Paradoxically, however, such opportunities came up against a lack of resources in a situation of falling oil revenues, with the private sector largely dependent on public orders.

In periods of financial affluence, such as those experienced by the country, thanks to the rise in oil and gas prices, the trade balance becomes strongly in surplus and large foreign exchange reserves (net international reserves as defined by the IMF, 2013) are built up. This was particularly the case during the 2000s and until the end of 2013, when they reached 194 billion dollars. But from that date onward, they gradually began to melt away, as the volume of imports remained high due to the effect of the hysteresis principle. In almost seven years (2014–2020), the country has lost almost 70% of its foreign exchange reserves (i.e., 135 billion dollars), with an annual average of around 20 billion dollars.[31] Successive governments have tried in vain to reduce the import bill in order to preserve foreign exchange reserves somewhat: from 9 billion dollars in 2000, this rose to 40 billion in 2010 and to more than 58 billion in 2014 according to ONS data (October 2015), only to begin a slow descent from 2015 (to more than 51 billion dollars) and finally to settle at almost 39 billion dollars in 2021 through regulatory contraction of imports.

The structure of imports (see Table 3.4) is stable overall, with a balanced distribution across the three main economic categories used by the Algerian statistics

Table 3.3 Growth in Total GDP and Non-Hydrocarbon GDP (%)

Year	*2016*	*2017*	*2018*	*2019*
GDP	3.2	1.3	1.2	0.8
GDP HH[30]	2.2	2.0	3.0	2.4

Source: ONS Les comptes économiques en volume no. 900: 2

agency (ONS), indicating that the country imports all types of goods and services. On the other hand, over 98% of exports (at least until 2018) are concentrated in the "Industrial supplies" category alone, and more particularly in the "Fuel and motor fuels" subcategory (over 93%), which in both cases is a sign of the virtual absence of economic diversification.

While, throughout the 2000s and until August 2014, the increase in imports did not affect foreign exchange reserves due to the country's rising oil revenues, the same has not been true since that date, as the aforementioned in figures later. Reduced to the bare minimum, foreign exchange reserves now represent just a few months' worth of imports, giving rise to tensions between rival factions within the ruling sphere itself on the one hand, and between these factions as a whole and society on the other.

Table 3.4 Changes in the Structure of Imports (M) and Exports (X) by Broad Economic Category (%)

Wording	*2013*		*2014*		*2015*		*2016*		*2017*		*2018*	
	M	*X*	*M*	*X*	*M*	*X*	*M*	*X*	*M*	*X*	*M*	*X*
Consumer goods of which	25.8	0.6	25.4	0.5	24.7	0.7	25.9	1.2	26.4	1.2	25.1	1.0
Durable goods	4.2	0.0	2.3	0.0	2.4		3.0		2.8		2.3	
Goods mainly intended for industry	5.1	0.0	4.9	0.0	5.8	0.0	5.1	0.0	5.2	0.0	5.8	0.0
Industrial supplies (including fuel and lubricants) of which	36.9	99.3	35.6	99.5	36.7	99.2	37.1	98.8	37.4	98.5	37.2	98.9
Fuel and motor fuels	8.0	96.9	4.9	95.8	4.6	94.4	3.4	94.0	4.3	94.5	2.3	93.0
Other capital goods (including transport equipment) of which	37.2	0.0	39.0	0.0	38.5	0.0	36.9	0.0	36.1	0.1	37.7	0.1
Transport equipment and accessories	17.8	0.0	16.3	0.0	13.8	0.0	11.6	0.0	11.2	0.1	14.4	0.0
Property not elsewhere specified	0.1	0.1	0.0	0.0	0.1	0.1	0.1	0.0	0.1	0.2	0.0	0.0
Total	100		100		100		100		100		100	

Source: Constructed by us from ONS data, 2019

Nevertheless, these tensions did not give rise to extreme violence as in the years 1986–1999, but rather to large-scale peaceful demonstrations which were exacerbated by the prospect of a fifth term for an elderly president severely weakened by illness. The crisis of governance linked to dwindling rents was thus brought out into the open, while the difficulties of life for whole sections of the population, which constituted the ferment of the mal vie, gave rise to rampant violence, which was further encouraged by the weakness of the institutions, even though the authorities continued to rely on the centrality of resources to perpetuate the externalized administrative mode of regulation of the economy and the associated methods of allocating rents.

Net Rent and the Crisis of Governance in Algeria

We have dealt earlier with the centrality of resources as a mode of economic regulation in a situation where rent prevails over profit within the formal framework of the market economy. It is now appropriate to examine the nature of the rent-resource centrality link as a diptych around which the mode of regulation of the economy is articulated.

A Look Back at the Concept of Rent

The idea of an organic link between rents and the centrality of resources leads us to examine the determinants of the current situation in Algeria, where the state, described by many authors as a rentier state because of the proportion of its income derived from oil and gas, enjoys a high degree of autonomy from society. It is not so much the existence of rents as the fact that they are centrally available (centrality of resources) that determines this autonomy. Although we have always been dealing with a hard authoritarian regime (State power) since independence, the State has experienced marked weaknesses linked to the dwindling of rents, while at the same time presenting itself as the guardian figure of society in a situation of financial ease resulting from the increase in revenues from hydrocarbons. The same type of state as that described by Douglass North et al. as the natural state is at work here, albeit with changing characteristics. It is therefore necessary to start again from the definition of rents given by the aforementioned authors in order to grasp its current forms in the case of Algeria.

On the basis of the definition of rent given earlier for social orders with limited access, we will refer to the gross annual rent as all the revenues from oil and gas exports generated in the course of a year, after deduction of ordinary[32] sectoral costs and benefits. The part of this gross annuity that exceeds the absorption capacity of the economy is referred to as the annual net annuity, and the cumulative net annuity at a given date is referred to as the cumulative net annuity.

The accumulated net pension increases or decreases depending on whether:

1) Oil and gas revenues rise or fall over the period under review;
2) Sector costs increase or decrease;[33]

3) Domestic spending by these incomes on imported consumer or capital goods rises or falls;
4) The result of these three factors is positive or negative, whether they operate in the same direction or in opposite directions.

Insofar as the net international reserves (i.e., the major part of the net rent) consist of temporarily dormant revenues,[34] they represent the main stake in the struggles between rival factions aiming to accede to State power in order to seize them according to the path described by Douglass C. North et al. for natural states, and make use of it to their advantage.

There are two situations to consider:

1) A significantly high net rent gives rise to a wide distribution of prebends including not only the direct clientele of the regime's supporters but also a more or less numerous social category with the power to cause harm through economic or institutional blocking actions. This covers a whole range of political practices, including granting virtually unlimited lines of credit or large-scale public contracts to investors born of spontaneous generation (Benachenhou, 2007)[35] or who have been around for a long time; buying votes in local and national elections (communal or wilaya people's assemblies, national people's assembly, presidency of the republic); in open or hidden support for the President of the Republic from employers' or employees' organizations and civil society associations in return for subsidies; in demonstrations of strength by social groups of various kinds in return for an increase in their income, etc. During Abdelaziz Bouteflika's last two terms in office, measures were taken to broaden the regime's clientele, resulting in a diversified arsenal of debt write-offs targeting farmers, beneficiaries of loans to set up small businesses under the auspices of public bodies promoting private investment (ANSEJ,[36] ANDI, . . .[37]), etc.
2) A significantly low net income gives rise to manifestations of violence that go beyond comprehension in certain circumstances, as if the social forces close to the regime were panicking at the prospect of seeing the undue income derived from their situation dry up; while the social forces further away from the regime would act in the same way because their income would dwindle to such an extent that they would find themselves in a state of unbearable impoverishment. This was the case at the end of the 1980s when, in the wake of the 1986 oil crisis, major demonstrations took place in most Algerian towns, sometimes for existential reasons, such as the sudden rise in the price of basic necessities, shortages of these same products, the absence of water in the taps for several days (or even weeks), etc. These demonstrations were followed by riots in the streets of the capital. These demonstrations were followed by riots bordering on unarmed insurrection, which were put down in bloodshed (October 1988), culminating in a whole decade of unprecedented violence (1990–1999) when the FIS began to harbor hopes of taking power. On a clear-cut ideological basis, the FIS built up a clientele among the socially deprived on the one hand, and an elite

practicing political Islam on the other, ending up leading an armed insurrection that resulted in tens of thousands of deaths among the population.

What should be noted about net income is that, insofar as it represents that portion of gross income which exceeds the absorption capacity of the economy, it is intended to be expatriated or not repatriated (in the case where it is directly denominated in foreign currency) or to be used to increase the property and real-estate assets of its beneficiaries (in the case where it is denominated in dinars). We are obviously only talking here about the portion of the net rent that escapes the public accounts, the part constituting the foreign exchange reserves being invested in US Treasury bills or stored in cash or gold in the vaults of the Bank of Algeria and the primary banks. As foreign exchange reserves, they are used to finance imports in excess of the country's foreign exchange earnings when the latter are insufficient, as has been the case during oil crises.

However, the very nature of imports is partly a source of hoarding of net income by the social actors who make up the regime's clientele. While benefiting from public credit lines in foreign currency for their import–export trade,[38] resort to various illicit practices of deception on the goods (nature, quality, quantity), on prices, or on the expiry dates of imported products. These practices give rise to the conversion of dinars into foreign currency or foreign currency into dinars on the informal foreign exchange market in Algeria itself (which exists unofficially but effectively) or abroad. It should be pointed out, however, that this dual informal market is also supplied from their own income by ordinary citizens in search of foreign currency to travel, for treatment abroad, or for any other urgent need, which can represent a considerable amount of money that does not enter fully into the composition of the net income.

Back to the Question of the Centrality of Resources

By resource centrality, we mean state ownership of subsoil resources, the exploitation of which generates income. The key element of resource centrality is the state's exclusive ownership of the country's subsoil, but this is not unique to the Algerian state: many other states around the world enjoy the same privilege. This prerogative is certainly inherited from the French colonial state (whose Mining Code dates back to 1810) but, in the case of Algeria, it has an irrefutable historical and sociopolitical reality: all the immovable property left by colonial France or the colonists passed all the more naturally to the Algerian state as, at independence, there were no Indigenous social or political forces able to claim legitimate ownership of it. Along with the land owned by the colonists and private French or foreign companies, the subsoil owned by the unitary French state was an integral part of this real estate.

What is specific to countries with a rentier economy, where the state relies on rents as its main source of revenue, is the autonomy enjoyed by state power in relation to society; an autonomy which places it outside society and which is reflected in an authoritarian mode of governance. In such a situation, it matters little whether or not the economy functions efficiently: as Ahmed Henni writes, "the performance that gives the social situation is not that which consists in having the maximum number of clients on the goods market, but the maximum number of clients on the situations market" (Henni, 1988, p. 24). It is therefore to governance that we should turn to locate the causes of the inefficiency of the Algerian productive system in relation to the status of rents and the centrality of resources.

Centrality of Resources and Governance

We have already mentioned some of the characteristics of governance in Algeria. Some authors have devoted their dissertations to the subject or produced academic studies dealing with the issue in relation to that of rents and the centrality of resources, without however analyzing the problem in terms of net rents and the exteriority of state power as we have just done: Smaïl Goumeziane, whose thesis on this subject is published under the title "Le mal algérien, Economie politique d'une transition inachevée" (1962–1994). Calling into question the centralized allocation of resources, the author denounces the "omnipresence of the state" (Goumeziane, 1994, p. 51), virtually repeating the litany of grievances that the MPAT report had already enumerated against the public sector. The author points out in detail the apparent causes of capital inefficiency (sic) (Goumeziane, 1994, p. 71) without questioning the economic status of the latter or that of rent: is rent capable of being transformed into capital so as to be subject to the same treatment as the profit generated by the productive assets that make up the latter? This is the question that he should have clarified at some point in his reasoning, as we have attempted to do in this study by associating annuities with dedicated assets. As a former minister in the so-called reformist government, his thesis consists of an almost emotional plea in favor of the reforms that the latter had unsuccessfully undertaken from 1988 onward. The author does not seem to have understood that it is not so much the central state as a collective being but rather the externalized power of the state and the mode of governance it establishes that are at issue. It does not occur to him that what he calls the inefficiency of capital is a form of distributive efficiency of rents, as Ahmed Henni suggests. However, other works on the subject do exist. In addition to the work mentioned here by Ahmed Henni, a seminal article by Djilali Liabès in 1986 outlined a political economy of rents applied to Algeria. Titled "Rente, légitimité et statuquo: quelques éléments de réflexions sur la fin de l'Etat-providence," the article posed the question: "under what conditions can distribution relationships, based on a state monopoly rent, take the place of production relationships, i.e. assume the structuring function of the entire social system?" (Liabès, 1986, p. 4). In response, the author argues that capital is subsumed under rent, which "fulfils a function . . . of legitimising the system of powers" (Liabès, 1986, p. 6).

Many other authors have pointed to the same characteristics of the Algerian economic system in different terms. Some have focused on the technical inconsistencies of the development project (some of which we have pointed out ourselves in this study), others on the managerial inconsistencies behind which they target the mode of governance (or public management as some of them call it). Abdelhak

Lamiri, for example, rightly speaks of an "economy of signatures" (1999) in relation to the forms taken by the distribution of goods and the granting of privileges: while distribution is subject to the signature of insignificant agents occupying subordinate positions but enjoying the right to sign purchase vouchers when goods are in short supply, the granting of privileges is part of a complex network of reciprocal influences. We are therefore dealing with a kind of institutional arrangement in which rents play the role of organizing agent, whatever changes are made to the mode of regulation. Rachid Boudjema (2011), speaking of the economic reforms for which Smaïl Goumeziane laments their incompleteness, points out that the economic role of the state can be read—like a palindrome (as the author puts it)—in both directions and according to the same logic: from the state to the market or from the market to the state.

In all cases, the net rent is at the heart of a perverse social, political, and ideological dynamic that leads to what Ahcène Amarouche (2015) has called "the spirit of rent," the effects of which are nothing less than a generalized social disempowerment of the players that has ended up breaking with homo algerianus as a product of the war of liberation. Despite the determination shown by the authorities in the wake of the crisis of governance following the rejection by the population of a fifth term for Abdelaziz Bouteflika, the same path seems to characterize what they call the "new Algeria."

A Critical Look at the "New Algeria"

"New Algeria" is the slogan that the country's current authorities have adopted to signify their break with the previous regime. However, despite the arrest of a string of key figures in the previous regime—including the president's brother, two former prime ministers, numerous ministers and advisers, and senior army officers—a large number of state clerks, magistrates, and high-ranking military officers with questionable links to the regime's players and businessmen are still in office or in the corridors of power. So, despite the efforts of the new authorities to legitimize themselves by holding a referendum on a new constitution (organized on the 66th anniversary of the outbreak of the war of national liberation), by holding new legislative elections, etc., the prevailing feeling among the population is one of mistrust or, at best, expectation. Distrust and expectation were reflected in turnout rates for the 2019 and 2021 presidential and legislative elections of no more than 40% and 23%, respectively, as well as in the turnout rate of less than 24% for the 2020 constitutional referendum.

On the economic front, however, and after the effects of the COVID-19 health crisis have faded, there has been a financial upturn as a result of the revaluation of hydrocarbon prices on the world market. The ongoing war between Russia and Ukraine has also greatly benefited oil- and gas-exporting countries other than Russia, due to the sanctions imposed on that country by Western countries.

Multilateral organizations such as the IMF and the World Bank, private French banks operating in Algeria such as BNP Paribas and Société Générale, and foreign risk assessment bodies such as Coface all point to a rebound in economic activity from 2021 onward, and forecast a clear improvement in macroeconomic indicators over the period 2020–2023, with the exception of inflation and, to a lesser extent, domestic public debt.[39]

This outlook is obviously not unrelated to the sharp rise in oil and gas prices on the world market since 2022: the improvement in macroeconomic indicators is commonplace when the country is in a comfortable financial position, as we have shown later.

In this characteristic context, the most significant element of this improvement is the upward trend (in both amount and proportion) in exports of non-hydrocarbon goods and services: according to figures from the National Statistics Office (ONS, no. 964, p. 8), they will account for 18% of total exports in 2020, or between six billion and seven billion dollars, compared with three billion in 2018. However, this high percentage is the result of the low level of hydrocarbon exports in that year compared with the years prior to 2014: it would fall by almost half if hydrocarbon exports had reached the 2013 figure, that is, 65.9 billion dollars. The increase in value is, in this case, more significant than the increase in proportion: if such an increase is not occasional, we can conjecture a substantial improvement in economic diversification insofar as the diversification of exports is a sign of it. But this view is undermined by the structure of non-hydrocarbon exports: the aforementioned documents from the National Statistics Office indicate that the bulk of the new performance is due to exports of services, which is corroborated by the positive but very slow trend in the country's industrial output.

In contrast to this set of data, those relating to other economic indicators leave us skeptical as to whether the country will emerge from the slump that has characterized the situation since the advent of the current regime. While the aforementioned bodies never fail to point out the shortcomings and weaknesses of the Algerian economy, such as its overdependence on hydrocarbon revenues, high youth unemployment, few job opportunities for young graduates, poor infrastructure and, more generally, a business climate that is hardly conducive to private investment, both domestic and foreign, the social situation is also extremely deleterious. We will mention here just a few of the problems faced by the population:

- The Bank of Algeria's concern to withdraw from circulation the mass of cash (four trillion dinars) injected by the last government of the Bouteflika regime in the form of unconventional credit to the economy led to a shortage of liquidity, which initially caused a stir among the population for several weeks before finally being resolved by reinjecting this manna into the money supply and fuelling inflation.
- Shortages of basic necessities such as semolina, milk, and oil (wheat and milk having been imported on a massive scale in the past) are a regular feature of the news, while the prices of other foodstuffs soar at the start of each Ramadan, only to fall back moderately by virtue of the principle of hysteresis.
- The abrupt halt to imports of private vehicles due to the poor state of the roads and the obsolescence of public transport equipment is putting pressure on

passengers and contractors in the sector, even after the constraints linked to the COVID-19 pandemic have been lifted.

- Endemic unemployment among young people in higher education provides opportunities for the services of French embassies and, to a lesser extent, Canadian embassies, to select the best-educated for quasi-definitive emigration, while the "harragas" movement[40] continues to lead to the death or detention abroad of many young people lacking prospects in their own country.

In terms of security, the country is being completely sealed off under the convenient pretext of the fight against terrorism, which the authorities believe to represent certain political organizations such as the Movement for the Autonomy of Kabylia (MAK) and the "Rachad" movement, as well as certain personalities affiliated or not to these organizations.

On the political front, the muzzling of the partisan opposition, autonomous trade unions, and other civil society organizations, dissolved[41] or forced into inactivity by regulations, contrasts with the official declarations associating the slogan "New Algeria" with the free exercise of democracy.

Finally, in the media, print newspapers and websites are regularly subject to explicit or implicit bans on publication or broadcasting, when they are not obliged to relay the official discourse, on pain of withdrawal by state institutions of their generally lucrative advertising.

In addition to all this, there is unbearable pressure on literary and cultural figures, radio broadcasters, and ordinary Internet users, who are sometimes sent to prison without trial for a simple statement they make or a post they make on social networks.

The combination of all these facts is obviously not fortuitous but reflects the same mode of governance as in the past, and one wonders what would distinguish the "new Algeria." The same clientelist practices associated with a State power that feeds on rents can be seen (e.g., in the awarding of public contracts by mutual agreement or in appointments to senior positions in the administration), and the same problems as in the past, where the denial of rights and physical or moral repression are used as weapons by an authoritarian regime. It is therefore doubtful whether there will be any substantial improvement in the situation until the mode of governance changes.

It is on this question of governance that we would like to conclude this study, as it seems to us to be of crucial importance in the course of past and future events in Algeria.

Conclusion: Is Rent a Socially Disempowering Factor?

The previous analysis of the role of rents in the economy needs to be supplemented by a sociological or even anthropological analysis: most of the authors cited in this study suggest or explicitly state that rents have a structuring role in the social body. We would add that it also structures mentalities in a way that runs counter not only to the economic rationality of the market economy but also to the ethos of the Algerian as forged by the war of national liberation and, even further back, by all the revolts and insurrections that marked the colonial period.

In one case, it disqualifies income-generating work and capital as the source of a dynamic of accumulation, and instead inscribes social groups and individuals in a logic of access to jobs and positions that provide prebends and privileges, the sociolinguistic expression of which is the barbarism recalled by Djilali Liabès in the aforementioned article–"Regda outmangé."[42] This has become the stereotype of social behavior in times of financial affluence, when money flows freely. In the other case, it disqualifies the political forces by establishing entitlement, corruption, and conformism as facts of society, while embedding them in a state of mind that feeds on tradition to which it adapts modernity (Henni, 1988) without the slightest reflexive hindsight and in a drive to disempower collective and individual social actors.

As if the very exteriority of state power in relation to society had externalized whole sections of the latter in relation to itself, it is hardly surprising that the antinomic phenomena identified by Slimane Medhar (1999) should emerge in situations of economic crisis, and that a nihilistic social and political crisis such as that which brought the country to the brink of collapse at the beginning of the 1990s should be the iterative outcome of governance in Algeria.

Notes

1 One example is the assassination of Abane Ramdane by his fellow soldiers in 1957.
2 Middle East and North Africa.
3 Insofar as virtually all industrial equipment had to be imported, the availability of foreign currency resources was an absolute necessity.
4 This is reflected in the type of technology used in imported equipment.
5 Société Nationale des Transports Ferroviaires.
6 On the subject of the first industrialized countries (England, Belgium, the United States), the author notes that: "it was on dry land that the real revolution had taken place, that of the railway" (Hobsbawm, 1975, p. 57).
7 Debt-annuity in the sense that future oil revenues are used to repay current debts.
8 Although the Dutch Disease theory, which Corden and Neary (1982) put forward to explain the de-industrialization of small oil- and gas-exporting countries (the case of Holland), is based on the tendency for the exchange rate to revalue automatically in an open economy, it can also be applied to the case of countries such as Algeria, whose exchange rate was administratively overvalued during periods when the country enjoyed financial prosperity following the appreciation of oil and gas prices on world markets.
9 No manager of a company or any other administrative structure was appointed without a prior police investigation by the security services.
10 As the World Bank notes (World Bank, 2018, p. 58), Arab countries have "abundant revenues from, among other things, the energy sector, which reduces the need to mobilise tax revenues."
11 Sentence pronounced by the former head of government during his speech at the symposium organized in September 2008 by the Algerian Association for the Development of

Social Science Research (AADRESS) in homage to M'hamed Boukhobza, assassinated on 22 June 1993, by the FIDHA terrorist organization affiliated to the FIS (Islamic Salvation Front).

12 Adam Smith wrote by way of definition of rent: "From the moment the soil of a country has become private property, the owners, like all other men, like to reap where they have not sown, and they demand a rent even for the natural product of the land" (Smith, 1976, p. 75). David Ricardo adds only that: "The rent from mining does not differ from the rent from land except that it has no relation to the natural and indestructible faculties of the soil" (Ricardo, 1977, p. 58).

13 See Capital, Book III, volume 3, sixth section: "Conversion of surplus profit into land rent" (Marx, 1971, p. 7). This same idea can be found in the work of authors such as Gilbert Abraham-Frois and Edmond Berrebi (1980) on the subject of an industrial production system where the introduction of a new technique would be the source of a surplus profit which would be transformed into a "quasi-rent"; the authors specify that the quasi-rent differs from the rent only in its provisional character (see chapter four, pp. 115 ff.).

14 In contrast, non-dedicated assets are assets employed under the competitive regime in non-annuity-providing sectors.

15 These countries, incidentally, are supplied with industrial equipment by the major industrialized countries.

16 From a very general point of view, we can agree with the aforementioned authors on the concepts of social orders with open-access and social orders with limited access, which they use to characterize the evolution of social formations over the last ten thousand years.

17 The same obviously applies to all the other producing countries, which does not rule out competition between assets on an international scale.

18 Algeria has never been so courted by European consumer countries as it is at the time of writing (September 2022), due to the effects of the Russia–Ukraine war and the economic sanctions imposed by the EU on these countries' gas supplies from Russia.

19 The first five-year plan (1980–1984) clearly reflected this reorientation through what the authorities called the Anti-Scarcity Programme (APP).

20 As R. Malek (1991) notes, the more backward society is, the greater the power of technocracy: "It is left in the hands of a layer of specialists who quickly become technocrats" (Malek, 1991, p. 147).

21 In a contribution to the press, the former Minister Delegate and Minister of the Interior under Bouteflika (2001–2013), Dahou Ould Kablia, boasted that the MALG had given Algeria more than 150 leading political figures (ministers, ambassadors, walis, etc.). But the regime has co-opted many other key figures for their technical expertise and know-how in implementing the development strategy it has adopted.

22 Ordinary taxation refers to all taxes and duties levied on domestic activities (as opposed to petroleum taxes). It does not, of course, include depreciation allowances, which are a fictitious charge on companies' operating accounts to finance future investment. In the case of Algeria, however, the dinar is a non-convertible currency, so these allowances can only be used marginally for this purpose, which no doubt explains why they are centralized. The result of this operation, however, is to place a heavy burden on company finances, which have already been weakened by charges on supplier loans taken out for imports.

23 The expression "supervising ministry," commonly used, clearly reflected the subjection of public companies to the central authorities represented by the ministries.

24 The lack of legitimacy is reflected in the fact that state power is external to society.

25 In his 1980 book, Abdellatif Benachenhou, a university professor who had held positions of responsibility within the FLN, outlined the organic and financial restructuring of public companies, as this ill-advised reform was known.

26 It should be noted that the capital in question, which was the exclusive property of the State, was neither transferable nor alienable, which are, so to speak, the natural characteristics of all capital.
27 Having worked in multi-disciplinary teams on strategic diagnostics of new companies in difficulty on behalf of public bodies in charge of these operations, the author of these lines has raised this issue in various committees without encountering any attention from other members with accounting or traditional management backgrounds.
28 Net assets are the total assets on a company's balance sheet, less its liabilities.
29 For an overview of this issue, see our contribution to the daily El Watan of 11 December 2004 titled "L'assainissement financier des entreprises publiques algériennes: l'arbre qui cache la forêt" ("The financial restructuring of Algerian public companies: the tree that hides the forest").
30 HH: excluding hydrocarbons
31 Data provided by the Minister for the Economy at several press conferences.
32 Although the oil and gas sector generates income, it operates according to market economy standards because it is part of the global economy.
33 On the one hand, the need to carry out new explorations, acquire new and more expensive equipment, etc.; on the other hand, higher yields than current standards, superior oil quality, etc.
34 It should be understood that we are not taking account here of the financial income from investments in US Treasury bills or other funds, but of the productive domestic use of the income that makes up international reserves.
35 Abdellatif Benachenhou (2007) classifies Algerian private entrepreneurs according to the length of time they have been in business or the origin of their wealth, and titles one of the chapters of his book "les enfants gâtés de l'ouverture" ("The Spoilt Children of Openness").
36 National Youth Employment Support Agency.
37 National Industrial Development Agency.
38 Algerians are well aware of the illicit practices involved in foreign trade, which is dominated by imports, and ironically refer to it as import–import trade.
39 External public debt has been virtually non-existent since Abdelaziz Bouteflika decided in 2004 to pay off the country's debt early.
40 Young Algerians leaving the country by sea in makeshift boats.
41 This was the case most recently (September 2022) with the Algerian League for the Defence of Human Rights (LADDH), despite its affiliation with the International Federation for Human Rights (FIDH).
42 A term made up of an Arabic word and an Arabicized French word that can be roughly translated as "to sleep and eat."

References

Abraham-Frois, G., & Berrebi, E. (1980). *Rentes, rareté et surprofits*. Éditions Economica.

Amarouche, A. (2015). *État-nation et économie de rente en Algérie: Essai sur les limites de la libéralisation*. Éditions Universitaires Européennes.

Belghenou, A. (1992). La gestion socialiste des entreprises en Algérie: Participation et conflit. *Relations industrielles/Industrial Relations*, *47*(2), 300–324. https://doi.org/10.7202/050768ar

Benabdellah, Y. (1999). *Économie rentière et surendettement* (Doctoral dissertation, Université Lumière Lyon 2).

Benachenhou, A. (1980). *Planification et développement en Algérie (1962–1980)*. Imprimerie Commerciale.

Benachenhou, A. (2007). *Les entrepreneurs algériens*. Alpha Design.

Boucekkine, R., & Bouklia-Hassane, R. (2011). Rente, corruption et violence: L'émergence d'un ordre nouveau dans les pays arabes? *Regards économiques*, *92*.

Boudjema, R. (2011). *Économie du développement de l'Algérie, 1962–2010: Volume 3: Des contraintes majeures du développement et des tares de la logique rentière*. Dar El Khaldounia.

Bouyacoub, A. (1984). *L'entreprise industrielle publique en Algérie et ses modes de gestion, 1962–1982* (Doctoral dissertation, University of Oran).

Claval, P. (2000). Réflexions sur la centralité. *Cahiers de géographie du Québec*, *44*(123), 285–301.

COFACE. (2021, February). *Algeria: Main economic indicators*. Paris: COFACE.

Corden, W. M., & Neary, J. P. (1982). Booming sector and de-industrialisation in a small open economy. *The Economic Journal*, *92*, 825–848.

De Bernis, G. (1971). Les industries industrialisantes et les options algériennes. *Revue Tiers-Monde*, *12*(47), 545–563.

Garon, L. (1994). Crise économique et consensus en État rentier: Le cas de l'Algérie socialiste (Note). *Études internationales*, *25*(1), 25–45. https://doi.org/10.7202/703278ar

Goumeziane, S. (1994). *Le mal algérien: Économie politique d'une transition inachevée (1962–1994)*. Fayard.

Henni, A. (1986). *État, surplus et société en Algérie avant 1830*. ENAG.

Henni, A. (1988). *Le cheikh et le patron: Usages de la modernité dans la reproduction de la tradition*. Office des Publications Universitaires.

Hobsbawm, E. J. (1975). *The age of capital, 1848–1875*. Weidenfeld & Nicolson.

International Monetary Fund. (2013). *International reserves and foreign exchange liquidity: Guidelines for use of the standard data reporting form*. Washington DC: International Monetary Fund.

Lamiri, A. (1999). *Crise de l'économie algérienne: Causes, mécanismes et perspectives de redressement*. Les Presses d'Alger.

Liabès, D. (1986). Rente, légitimité et statu quo: Quelques éléments de réflexion sur la fin de l'État-providence. *Cahiers du CREAD*, *6*(2), 129–164.

Malek, R. (1991). *Tradition et révolution: Le véritable enjeu*. Éditions Bouchène.

Marx, K. (1971). *Le capital*. Éditions Sociales.

Medhar, S. (1999). *L'échec des systèmes politiques en Algérie*. Éditions Chihab.

Ministère de la Planification et de l'Aménagement du Territoire. (1980, May). *Synthèse du bilan économique et social de la décennie 1967–1978*. Algiers: MPAT.

North, D. C., Wallis, J. J., & Weingast, B. R. (2010). *Violence et ordres sociaux*. Gallimard.

Office National des Statistiques. (2015). *Collection statistiques n°194/2015. Évolution des échanges extérieurs de marchandises de 2004 à 2014*. Algiers: Office National des Statistiques.

Palloix, C. (1980). Un essai sur la formation de la classe ouvrière algérienne (1963–1978). *Revue Tiers-Monde*, *83*.

Ricardo, D. (1977). *Principles of political economy and taxation*. Éditions Flammarion.

Smith, A. (1976). *Recherches sur la nature et les causes de la richesse des nations*. Éditions Gallimard.

Société Nationale des Transports Ferroviaires. (2012). *History, modernity and challenges*. Algiers: Société Nationale des Transports Ferrovaires.

United Nations, Economic Commission for Africa. (2019). *Structural transformation, employment, production and society*. New York: United Nations Publications.

World Bank. (2018). *A new economy for the Middle East and North Africa: Middle East and North Africa economic situation monitoring report*.

4 The Role of Actors in the Institutional Dynamics of the Rentier Regime in Algeria

Samir Bellal

Introduction

Economic activity in a rentier country like Algeria bears the stamp of state intervention. As the country's economic performance (like that of many other rentier countries) remains mediocre, a credible economic development project currently requires systemic and structural reform of the economy's workings, which in turn demands profound political choices. However, the facts show that the autonomy that politicians acquire in the management of economic affairs often proves a barrier to change. In one of his contributions on the economic situation in Algeria, the economist Ahmed Dahmani stressed the weight of the political factor, which, in his view, is the main obstacle to the country's economic recovery, since, once it has freed itself from the constraints of the conflictual economic dynamics that drive civil society, politics has ended up autonomizing itself, giving rise to practices that become a real blocking factor and inhibit any enterprise (Dahmani, 1999).

Although, like many other analysts, he has frequently framed his speeches in terms of the recurring and generic theme of "the transition to a market economy," Dahmani offers a reading which has the particular interest of highlighting the role of the State, and therefore of politics, which can be an initiator and catalyst of a virtuous economic dynamics or, on the contrary, a blocking factor.

This chapter examines the role of politics in Algeria's economic trajectory. More specifically, it examines the roles of the various political and economic players in shaping the country's economic direction through fundamental institutional choices. It is structured around three points. The first is devoted to a reminder of the terms in which the question of institutional change arises in the case of a rentier economy such as Algeria's, a reminder which emphasizes the political dimension of the obstacles preventing Algeria from ridding itself of the "oil intoxication" (Ominami, 1986) to which its economy has fallen victim. The second will focus on the autonomy of the political sphere and its manifestations in the behavior of economic and political actors. The last point will focus on the pre-eminence of populist ideology, the veritable "software" that guides the economic action of the state in Algeria, an action which, it should be emphasized, is virtually unchallenged by the main economic and political players.

DOI: 10.4324/9781003730750-4

The Question of Institutional Transition

The rentier nature of the Algerian economy—and this cannot be stressed enough—means that the issue of economic and social transition in the country must be formulated in terms that are necessarily specific, in terms of both content and objectives. Today, some people believe that the Algerian economy, in its successive configurations of "statist" and "liberal," is best understood as a transition to a productive economy. The essential challenge is to encourage the creation, within the national community, of a surplus other than mining (Ricardian rent), and this can only result from an appropriate "institutional" compromise, the configuration of which depends largely on the State's actions.

The state is recognized here primarily for its capacity to define and implement economic policies. But once we recognize that politics has a degree of autonomy, a fortiori in the context of a rentier regime of accumulation,[1] we can consider the possibility of the state playing the role of promoter of a specific national form of integration into the global economy to be entirely possible from a political point of view.

Historically, the Algerian state has demonstrated such political capacity, even if the implemented project (known as the Algerian Development Strategy), because it was built in isolation from and against the objective laws of the market, ended, if not in failure, at least in a dead end. In the new international context, characterized by the deepening of international economic relations in the form of increased commercial and financial liberalization, many analysts consider such an undertaking to be extremely difficult, not to say futile. Globalization is often presented, in this respect, as a factor inhibiting any attempt to define an autonomous national development trajectory.

What is the reality? It would seem that globalization is often presented as a discourse that glorifies a (liberal) political project, the realization of which, as with any project, is uncertain. For many "heterodox" analysts, globalization can be understood as a discourse through which the social and economic groups that benefit from the process of external opening and liberalization try to obtain from governments and states revisions in their favor of economic legislation relating to labor, taxation, competition . . . in short, domestic institutional arrangements favorable to the safeguarding of their group interests (Boyer, 2002). From this point of view, globalization appears, paradoxically, to be above all a domestic affair.

Moreover, the experience of the last three decades shows that, far from leading to the generalization of a single, standard model of capitalism, the deepening of international economic relations has strengthened national institutional compromises (and therefore accentuated national specificities). This strengthening of national institutional compromises, manifested in the coexistence of contrasting national trajectories, no doubt explains why globalization has not led to the synchronization of macroeconomic conjunctures, as predicted by economists and financiers committed to the idea that accumulation now operates on a global scale. The 2008 financial crisis is a perfect illustration of this, since at a time when growth was faltering in all the advanced capitalist economies, China and certain so-called emerging countries continued to record highly enviable growth rates.

Faced with the constraints posed by globalization, the range of political choices available to the state remains very broad, especially since, contrary to the teachings of orthodox international trade theory, international relations are not reduced to market relations but often involve decisive political negotiations between states. As in the case of money and the budget, almost all the components of a country's international integration are subject to political arbitration.

In addition to the weight of the external context, usually referred to as "globalization," internal considerations are cited to support the argument that it is uncertain whether the State can promote a specific national form of integration into the global economy.

Thus, for some, the State's economic policy faces the difficulty of reconciling the interests of different social categories. In this context, F. Yachir writes:

> *Economic policy is neither a concentration of pure knowledge nor the execution of an abstract rationality. It involves arbitration between conflicting social demands, between multiple and divergent configurations of interests. It is marked by the imprint of social positions determined by the economic and political system.*
>
> (Yachir, 1990, p. 29)

This is an important political prerequisite for fruitful economic change: the creation of an institutional configuration that favors the development of productive activities over rent-seeking. According to this approach, as long as the social strata whose interests align with those of previous economic policies hold power in political decision-making, change is unlikely to occur.

In Algeria, we might consider the best illustration of this impossibility to be the presence of institutional regulation whose configuration gives pride of place to "economic populism" to the point of defining it. Generally speaking, this regulation, which is characterized by its "umbilical" dependence on the circulation of rents, can be seen in specific configurations:

- Structural overvaluation of the national currency, favoring imports and consumption to the detriment of production and hindering the export of products other than mining.
- The country's economic borders were opened wide, and a rapid and abrupt process of customs dismantling began, often as a result of external pressure. The state monopoly on foreign trade was abolished in 1991. This opening was reinforced by the agreements on the rescheduling of foreign debt (1994–1998), which forced the country to liberalize its foreign trade considerably.
- The latter, which is crumbling under the weight of a structural deficit and a bloated workforce, is more akin to a political market, not only because its managers are often appointed on the basis of patronage but also because its recruitment, operation, and activities are governed less by the economic imperatives of

profitability than by political interference and intervention. Over the long term, such a situation is only tenable if considerable external resources are mobilized to finance the resulting structural deficits (Bellal, 2014).

- An allocation of public spending that is more in line with a "political" logic of redistribution than with an economic logic of supporting accumulation. In general, the economic imperative of financing accumulation and the political imperative of redistribution often find themselves in competition, and the balance between the two is resolved, in practice, according to the degree of intensity of the imperative of legitimizing the political regime in place, on the one hand, and the degree of that regime's ability to control and mobilize society, on the other. While during the 1990s it was the economic imperative of adjustment that prevailed over the rest,[2] from 2000 onward, the distributive logic seems, thanks to the continuing recovery in oil prices, to have gained a clear advantage.
- Structuralist management of money, based on an ex-post settlement of the conflict over the distribution of rents, according to the clientele game, implying a process of inflationary redistribution which requires the permanent manipulation of the monetary variable (through money creation). This type of management corresponds, in fact, to the clientelist method of resolving the distribution conflict.
- Restriction of competition through restrictive regulation of market access for factors of production and maintenance of administrative control of prices for a wide range of products and services. The regulatory role of prices is continually called into question. In reality, the scope of market exchange is a function of the availability of rents: the expansion of market exchange during the 1990s followed the drying up of rents during that period, which led to the abolition of the various subsidies that maintained administered prices. With the sustained recovery in oil prices since 1999, the State seems to have regained the financial resources to enable it, if not to reduce, at least to contain the extent of the market exchange sphere.[3]

This institutional architecture[4] is characterized by its permanence. Over almost four decades, it has undergone very few changes. With the exception of a few marginal changes in specific political contexts, the overall configuration has remained fundamentally the same since the 1970s. Despite the combined and recurring effects of oil shocks and counter-shocks, and of changes in the international economy, the institutional forms of the rentier system remain fundamentally unchanged, insofar as their concrete configurations constantly involve price controls, overvaluation of the currency, clientelist management of the public sector, control of access to the factors of production, and so on. Overall, this architecture is a perilous combination of childish liberalism on the one hand and sterile statism on the other. The liberalization that began in the wake of the crisis at the end of the 1980s ended up giving substance to a new mode of regulation, the essential consequence of which is to perpetuate and reinforce the rentier (extractivist) nature of the economic system. By favoring external openness in its various forms (customs dismantling, foreign direct investment (FDI), free trade agreements, overvaluation of the dinar, etc.), the new regulation sidelines the internal dimension of adjustment. In so doing, it creates the objective conditions for the perpetuation of the rentier regime and, at the same time, rules out the prospect of building a productive economy.

The institutional compromise expressed by the mode of regulation conveyed by the specific figures described earlier (which would benefit from greater detail) also contains several ambiguities that should be noted. The previous discussion does not account for the complementarities and hierarchies that link the various partial regulations. Very often, the relevance of a mode of regulation depends less on the content of the concrete configurations that each partial regulation assumes than on its ability to form a system (Bellal, 2022). Partial regulations are, in fact, the complementary elements of a combination, the effectiveness of which is measured in terms of the degree of achievement of the objectives, formal or informal, assigned by the community (the State) to economic regulation as a whole. It is therefore necessary to consider the mode of regulation as a set of rules that constitute a system with its own purpose. From this perspective, economic regulation in Algeria appears to be an instrumentalization of the economy to achieve political goals. This regulation has only served to consolidate the rentier basis of the national economy, a consolidation which takes various forms: maintenance of the crushing weight of the hydrocarbons sector in the structure of exports, GDP, the State budget, etc.; accelerated de-industrialization of the country, which for the moment nothing seems able to stop; an explosion in imports, and the ultimate consequence, a worsening of unemployment and social inequalities, phenomena which are currently taking on proportions seriously threatening the fragile internal cohesion.

There are many ambiguities. To mention only the most important, we should say, first, that the minor and auxiliary status of the wage relationship in the economic reproduction of society as a whole is based more on external rent than on work (or productive effort). In fact, the wage relationship, which is a central institution in market economies, occupies only a secondary place in Algeria; moreover, in a fragmented configuration. It is not at the center of overall economic regulation. This seems to be dominated by the way in which the national economy is integrated internationally (through the variable of oil revenues) and by the State (through the Budget). Second, the persistence of incompatibility between partial regulations deprives the State's economic policy (and therefore the country's) of the coherence that would have given it the contours of a development project. In short, the State's economic practice lacks visibility and its economic project, if there is one, is, to use R. Boudjema's expression, devoid of the elements that would make it scientifically identifiable (Boudjema, 2012). Finally, a proven inability of the institutional arrangement in place to generate a dynamic of productive accumulation, as a consequence of the incompatibility of partial regulations. This inability stems from the fact that the institutional hierarchy remains marked by the State and international integration. In a rentier regime such as the one in place in Algeria, the basic rent has the capacity to "intoxicate," through institutional forms, the behavior of agents and actors in such a way that the latter are encouraged to seek to transform the opportunities that present themselves into places and forms of rent capture. Rent-seeking behavior is a result of the institutional environment. This is an idea that is widely shared today. Using an image, D. North writes that if the most profitable activity in an economy is piracy, we can expect agents and players to invest in the skills and knowledge that will make them better pirates (North, 2005). This seems to be the main difficulty facing productive activity in a rentier country like Algeria: how can we ensure that high returns are generated by production? In other words, what can be done to ensure players focus on production activities rather than speculative or service activities?

In addition to discouraging production and favoring imports and consumption, this specific configuration is therefore at the root of a system for capturing rents.

Does this mean, according to a widespread thesis, that the economic trajectory of the last three decades, which has led to the concentration of economic power in the hands of a privileged stratum, has resulted in the subordination of political power to the economic power of this same privileged stratum? According to this assertion, the concentration of economic power renders illusory any possibility of autonomizing political power from the emerging economic power.

The advent of the popular movement of 22 February and the politico-economic consequences that have flowed from it today provide a stinging rebuttal to this assertion. The politico-judicial treatment of the excesses attributed to the "oligarchs" and other politically prominent local capitalists clearly shows that economic power remains subject to the omnipresence of political power, and that the former can only develop and flourish with the blessing and support of the latter. Without the protection and support of political power, there is no economic power.

There is a reason the economy is effectively subservient to politics: emerging economic power is closely linked to rents held by the state. As a result, we can see that most large private groups (by sales or the number of employees) often operate in areas where proximity to political power is a key factor. This is particularly true of activities linked to imports, public works, and construction, and public facilities in general. And when this presence becomes apparent in the industrial sector, which is less frequent, it is often as a result of largesse granted in various forms: tax exemptions, easier access to credit, land, etc.

Political Autonomy and the Role of the Players Involved

The economic experience of recent years suggests that starting from the idea of the autonomy of politics in relation to economics is a more relevant way to understand the issues than the ones we just briefly identified. A historical analysis of the state's economic practices in Algeria shows that the state is a fairly autonomous body in terms of the institutional compromises it codifies. This autonomy does not, however, mean absolute independence: it is relative to the historical process of the differentiation of the two orders: the political order and the economic order (Théret, 1992).

The process of differentiation between the political and economic spheres is the work of actors whose actions are deployed in both fields, in different but not necessarily divergent ways, in terms of the respective consequences they have on the nature of the articulation between the political and economic spheres, and hence on the institutional dynamics at the root of the change (or blockage). Although identifying these actors is not easy for analyzing the dynamics of institutional change, in the specific context of Algeria, a certain number of actors can be readily identified through a Northian reading.

Thus, in the economic field, we distinguish:

- The public industrial and commercial sector, which functions more as a place for sharing oil revenues: public industrial and commercial companies are largely unstructured, and a large number of them are structurally loss-making.[5] If they manage to stay in business and finance their operating cycle, it is, as in the past, thanks to systematic recourse to financial support from the Treasury;[6]
- Private capital, which has a clear predilection for protected sectors.[7] It should also be pointed out that, in reality, most of the sector's turnover is generated by a small number of groups that thrive in the vicinity of political power, in "grey" areas, and under conditions that are far from those that characterize free competition;
- Foreign capital, or FDI. In addition to its small contribution, akin to a defection, foreign capital in Algeria, when deployed, is part of a clearly extractive logic in both senses of the term (Bellal, 2015). Indeed, its presence is mainly confined to hydrocarbons, telecommunications, public works, and construction. Industrial investment (excluding the mining sector) is modest, to say the least.

Overall, these players do not behave as centers of accumulation in an economy seeking dynamism and performance, but rather as centers of rent capture.

In the political arena, the following points can be made:

- At the forefront is a more or less small, homogeneous military hierarchy, whose ideological preferences are more clearly focused on limiting (economic and political) access than on opening it up.[8] The army is an integral part of the state and has played a decisive role in the country's political, strategic, and economic policies since independence. It is this military hierarchy that is at the helm of political and economic society via the State.
- A trade union technostructure, made up of the official trade union (the *Union Générale des Travailleurs Algériens* (UGTA)) and a plethora of supposedly autonomous trade unions. Politically or financially linked to the state, this technostructure is supposed to represent the wage-earning society as a whole. In reality, only public sector and civil service workers are formally represented and therefore relatively protected. In the private sector, this technostructure is totally absent. The blocking of trade union action has a number of perverse effects on the effectiveness of economic and social change.[9]
- A private "monetary bourgeoisie," linked to political networks, operating in import activities or in activities directly linked to public contracts (public works, services). The economic profile of the private bourgeoisie is limited to rent-seeking activities. The industrial profile is an exception.

- A technostructure of managers of public enterprises and the administration, linked organically and financially to the state. In recent years, this technostructure has served as a reservoir from which most of the civilian political staff assigned to run the State, or more precisely the State–Class, are drawn (Ouaissa, 2010; Elsenhans, 1982).

This summary typology of players has not fundamentally changed with the process of relative economic opening that has been underway since the end of the 1980s. However, the predominance index appears to have shifted slightly in favor of an increasingly assertive hegemony of the military hierarchy, due to the political crisis, the rise of private interests, and, above all, the weakening of the trade union technostructure. It is therefore clear that political deliberation takes place above all at the level of the military hierarchy. Consequently, if there is to be change, it is at this level that the impetus must be given. In an article with a very suggestive title, F. Ghilès had already emphasized the inability of the military hierarchy, during the 1990s, to define the contours of a new institutional compromise (Ghilès, 1998). The persistence of the status quo since the end of the 1990s is indicative of this inability to conceive of a substitute for what Lahouari Addi called, in *L'impasse du populisme*, the "global regulating tacit compromise," a compromise which characterized the economic trajectory of the 1970s and 1980s and on which the rentier model of accumulation was based (Addi, 1990).

Originally defined in these terms: relaxed discipline inside the factory—political control outside, the compromise in question seems to have been reduced, thanks to the extreme trade opening imposed by the structural adjustment of the 1990s, which removed the factory's raison d'être, to the second term.

The political control exercised over society has recently been accompanied by a narrowing of economic openness and a reintroduction of bureaucratic controls on economic activity. All these considerations lead us to emphasize the role of politics in economic and social change. The idea is that, over and above the diversity of national trajectories observed elsewhere, it is mainly in the dominant features specific to the state's history and its relationship with civil society that lies the source of the direction of the national economic trajectory since independence.

From this point of view, especially since the Structural Adjustment Plan (SAP) was launched in the 1990s, Algeria does not seem to have drawn up a real program for its economic development. It was only in the 1970s that it had a project, with the results we know. The absence of a plan explains why the opening up of trade to the world market has proceeded so smoothly, almost "naturally."

Paradoxical as it may seem, successful institutional transition in a rentier regime such as Algeria's, requires state intervention. The uncontrolled external liberalization over the last two decades has only made the country even more dependent on hydrocarbons. If it is to have any chance of ending this dependence, state intervention must, needless to say, take different forms from those it indulged in during the 1970s and 1980s. Bresser-Pereira, Brazil's former finance minister, refers to this as a new developmentalism, as opposed to the old developmentalism (Bresser-Pereira, 2009). While it is now accepted that the price system can only be controlled by obeying it, State intervention cannot be reduced to blind and naïve obedience to the laws of the market. To take just one example, it is clear that the question of the national currency's exchange rate requires, in the case of the rentier system of accumulation, a specific state intervention that must necessarily run counter to the prevailing liberal discourse.[10] The same applies to the management of the currency, the budget, and other areas of regulation, which must, in all cases, operate in accordance with the principle of complementarity that links partial regulations.[11]

But, beyond its formal or conjunctural expressions, the problem with the link between politics and the economy (in other words, between the State and society) is that it enshrines clientelism as a mode of political action in the economic sphere. In so doing, it removes from the scope of the State's economic action the objective of rehabilitating productive activity, which is the only way to ensure a lasting rise in the standard of living, in favor of a rationale based on the "political redistribution" of oil revenues.

Here, we find elements of the problem already formulated by L. Addi in *L'impasse du populisme* (Addi, 1990). Three decades later, it is easy to see that the terms of the problem remain essentially the same, although the mechanisms of redistribution have changed considerably in the meantime. The political redistribution of rents was to benefit, albeit unevenly, various social categories and groups likely to support the legitimacy of political power: the army, the revolutionary family, the judiciary, the upper echelons of the administration, etc., as well as all the categories that had invested the political framework with formal expression (parties, official unions, mass organizations, various associations).

On the other hand, the subjugation of economic society to political power also manifests itself in the fact that economic relations are often interwoven with political networks, rendering the very notion of competition meaningless. As a result, the economic performance of private enterprise depends more on its belonging to a clan and its clientelist relations with the political elite in power than on its productive efficiency. Under these conditions, the challenge of economic and social change would be to establish competitive economic relations that free the market sphere from any subordination to political hierarchies.

Economic activities and political networks may be intertwined to varying degrees, but, contrary to what is suggested by the classic debates between "liberals" and "statists," the question is not so much whether we need more or less government.

The real question concerns the nature of links between the State and the economy, between politics and economics: as long as the configuration of the private–public relationship is based on clientelist relations, the State will inevitably represent the ideal place for inefficiency and waste. From this point of view, the project of liberal reform in Algeria refers, in terms of the meaning to be given to it, to Europe's historical experience of the emergence of capitalism: instituting the competitive market by freeing individual entrepreneurs from the relations of dependence that bind them to politics. This liberation would go hand in hand with submission, not to individuals, be he the *Prince* of the moment, but to rules, those of competition, which would tend to force economic efficiency.

The Pre-Eminence of Populist Ideology

To understand the reasons for the institutional deadlock in Algeria, we need to look at the weight of ideological preferences in political deliberation. Ideology is at the root of the permanent institutional configuration described earlier. From this perspective, it should be noted that populism, as the dominant ideology, has always accompanied Algeria's development policy since independence. Having first fallen into crisis toward the end of the 1980s, to the point where many observers were predicting its imminent extinction, the populist ideology seems to have succeeded, thanks to the sustained recovery in hydrocarbon prices, in regaining ground for the long term.

Although populism is essentially a political ideology, it is in the economic sphere that its manifestations are, in Algeria, the most obvious and the most harmful. By refusing to arbitrate distribution conflicts in accordance with the laws inherent in the economic reproduction of any society, populist economic practice ends up establishing as a rule of conduct the negation of the conflict itself. The result of this permanent denial is an economic impasse whose gravity continues to be underestimated.

By denying political conflict and refusing to see society through the conflicting interests that run through and divide it, populist ideology continues to shape the state's economic policy, which also serves as the main source of legitimacy for the ruling political elite.

However, it should be noted that if populist ideology has left its mark on the entire economic and social trajectory of the country, a trajectory that can be summed up as an attempt to build an economy sheltered from and against the laws of the divisive market, it is undoubtedly because the country had sufficient resources to meet the costs that the denial of economic conflict inevitably generated. As long as oil revenues were available in sufficient quantities, the state saw no need to reform the way it conducted the country's economic affairs, and populist ideology continued to serve as a solid and exclusive foundation for development policy.

Fundamentally, populism wants to remove the market's role in regulating trade, because the market is seen as a source of exclusion and antagonism. Populism would like to abolish all prices so that people obey politics.

From this perspective, the 1986 crisis was a major event in the country's economic history. It inevitably led to the abandonment of systematic price controls and a series of painful adjustments that ran counter to the populist conception of the economy. The economic difficulties of the time soon put the entire political and ideological balance that had prevailed up to that point in question, leading some to see the adjustments that followed as a systemic break with the previous economic model. Although the period was, in many respects, highly fertile in terms of economic and social change, the official discourse was struggling to take on new contours in its formal expression. Populist ideology had undoubtedly lost ground, but its transcription into the economic debate still maintained the theme of safeguarding national economic independence against external threats. Throughout the 1990s, populism was in real trouble. But that was without accounting for the turnaround in the global oil and gas market, from which populism draws all its economic resources.

The intrusion of the market into social regulation has exacerbated the conflict between the various protagonists over the sharing of the economic surplus, in this case, rents, and has forced populist ideology into its ultimate entrenchments in symbolism and representation. But this conflict between the economy and populism is dynamic, and its outcome is uncertain. The experiment in reform attempted during the 1990s and the institutional immobility that succeeded it during the 2000s clearly indicate that populism has not been defeated as the pre-eminent political ideology. With the abundant resources that the country has reaped from oil, it seems that in recent years, this ideology has regained the financial means to continue to leave its mark on the economic activities of the state.

With the increased availability of financial resources from hydrocarbon exports, the State is inevitably led to reaffirm its congenital desire to restore its control over aspects of economic activity it considers a source of conflict or a threat to civil peace. The widespread practice of price subsidies, the systematic financial support for state-owned industrial enterprises (which are structurally loss-making and a veritable money sink for the community), the plethoric recruitment of civil servants, the unjustified and ill-considered public spending on equipment, and the maintenance of an overvalued exchange rate are all manifestations of this political will to shield society from divisive conflicts. In *L'impasse du populisme*, Lahouari Addi sums up the situation by referring to a political rejection of economic regulation.

Populist practices generate structural economic problems. The country is regularly called upon to face crises, the resolution of which is all the more painful as marginal adjustments often prove insufficient to deal with the multiple economic imbalances.

A few factors are enough to give an idea of the scale of the adjustments needed. We could mention the enormous imbalances which characterize the sphere of commercial exchange, the catastrophic (and emblematic, we would be tempted to add) situation which prevails in the industrial public sector,[12] as well as the eminently social role, through extremely costly over-recruitment, conferred on the Civil Service. It is in these areas in particular that the adjustment is proving the most difficult to implement.

Other elements can be added to those mentioned earlier, all of which illustrate that while populism is political in essence, it is in the economic sphere that it produces the most damaging effects on the country's economic future. In Algeria, the populist ideology seems to have found in the income from the export of hydrocarbons the resource that allows it to do as it pleases, and to establish a lasting hold over all aspects of social life in general, and the economy in particular. This undoubtedly explains why, since it emerged from the SAP of the 1990s, the country seems content to tread water in terms of economic and social policy.

In short, rents create the objective conditions that allow populism, the ideology that justifies their use, to have sufficient means to impose itself, thus "fossilizing" the social dynamic, and at the same time delaying the inevitable and necessary break with the rentier regime.

Conclusion

By way of conclusion, the foregoing considerations underscore the importance of political deliberation in shaping economic and social change. In the specific context of Algeria, the question of the political prerequisite for a fruitful institutional transition is justified as soon as we recognize a certain autonomy for politics, hence the conclusion that the State is in a position to play the role of promoter of a specific national mode of integration into the global economy. However, the exercise of political power must in turn be institutionalized, not necessarily in the sense of a "formal" or "morphological" democratization, which in our case would probably only reinforce the many and varied populist temptations, but above all in the sense of giving credibility to political action. The lack of credibility, which affects both the political institutions in charge of the country's affairs and the formal actions of the players, renders any political discourse advocating change futile and, more seriously, confers a purely formal character on the institutional compromises that are supposed to promote change.

Notes

1 It should be pointed out that the notion of a rentier regime is often used in quite different senses. One definition (Lanzarotti, 1992), based on Marx's sectional division, identifies the rentier regime as one in which the import of capital and technological goods (Section 1 goods) is financed by the export of primary products. Another definition would be to consider the rentier regime as one in which accumulation is financed by a transfer, in the form of Ricardian rents (mining, oil, agricultural, etc.), of external origin. In empirical terms, the rentier nature of the accumulation regime can be seen in the statistics relating to the resource structure of GDP, the share of external rents in state budget resources, and the structure of exports.
2 No doubt because of the external constraints facing the country at the time.
3 The State devotes considerable sums to direct or indirect subsidies, financed by the State budget in the form of social transfers. Targeted subsidies (housing, health, etc.) and general subsidies (price subsidies for basic products, food, energy, and water) account for a considerable proportion of State expenditure. By 2023, these transfers will account for roughly a quarter of GDP, or the equivalent of 5,000 billion dinars (35 billion dollars)!
4 We use the expression "institutional architecture" to emphasize the importance of taking account of the principles of hierarchy and complementarity which link the institutional forms in the dynamics of the mode of regulation. Similarly, the use of the expressions "institutional compromise" and "institutional arrangements," which refer to nothing other than the mode of regulation, emphasizes the conflictual nature of social relations and the diversity of modes of regulation, respectively.
5 According to statistics published in the press, out of around 1,000 public companies, 95% are in permanent deficit. We do not have reliable figures on the amount of these deficits. It should be pointed out that the industrial public-sector employs more than 600,000 people.
6 The government regularly writes off all or part of the debts of public companies.
7 The private sector, 90% of which is made up of micro-businesses, often family-owned, operates mainly in the agri-food, land transport, public works, and services sectors. This sectoral presence, which is not unrelated to the institutional configuration mentioned earlier, clearly shows that private capital is directed toward activities that are naturally not very open to foreign competition (the non-tradable goods sector, to use the terminology used in the famous Dutch disease theory) and where payback periods are very short.

8 In the words of Lahouari Addi, the Algerian army is driven by an "obsessive need for unity," an attitude he sees as inherited from the national movement (Addi, 1999).
9 In addition to over-protecting unionized workers (in the public sector, in particular), the blocking of union action has resulted in the development of strategies of collusion or connivance between the UGTA and the public authorities, the obvious result of which is the maintenance of the status quo; an increase in "illegal" strikes, often initiated by "non-approved" or "autonomous" unions; and violent action, in the form of riots, which have inevitably become a means of expression of last resort. The proliferation of "illegal" strikes reflects the lack of credibility of formal institutional compromises.
10 This is illustrated by the IMF's call in 2008 for a revaluation of the dinar.
11 By the principle of complementarity, we mean that each arrangement in one area of regulation is more or less reinforced in its existence and operation by other arrangements in other areas.
12 The recurrent rehabilitation of this sector only makes sense if it is in line with the populist-clientelist logic that drives state action, a logic according to which the existence of a public sector is only of interest if it is used as an instrument for distributing prebends to political clientele, a place for negating the capital–labor conflict and a window that serves as a place for the indirect distribution of rent, in the form of "salaries" and other benefits.

References

Addi, L. (1990). *L'impasse du populisme*. ENAL.
Addi, L. (1999). L'armée, la nation et l'État en Algérie. *Confluences Méditerranée*, *29*, 39–46.
Bellal, S. (2014). Rapport salarial et régulation économique en Algérie. *Revue Tiers Monde*, *217*, 199–215.
Bellal, S. (2015, June 24). L'investissement direct étranger en Algérie: La pompe à aspirer les ressources en devises du pays. *Le Soir d'Algérie*, 6.
Bellal, S. (2022). *Rente, populisme et question économique en Algérie: Réflexions sur un système en crise*. Editions El-Amel.
Boudjema, R. (2012). *Économie du développement de l'Algérie 1962–2010*. Dar Al-Khaldounia.
Boyer, R. (2002). Variété du capitalisme et théorie de la régulation. *L'Année de la régulation*, *6*, 125–194.
Bresser-Pereira, L. C. (2009). *Mondialisation et compétition: Pourquoi certains pays émergents réussissent et que d'autres non*. La Découverte.
Dahmani, A. (1999). *L'Algérie à l'épreuve: Économie politique des réformes 1980–1997*. Éditions Casbah.
Elsenhans, H. (1982). Capitalisme d'État ou société bureaucratique de développement. *Études internationales*, *13*(1), 3–22.
Ghilès, F. (1998). Does the army have an economic policy? Chronicle of twelve years of uncertain compromises. *Pouvoirs*, *86*, 85–106.
Lanzarotti, M. (1992). *La Corée du Sud: Une sortie du sous-développement*. Presses Universitaires de France.
North, D. C. (2005). *The process of economic development*. Éditions d'Organisation.
Ominami, C. (1986). *Le tiers-monde dans la crise*. La Découverte.
Ouaissa, R. (2010). *La classe-État algérienne 1962–2000: Une histoire du pouvoir algérien entre sous-développement, rente pétrolière et terrorisme*. Publisud.
Théret, B. (1992). *Régimes économiques de l'ordre politique: Esquisse d'une théorie régulationniste des limites de l'État*. Presses Universitaires de France.
Yachir, F. (1990). L'ajustement structurel dans le tiers-monde. *Cahiers du CREAD*, *21*, 15–41.

5 Resource Nationalism, Extractivism, and Protest in the Maghreb

Kressen Thyen

Introduction

Since the 2000s, Maghrebi societies have witnessed a stark rise in resource protests. These protests not only have an economic impact, with strikes and occupations regularly putting production on hold, but also exacerbate socio-spatial cleavages and political instability. The region-wide uprisings of 2010/2011 were triggered in Sidi Bouzid, a region in Tunisia heavily affected by agricultural extractivism, then spread into the mining areas before finally reaching the country's capital. Since then, resource protests have grown rather than decreased. This new politicization of the resource question is no exception to a worldwide trend, with protests at extraction sites becoming an everyday feature of global politics. At the same time, resource protests in the Maghreb are carried by ambiguous claims against the state, alternating narratives of rebellion against central power with that of nationalist resistance (Allal & Bennafla, 2011). Quite obviously, the protests are thus about more than opposing extraction or negotiating the economic and social benefits. They are indicative of a larger state–society conflict, decrying social exclusion, exploitation, and repression by the state and those who run it. What accounts for these particular dynamics? And what consequences does this have for resource politics in the region?

Based on a historical contextualization of current resource politics in the Maghreb, this chapter argues that these are strongly influenced by divergent, historically constituted understandings of resource sovereignty and, in extension, varying forms of resource nationalism. In the Maghreb, the timely coincidence between decolonization and the declaration of the international principle of Permanent Sovereignty over Natural Resources (hereafter "resource sovereignty") gave way to strong resource nationalism that would be constitutive in postcolonial state-making both in its political, economic, and cultural symbolic form.[1] While the discourse of resource nationalism is used by groups with strongly contrasting political agendas, it generally converges on the argument that the people, instead of foreign entities or corporations, should benefit from the resources within the territories of their respective nation-states (Koch & Perreault, 2018). Accordingly, the meaning and implementation of resource nationalist policies vary over space and time (Ostrowski, 2023). In the Maghreb, its emergence in the specific historical context of

DOI: 10.4324/9781003730750-5

decolonization gave way to a state-centric understanding of resource governance that has remained hegemonic to this day.

The central role acquired by the Maghreb states in resource extraction and management had important consequences for resource politics. As such, states not only gained control over the exploitation, redistribution, and allocation of key resources but also became directly responsible for managing the socio-environmental consequences and conflicts. This became a problem once the central appropriation of land and natural resources did not result in equal rights and welfare for all but facilitated the emergence of (semi-)rentier economies in which resource revenues were increasingly turned away from the lands generating them. State-led extractivism exacerbated tensions between the "losers" and the "winners" of the postcolonial development model. As a result, negatively affected parts of the population began to challenge resource nationalism in its state-centric understanding, engendering claims of "resource regionalism" (Mills & Alhashemi, 2018; Ghanem, 2021) or local "land sovereignty" (Salime, 2022). Understanding these narratives and representations in addition to the material dimensions of resource nationalism enables us to better capture the complex realities of resource politics and extractivism in the Maghreb. It also helps to deconstruct protesting communities as simple rent-seekers primarily interested in increasing their share of benefits. Indeed, their demands for access and control over resources are intrinsically linked to claims for equal citizen rights and social justice in centralized and divisive states (Mills & Alhashemi, 2018).

Empirically, I will draw on paradigmatic examples from Algeria, Morocco, and Tunisia. Although their economies and respective degrees of resource nationalization vary, the three countries share several commonalities regarding their development models and resulting socio-spatial cleavages. The empirical analysis is based on a thorough reading of the literature and newspaper articles in French and Arabic, completed by informed conversations with researchers and activists during research stays in Tunisia (October—November 2022; April—May 2023) and Morocco (November—December 2023). The remainder of the chapter will proceed as follows: the next section outlines the historical context to understand the linkages between the moral principle of resource sovereignty, resource nationalism, and extractivism in the Maghreb. I will then present the two main forms of resource conflicts emerging from this linkage. Finally, the conclusion considers broader theoretical and practical implications.

From the Principle of Resource Sovereignty to the Extractivist State

To understand the specificities of resource politics in the Maghreb, it is important to recall the centrality of resource sovereignty and its translation into resource nationalism in the debates accompanying decolonization. The combination of national sovereignty and resources was widely considered key to liberating the newly independent states from their economic dependence on colonial powers and bringing welfare to their impoverished populations (e.g., Khoday, 2013). In this context, emergent discourses of resource nationalism merged notions of sovereignty, the state, and territory, as well as national identity, citizenship rights, collective welfare, and the value of natural resources in achieving these aims. In 1962, the UN General Assembly Resolution 1803 elevated resource sovereignty to a moral principle, allowing governments to expropriate foreign investors' assets for public benefit and in exchange for "adequate compensation" (UN, 1962). This timely coincidence between political and resource sovereignty advanced a state-centric understanding of resource governance throughout the Maghreb, irrespective of political agenda and ideological inspiration. All governments—whether monarchist as in Morocco or socialist-inspired as in Algeria and Tunisia—nationalized crucial natural resources, including agricultural land, hydrocarbons, and mineral reserves. With this, they aimed to end siphoning off local resources to benefit colonial metropoles and, instead, to use them for national development and their impoverished populations' well-being.

Resource nationalization was thus a direct reaction to colonial economic policy, which rested on two pillars: the development of export-oriented agriculture and the exploitation and export of mineral resources (Saul, 2016). Geared to the provision of goods to the colonial metropolis, this predominantly privatized export strategy was dominated by French investors, settlers, and national elites who appropriated the economic benefits for themselves. It was supported by the colonies' economic-administrative division into economically "useful" and "useless" regions. Hosting important settler communities, the former benefitted from a disproportionate share of investment and infrastructure as well as colonial tax systems that diverted fiscal resources away from local investments toward capital regions. Resource discoveries in "useless" regions engendered the emergence of geographical enclaves of economic development, accompanied by an influx of foreign staff, goods, and services with limited impacts on the surrounding economy. This economic dualism was mirrored in a twofold political administration, with the "useful" areas subject to civilian management and the "useless" areas declared Berber land, zones of military supervision (Rousseau & Harroud, 2021). The politically enforced redistribution of colonial state resources from the rural, interior regions to the wealthy, coastal cities produced significant socioeconomic cleavages and important politico-spatial inequality best summarized in Mamdani's (1996) distinction between "citizens" and "subjects."

Before this background, discourses of resource nationalism and the right to development strongly resonated in the independence movements, which heavily relied on the impoverished rural populations as their popular base (Henry, 2010). Consequently, all postcolonial governments, irrespective of their political orientation, elevated the principle of resource sovereignty to a program. This included land reform, as much of the most valuable land had been appropriated by French settlers. Starting in Algeria in 1962, Morocco in 1963, and Tunisia in 1964 (El Nour, 2021), all states expropriated or enforced the sale of settler farms to return land to national hands. In Algeria and Tunisia, the nationalization of large agricultural holdings was coupled with collectivization and resettlement policies, though in Tunisia, the latter was quickly abandoned due to massive resistance from peasants and landed elites alike. In Morocco, where the emerging nation-state was less monolithic, the *makhzen* (the institutions of government associated with the King) enjoyed relative autonomy and selectively procured settler property to distribute it among strategic clients. Accordingly, the state took over a much smaller share of French properties, while the King became the monarchy's largest landowner. Regardless of these different trajectories, all governments gradually side-lined the agrarian issue, instead focusing on agricultural modernization according to the interests of landed notables, rural entrepreneurs, and new urban and rural elites.

The main focus of resource nationalization quickly shifted to key mineral and hydrocarbon resources, reflecting their strategic economic and political importance. This included the nationalization of phosphate mines in Tunisia in 1961 and oil fields in Algeria in 1971 (Naylor, 2000; Ghilès & Woertz, 2018). In Morocco, where the colonial state had nationalized all phosphate reserves in 1920 to end the rush for concessions and guarantee French supremacy, ownership passed from the colonial to the Moroccan state (Avermaete, 2012). Other industrial properties were nationalized after 1973, whereby the proceeds went mainly to royal holdings and various groups of private entrepreneurs. Despite the varying extent to which hydrocarbon and mineral reserves passed into state ownership, the aim of their centralized appropriation and redistribution remained the same: withdrawing the resulting revenues from foreign investors and using them for national development instead. As such, the newly independent states promised to use large parts of the rents generated through the export of hydrocarbons and minerals to diversify their respective economies and to deliver on their welfare promises. Especially Algeria and Tunisia, where socialist orientation coincided with a rise in international oil prices, witnessed an impressive expansion of public infrastructure, education, and health services.

However, this post-independence development model soon reached its limits and did not overcome the structural heterogeneity and rent dependency of Maghrebi economies and societies. With the fall of resource revenues, states became increasingly dependent on foreign lending and external grants to fulfil their economic and welfare promises. This ultimately prevented a widening of the ruling elites' social base, who developed a preferential treatment policy for strategic clientele and support groups. Instead of fully breaking with colonial economic policy, as initially intended, the highly centralized governments continued to favor spatially biased development policies capitalizing on commercial export-oriented agriculture and the export of largely unprocessed minerals and hydrocarbons to increase export revenue, that is, rents. Over time, this rent dependency even strengthened the role of foreign capital in the region, as countries went through periodic economic crises due to their overreliance on and exposure to fluctuating world market prices. Only in exceptional cases did producing states determine these prices unilaterally, such as the OPEC after 1973. Eventually, the establishment of the World Trade Organization (WTO), liberalization of the international trade regime, and binding standards for export products effectively limited the postcolonial states' recently won resource sovereignty (Feichtner, 2016).

These economic dynamics were accompanied by domestic changes that translated global economic inequalities into local ones. After the failure of import-substitution economic models in the 1970s, all governments swung to a new economic-liberal and domestically authoritarian course, albeit at varying degrees and speeds. This shift, accompanied by growing state–business interdependencies (Hibou, 2008), entrenched and, in some cases, exacerbated the colonially induced politico-economic bias between rich (coastal) cities and marginalized interior regions (Mills & Alhashemi, 2018). Despite development-oriented discourse, policies were increasingly oriented away from the majority population's economic and social needs. Following the collapse of commodity prices and mounting debt amplified by the drying of foreign lending in the 1980s, this discrepancy was amplified as state structural adjustment programs called for (partially) privatizing cumbersome sectors and decreasing trade restrictions. The reforms not only reduced job opportunities in the extractive industry but also deprived many workers of the comparatively generous social security they had enjoyed as public-sector employees (Camau, 1997). The Tunisian state-owned company *Compagnie des Phosphates de Gafsa* (CPG), for example, employed only one-third as many workers in 2010 compared to the 1980s (Allal & Bennafla, 2011). This significantly reduced rent redistribution through state employment, particularly in the mining areas themselves.

Contrary to the welfare promises connected to the discourses of resource nationalism, these changes in the economic environment favored the concentration of national capital in the hands of a few entrepreneurs with close connections to state elites. They further allowed resource extraction and commercial agriculture to reopen to transnational investment. Combined with the technological and financial upgrading of extractive industries, this resulted in an ever-closer intertwining of state, corporate, national, and transnational interests. In Morocco, the lines became particularly blurred, as the *makhzen* and state institutions serve as the primary intermediaries for privately owned royal holdings. The formerly state-owned OCP became a joint stock company under the name OCP Group in 2008, developing into the world's largest phosphate producer boasting 12 subsidiaries on the African continent (OCPA, 2019) and several joint ventures with companies from Belgium, Germany, Spain, the United Emirates, and the United States (OCP, n.d.). In the 2010s, the fall of commodity prices ushered in further intensification and expansion of resource extraction to compensate for the loss of export earnings. In consequence, Maghreb states have today become driving actors in the expansion of transnational extractivist activities.

Rural populations have principally borne the costs of this shift toward extractivist economic models in the Maghreb, as they have been dispossessed or displaced to make way for agricultural modernization projects, expansion of conventional resource extraction, polluting processing industries, and, most recently, renewable energy installations. Despite the visible increase in socio-environmental crises, the development model of the independence era remains little challenged beyond grassroots mobilization—both internationally and nationally. State control over resources was confirmed and even reinforced in the post-2011 constitutions (Algeria 2016, Morocco 2011, Tunisia 2015 and 2022). The Algerian and Tunisian constitution accord ownership of natural resources to the people, explicitly mentioning the state as exercising this sovereignty in its name (Arts. 18–19 and Art. 13, respectively), while the Moroccan constitution, which confirms ultimate authority with the King, speaks more vaguely of "national natural resources" (Art. 35). Upholding the central(ized) state as the locus of resource nationalism rehearses long-standing power imbalances for the benefit of private corporation and state power.

Current Resource Conflicts in the Maghreb

The tension emerging from the expectations of resource nationalism and the reality of extractivist development in the Maghreb broadly produces two types of resource protests:

(1) Demonstrations, strikes, and sit-ins in hydrocarbon and mineral extraction sites. These protests center around claims for a specific resource and the revenues from its extraction. Carried by workers, unemployed, and the general population, they mainly focus on improving regional economic conditions, providing employment, enhancing public and social infrastructure, and mitigating environmental impacts.
(2) Rural protests and movements carried by smallholder farmers and Amazigh communities threatened by the loss of land and hydric resources. These protests are primarily carried by claims to a given territory as a whole. They combine demands for greater autonomy, local control over land and water, and entitlement to a share of revenues in the case of resource extraction.

While the two types of protests are carried by different and sometimes even conflicting agendas, that is, more versus less resource extraction, they have one thing in common: the coupling of demands for co-determination or local control over resources with demands for equal rights and social justice. As such, most protests explicitly express experiences of *hogra*, a term from the Maghrebi dialect of Arabic describing oppression, unequal treatment, and humiliation of the powerless by the powerful (Hannoum, 2020, p. 35). Doing so, they are very much reminiscent of the claims formulated by the postcolonial governments when they nationalized natural resources. However, whereas protests were then directed at colonial governments and corporations directing revenues away from the lands generating them, they are today directed at the states depriving parts of their population of locally generated resource revenues. Little surprisingly, it is thus not uncommon for protesters to draw parallels between colonial exploitation and current resource policies, hereby expressing frustration that for many people, independence did not result in tangible sovereignty in the sense of self-determination and co-determination (Allal & Bennafla, 2011; Belakhdar, 2015; Hamouchène, 2019). Protest demands and dynamics are very similar regardless of whether extraction sites are privately owned or (para-) state investments due to how state and private sectors blur their roles and lines of authority (Rignall, 2021).

Protests at Sites of Hydrocarbon and Mining Extraction

Because of their strategic economic and political importance, hydrocarbons and minerals have been at the center of Maghrebi resource politics. Clashes between protesters and state authorities are amplified by the potentially high financial losses for the state and because their extraction requires high social and economic coordination. As such, their dependence on a concentrated workforce on fixed production sites renders them particularly vulnerable to strikes and production blockages (Mitchell, 2013). Protesters have used this to their advantage, organizing protracted sit-ins and occupations halting production to press for their demands in the form of employment, nationalizations, equal distribution of wealth, and accountability. However, the central states have resisted all calls for greater local control over resources, relying on a combination of concessions and repression instead.

In Algeria, conflicts around the exploitation of hydrocarbons and the distribution of benefits are particularly salient. This is due to their symbolic relevance to national identity and their economic significance. Algeria is among the largest energy-producing exporting countries in the world, providing the third largest amount of proven reserves of conventional crude oil in Africa and the 15th in the world. It also possesses the tenth-largest amount of proven gas reserves and the third-largest shale gas (Abada & Bouharkat, 2018). Between 2016 and 2021, the hydrocarbon sector accounted for 19% of GDP, 93% of product exports, and 38% of budget revenues (World Bank, n.d.). Yet the inhabitants of the Algerian Sahara, the region hosting the main deposits of raw material, are disproportionately affected by poverty.

In 2004, a delegation of representatives from several cities in the Sahara formulated a list of demands: the prioritization of residents in the allocation of jobs, a development program for the region controlled by elected representatives, and an end to the partial privatization of the state oil company Sonatrach. To underline their demands, the "Movement of the Sons of the South" organized several protests across the region. The Algerian authorities responded with harsh repression, provoking ever-stronger tensions. In 2013, the movement received nationwide attention when it organized a mass demonstration in Ouargla against *hogra,* unemployment, and social injustice (Belakhdar, 2015). The subsequent year, the protests gained an environmental dimension when the government announced plans to develop shale gas fields in In Salah in December 2014. Local populations feared the threat to the fossil groundwater reserves at the basis of oasis agriculture, and thus their very survival in the semi-arid region. Slogans accusing the state of putting their lives at risk spread through the region, including "Nature's ruthlessness is enough for us" and "Leave us alone, (but) don't kill us!" (Echorouk Online, 2015).

In 2019, the nationwide Hirak movement took up opposition to fracking when amendments to the Hydrocarbon Law allowed not only the exploitation of shale gas but also greater space for multinational companies. The Hirak movement accused the government of undermining national sovereignty by selling the country's resources to foreign interests, ultimately forcing long-term president Bouteflika out of office in 2020. While the new government took advantage of the COVID-19 pandemic to repress the Hirak movement, a renewed wave of protests emerged in the Sahara during the summer of 2021, when Sonatrach signed new cooperation agreements with transnational companies. The initially peaceful protests developed into violent riots after a leading activist was convicted of alleged incitement to terror. The government called in a national ombudsman to negotiate a solution with the protesters (Daoudi, 2021). Despite the mediation efforts, hydrocarbon protests in Algeria are increasingly accompanied by state repression on the one hand and militancy within the social movements on the other hand (Ghanem, 2021).

Hydrocarbon protests also occur in Tunisia, yet they are less disruptive to the economy than Algeria due to the country's limited oil production, which amounted to 1.5% of GDP in 2021 (World Bank, n.d.). Most platform operators are private transnational companies, with the state-owned *Entreprise Tunisienne d'Activités Pétrolières* (ETAP) holding 50% of the shares. However, contestation became more conflictual when the 2015 constitution introduced parliamentary oversight of resource extraction. Major protests erupted on the Island of Kerkennah, which had been affected by hydrocarbon extraction since the 1990s when a resident oil company stopped paying to a development fund to create local jobs (Feltrin, 2018). The protests amplified following an oil spill that threatened local fishermen's and their families' survival. The government sent the minister of the environment to the islands in person to prevent the conflict's escalation and radicalization (Robert, 2021). Around the same time, residents in the southern region of Tataouine started the *Finou el petrole?* (Where is the oil?) campaign, which accused private oil and gas companies of nepotism and concealing the true value of their extraction sites. Two years later, protesters occupied an oil facility in Kamour and demanded a fair distribution of revenues. In particular, they demanded reinvestment of 20% of profits in the region, a legally binding requirement for companies to create at least 4,500 jobs, one-time investments equivalent to 40 million euros in public and social infrastructure, a development fund, and the review and renegotiation of all concessions (Altarhoni, 2017). After three months of blockade, which resulted in significant economic losses, the Tunisian government declared all strategic oil extraction sites military zones. After military officers killed a protester, the government agreed to the protest movement's demands but eventually failed to fulfil them (McCarthy, 2022). In 2020, a new wave of protests and blockades emerged. It only ebbed off when transnational oil companies threatened to return their concessions and effectuated wage cuts (Meddeb, 2021).

In Morocco and Tunisia, protests are further common in the mining sector. While less lucrative than hydrocarbons, phosphate mining is particularly important for both countries due to the sheer size of their deposits and employment in the sector. Morocco has the world's largest phosphate deposits and ranks second behind China in production volume. Tunisia ranked fifth in production volume before 2011 but dropped to tenth place after protests led to production stoppages (Pistilli, 2022). In Morocco, the mining sector represents 10% of GDP, with 90% coming from phosphates. Phosphate production is monopolized by the OCP Group, which accounts for 20% of Morocco's exports. The largest non-phosphate producer is Managem, a private royal holding company Al Mada subsidiary. In

Tunisia, phosphate production and transformation are in the hands of the CPG and the adjoined *Groupe Chimique Tunisian* (GCT). It presently accounts for 4% of GDP and 10% of export revenue. Despite the weight of the mining sector in both countries, mining generates only limited wealth for local populations while its socio-environmental costs are particularly high. People living in mining regions are disproportionately affected by health problems. The industry's high water consumption and pollution obstruct alternative income sources such as farming and fishing, especially since the conversion from underground to surface mining in the 1990s (Hibou, 2015).

In Tunisia, the Gafsa Uprisings between 2008 and 2009 initiated a wave of major phosphate protests in the countries. They erupted as spontaneous protests over allegations of corrupt hiring practices, then grew into veritable upheavals. Surprised by the protests' ferocity, the police sealed off the communities involved in a quasi-state of siege for six months (Chouikha & Gobe, 2009). The hopes for political and economic change raised by the 2010/2011 "revolution" increased the willingness to protest, motivating regular sit-ins and occupations of mines and factories in the region. The mines in Oum Laarayes and Redeyef were at a standstill for almost half a year, affecting phosphate production to such an extent that the raw material had to be temporarily imported (Blaise, 2020a). To pacify the protests and resume production in economically difficult times, the Tunisian government relied on long-established co-optation strategies in rentier economies. It hired thousands of young unemployed people in fictitious positions, that is, without concrete work tasks. The state-owned CPG alone created 8,000 such jobs, employing an estimated 13,500 workers in 2018 without economic justification (Boumiza, 2018). In Gabès, once a unique coastal oasis and now one of the most polluted cities in the country due to the construction of a phosphate processing plant. According to official reports, CPG pumps up to 14,000 tons of phosphogypsum per day into the Gulf of Gabès (Arab News, 2017). The pollution has led to protests not only by the city's population but also by farmers and fishermen from the surrounding countryside who have been demanding compensation for contaminated and, therefore, unsellable products for over 30 years (Blaise, 2020b; Robert, 2021). However, given their limited potential for disruption, the government has been much less reactive to their demands and fluctuated between ignorance and repression.

A similar dynamic can be observed in Morocco. Khouribga, where the country's largest phosphate mine is located, became the stronghold of protests against the OCP Group after 2011 (Bogaert, 2015). Since then, initially, peaceful demonstrations by mainly young unemployed people have repeatedly turned into violent riots and blockades of the central freight railroad lines. As in Tunisia, the government has to this day reacted with a mixture of repression and the creation of (partly fictitious) jobs. It created OCP Skills, the most comprehensive recruitment program in Morocco's history (Harroud, 2020). As in Algeria and Tunisia, anti-pollution mobilizations have also gained in traction. In Safi, the site of a processing phosphate factory, recurring chemical spills have caused significant environmental damage. This has serious consequences for agricultural activities, including fishing. Moreover, the local population suffers from high levels of cancer, kidney failure, and bone disease (White, 2015). In 2014, particularly fierce protests broke out when the government announced the construction of an additional thermal power plant in the city's surroundings. Despite resistance, the plant was completed in 2018 (Bouraque, 2014). In all Maghrebi countries, however, the impact of anti-pollution protests has been limited to this day as governments repeatedly ignore environmental studies. Instead, hydrocarbon extraction and phosphate mining are further expanded, not least to compensate for the economic crisis that followed the COVID-19 pandemic and the Russian–Ukrainian war.

Rural Protest Movements

A second type of resource protest has emerged in rural communities over the effective access to, use of, and control over land and water resources. While some experiences and demands are similar to the protests carried by workers and unemployed at hydrocarbon and mineral extraction sites, these protests are less about redistribution but retribution. They are mainly carried by groups of small-scale and landless farmers who see themselves deprived of their territories, source of livelihoods, and socio-cultural identity. These protests often carry an ethnic component, as the affected communities identify as Amazigh. While some protests emerge as a direct response to past and current processes of dispossession, others contest disproportionately high levels of water consumption by the mining industry and export agriculture, which significantly contribute to declining groundwater levels, salination or pollution, and failures of drinking water supplies (Mayaux & Rousseau, 2021).

The most radical form of land protest of the past decades has emerged in Tunisia. The protests are reminiscent of the agrarian question as it posed itself in the immediate postcolonial period and its subsequent abandonment by the Tunisian state privileging industrial and capital-intensive agriculture (Ayeb & Bush, 2019). With the 2010/2011 "revolution," many rural communities gathered hope to recuperate farmland that had been expropriated from their relatives during the colonial period and nationalized after independence. Over a few weeks, smallholders occupied more than 70,000 hectares of state-owned land, some of which were leased to private investors at favorable prices (Elloumi, 2013). These protests were justified with narratives of a historical right to the land and references to experiences of oppression by colonial power and the nation-state (Gana & Taleb, 2019). While individual families carried out most occupations, several collective actions lasted from a few days to several years. In one case, the oasis of Jemna in southern Tunisia, the community succeeded in maintaining an occupied date farm to this day due to specific circumstantial factors (Kerrou, 2021). While initially little successful, the land occupations formed the basis for the emergence of a smallholder movement carried by more local understandings of land sovereignty. To appease rural discontent and "correct" the course of Tunisia's "revolution," President Kais Saied issued a decree creating so-called *sociétés communautaires* in 2022.[2] These enterprises, comprised at least 50 individuals from one community, can access state land or commons managed by the state. While superficially acknowledging historical claims to territories, the decree confirms state control over land and resources as ownership remains with the state and the enterprises are subject to government control.

In Morocco, land protests have taken a different dynamic, as the King—not the state—is the kingdom's largest landowner. Further, in the absence of collectivization, collective land use remained much more widespread than in the neighboring countries. In this context, current land protests primarily respond to the privatization and re-allocation of communal land for agricultural, industrial, or urban development. In the past 20 years, the largest share was phosphate exploitation, followed by real-estate investments and large-scale commercial agriculture (Mahdi, 2018). One of the most visible protests occurred between 2009 and 2021 when families from the Guich Oudaya tribe were evicted from their land to make way for a real-estate project close to the capital city of Rabat. Approximately a hundred families resisted and remained on their land for almost five years following the evacuation order. In 2014, state authorities went in with bulldozers, tearing down their houses. The people did still not leave but built a camp made of tents and barracks on the lands, which was ultimately cleared by police forces in 2021. In the *same period*, the Soulaliyate women's struggle claiming equal shares and rights when their land was privatized or divided grew from grassroots into a nationwide protest movement against land dispossession. Since 2018, the Amazigh Akal (land) movement has been self-asserting the right to land, with protestors demanding that the state repeal all laws dating back to the colonial period that authorize expropriation on grounds of public interest and to subject future laws on pastoral management to collective consultation.

Moreover, rural protests increasingly combine territory and resource use issues with demands for equal rights and social justice. Here, the protest of the agro-pastoral population in Imider, Bouazzer, and Bleida is emblematic. It is directed against Managem, the operator of Africa's largest silver mine. While generating no significant wealth for the local population, the mine's water wells have drained the traditional irrigation system, and the chemicals used to extract the silver contaminate the surrounding soils (Bouhmouch & Bailey, 2015). In a sit-in that lasted almost ten years, the population of Imider initially demanded reparations for environmental damage, scholarships for study purposes, an improvement in educational opportunities, and a fair share of the profits generated by silver mining. As the protests developed and spread to other mining sites, local sovereignty claims increasingly took on an ethnic component, fueled by narratives of centuries of oppression of the Amazigh through colonialism, Arabization, and central government (El Khalaoui & Bogaert, 2019). Similar dynamics were visible in connection to the prestigious, semi-governmental Noor solar power plant in Ait Oukrour, built on formerly collective land and co-financed by transnational investors. Here, local residents engaged in demonstrations and hunger strikes against insufficient compensation, increased water stress, and local impoverishment (Rignall, 2021). While the protests did not successfully challenge long-established power imbalances, governments find it increasingly difficult to ignore increasing Amazigh mobilization and self-assertion.

To complete, in all countries, rural protests emerge in response to declining access to water for drinking and irrigation. In Zagora, a Moroccan town near the Algerian desert, inhabitants have been mobilizing in so-called thirst protests. The reason for the water shortage in the semi-arid region is the cultivation of watermelons for the European market, which takes up almost all of the water reserves. It hereby directly threatens the survival of the local population (Bossenbroek et al., 2023). In the Algerian Tin-Zaouatine, citizens protested the erection of a fence prohibiting them from accessing the local river. The protests took a violent turn when a protester allegedly died after being shot by Army forces (Ait El Kaid, 2021). Water stress is also a major issue in Tunisia, where entire swaths of formerly agricultural land have become worthless due to salination and lack of water for irrigation.[3] Moreover, public water supplies in rural areas are often interrupted for weeks. Yet governments have consequently denied the impact of mining and commercial agriculture on declining water reservoirs and groundwater levels, pointing to draught and problems of local water mismanagement as a primary cause.

Conclusion

The intensification of resource protests in the Maghreb reveals what resource nationalism failed to achieve: dissolving the hierarchy between exploiters and exploited and bringing prosperity to the postcolonial societies. Narratives of *hogra*, social, and ethnic oppression illustrate the post-independence development models' inability to sustainably improve the living conditions in rural areas and sites of resource extraction. By privileging the coastal urban centers, state-centered resource policies reproduced and sometimes even reinforced colonially induced socio-spatial inequalities. Moreover, instead of protecting their populations from transnational extractive business, states themselves turned into central actors of extractivism, including its inherent violence against territories and populations. As a result, what began as resistance against colonial exploitation has today turned into state–society conflicts.

While the Maghreb displays some similarities to other world regions regarding the socioeconomic consequences of extractivism, narratives, representations, and dynamics of resource protests diverge. This is principally due to the state's dominant role in resource extraction and redistribution. As such, it is much more difficult to develop claims for local control over resources in contexts where a state-centric understanding of resource nationalism prevails. While local demands for social justice and local or regional development are generally perceived as legitimate, communities' historically founded claims to territories and the resources they entail are quickly perceived as undermining national cohesion. Indeed, local resource-related demands are perceived as legitimate only as long as they are reconcilable with the "common good" as defined by the state. In other words, protesting resource extraction and protesting the state are only divided by a narrow line.

While this poses a serious problem for communities involved in the fight for co-determination over resources, equal rights, and the protection of nature, it also creates a dilemma for the states themselves. Their external and internal dependence on economic rents, derived from state monopolies over crucial resources and the concentration of political power, seriously limits their capacity to diversify their economies and reel back on the extractivist development increasingly destructive to their societies. While rents could be distributed more equitably, this is ultimately limited by the transnational dimension of extractivism. Global North countries largely benefit from resource extraction, yet the extracting state carries the costs of securing the investments and managing the socioecological consequences. As world market prices decrease, so do their repertoires of action vis-à-vis protesting populations. Irrespective of the form of government, responses fluctuate between buying peace where the pressure becomes untenable (including the creation of fictitious jobs and punctual investments) and outright repression. This renders them vulnerable from within, as they are forced to coerce increasing parts of their population to maintain their extractivist development models.

Ultimately, the analysis of resource protests in the Maghreb reveals a blind spot in the debates of the 1960s and the principle of resource sovereignty itself, namely the omission of the question of whether and to what extent national resource sovereignty would also lead to socially just redistribution, the protection of local livelihoods, and social recognition. The idea of resource sovereignty, as defined by the UN, primarily reflects the postcolonial state classes' desire to renegotiate their influence within the Global North-dominated world economy. Little thought was given to aspects such as internal democracy, local autonomy, or self-determination raised by affected communities. However, especially for rural populations, local control over resources constitutes an existential issue: being a citizen means little if the state can expropriate vital resource space for a self-defined "public benefit," or collective land can no longer be used to grow food because of environmental degradation or water shortages caused by extractivist "development" projects. The current re-politicization of resource use and ownership across the Maghreb is crucial for exposing this tension and initiating discussions over alternative development models.

Notes

1 The extent to which the independent states appropriated natural resources as well as their significance in state-making varied: the postcolonial Algerian nation-state was primarily legitimized by geographical weight and wealth of natural resources, whereas the Moroccan nation-state was built on its precolonial history and the monarchy's continuous existence (Stora, 2003). Yet national sovereignty over territory and resources played a significant role in the emerging national identities across the Maghreb.

2 Presidential decree n°15–2022 effective on 21.03.2022.

3 Interviews with an activist farmer and a local representative of the Tunisian Farmers' Union (SYNAGRI) in Kairouan, Tunisia, October 2022.

References

Abada, Z., & Bouharkat, M. (2018). Study of management strategy of energy resources in Algeria. *Energy Reports*, *4*, 1–7.

Ait El Kaid, H. (2021). Bottom-up protests in Morocco, Tunisia, and Algeria: A struggle against "inherited" socio-spatial inequalities. In Z. Szerényi, G. Salamin, & Z. Nemes (Eds.), *Environmental, social and economic sustainability in the light of the geopolitical challenges of our age*. Corvinus University of Budapest.

Allal, A., & Bennafla, K. (2011). Les mouvements protestataires de Gafsa (Tunisie) et Sidi Ifni (Maroc) de 2005 à 2009. *Revue Tiers Monde*, *HS*(5), 27–45.

Altarhoni, S. (2017, May). الكامور اعتصام: الرافضون لعرض الحكومة يعتصمون قرب محطة ضخ البترول [Sit-in in El Kamour: Those refusing the government's proposal are protesting near the oil pumping station]. *Tunesien.tn*. Retrieved March 2, 2023, from http://www.tunisien.tn/

Arab News. (2017, August). Tunisian beachside town fights industrial pollution. *Arab News*. Retrieved March 2, 2023, from https://www.arabnews.com/

Avermaete, T. (2012). Excavating the company town: Small Moroccan mining cities in European archives. In E. Godoli, D. Peyceré, & C. Piaton (Eds.), *Building beyond the Mediterranean: Studying the archives of European businesses (1860–1970)* (pp. 118–125). Publications de l'Institut national d'histoire de l'art.

Ayeb, H., & Bush, R. (2019). *Food insecurity and revolution in the Middle East and North Africa: Agrarian questions in Egypt and Tunisia*. Anthem Press.

Belakhdar, N. (2015). L'éveil du Sud' ou quand la contestation vient de la marge. *Politique Africaine*, *137*(1), 27–48.

Blaise, L. (2020a, February). Les habitants meurent à petit feu. En Tunisie, le phosphate pollue l'air de Gabès. *Le Monde*. Retrieved March 2, 2023, from https://www.lemonde.fr/

Blaise, L. (2020b, October). La Tunisie, autrefois leader dans le phosphate, doit désormais en importer. *Le Monde*. Retrieved March 2, 2023, from https://www.lemonde.fr/

Bogaert, K. (2015). The revolt of small towns: The meaning of Morocco's history and the geography of social protests. *Review of African Political Economy*, *42*(143), 124–140.

Bossenbroek, L., Ftouhi, H., Kadiri, Z., & Kuper, M. (2023). Watermelons in the desert in Morocco: Struggles around a groundwater commons-in-the-making. *Water Alternatives*, *16*(1), 87–107.

Bouhmouch, N., & Bailey, K. D. (2015, December). A Moroccan village's long fight for water rights. *Al Jazeera*. Retrieved March 2, 2023, from https://www.aljazeera.com/

Boumiza, K. (2018, February). Tunisie: 13.500 reçoivent rémunération sans travailler et 113 plaintes déposées. *Africa Manager*. Retrieved March 2, 2023, from https://africanmanager.com/

Bouraque, T. (2014, July). Safi, ville polluée, lutte pour sa survie écologique. *TelQuel*. Retrieved March 2, 2023, from https://telquel.ma/

Camau, M. (1997). D'une république à l'autre. *Maghreb–Machrek*, *157*(3), 3–16.

Chouikha, L., & Gobe, E. (2009). La Tunisie entre la "révolte du bassin minier de Gafsa" et l'échéance électorale de 2009. *L'Année du Maghreb*, *5*, 387–420.

Daoudi, A. (2021, July). الجمهورية وسيط مندوب: شباب مطالب على وافق تبون الرئيس بورقلة. ورقلة *Ennahar Online*. Retrieved March 2, 2023, from https://www.ennaharonline.com/

Echorouk Online. (2015, January). الحكومة تعجز عن تحويل الجنوب إلى دبي أو كاليفورنيا الجزائر. *Echorouk Online*. Retrieved March 2, 2023.

El Khalaoui, S., & Bogaert, K. (2019). Politiser le regard sur les marges: Le cas du mouvement "sur la voie 96" d'Imider. *L'Année du Maghreb*, *21*, 181–191.

El Nour, S. (2022). Towards a just agricultural transition in North Africa. *Transnational Institute*. Retrieved December 15, 2021, from https://longreads.tni.org/

Elloumi, M. (2013). Les terres domaniales en Tunisie. *Études rurales*, *192*, 43–60.

Feichtner, I. (2016). Der Kampf um Rohstoffe im Völkerrecht. *Verfassung und Recht in Übersee*, *49*(1), 3–15.

Feltrin, L. (2018). The struggles of precarious youth in Tunisia: The case of the Kerkennah movement. *Review of African Political Economy*, *45*(155), 44–63.

Gana, A., & Taleb, M. (2019). Mobilisations foncières en Tunisie: Révélateur des paradoxes de l'après "révolution". *Confluences Méditerranée*, *108*(1), 31–46.

Ghanem, D. (2021, March). Algeria's Achilles' heel? Resource regionalism in Ouargla. *Carnegie Middle East Center*. Retrieved February 2, 2023, from https://carnegie-mec.org/

Ghilès, F., & Woertz, E. (2018). Tunisian phosphates and the politics of the periphery. In H. Verhoeven (Ed.), *Environmental politics in the Middle East* (pp. 53–74). Oxford University Press.

Hamouchène, H. (2019, November). Extractivism and resistance in North Africa. *Transnational Institute*. Retrieved March 2, 2023.

Hannoum, A. (2020). *Living Tangier: Migration, race, and illegality in a Moroccan city*. University of Pennsylvania Press.

Harroud, T. (2020). "Sustainable" entrepreneurial urbanism in Morocco: What change(s) for mining cities? *Justice spatiale/Spatial Justice*, *15*, 1–23.

Henry, C. H. (2010). Political economies of the Maghreb. In D. Sorenson (Ed.), *Interpreting the Middle East* (pp. 185–212). Routledge.

Hibou, B. (2008). Nous ne prendrons jamais le maquis: Entrepreneurs et politique en Tunisie. *Politix*, *84*(4), 115–141.

Hibou, B. (2015). Le bassin minier de Gafsa en déshérence: Gouverner le mécontentement social en Tunisie. In I. Bono, B. Hibou, H. Meddeb, & M. Tozy (Eds.), *L'état d'injustice au Maghreb: Maroc et Tunisie* (pp. 301–377). Karthala.

Kerrou, M. (2021). *Jemna: L'oasis de la révolution*. Cérès éditions.

Khoday, K. (2013). The emerging South and the evolution of sovereignty over natural resources. In M. C. Bassiouni et al. (Eds.), *The global community yearbook of international law and jurisprudence* (pp. 41–56). Oxford University Press.

Koch, N., & Perreault, T. (2018). Resource nationalism. *Progress in Human Geography*, *43*(4), 611–631.

Mahdi, M. (2018). Les campagnes marocaines . . . ces marges convoitées. *Revue Marocaine des Sciences Politiques et Sociales*, *11*(XVI), 111–133.

Mamdani, M. (1996). *Citizen and subject: Contemporary Africa and the legacy of late colonialism*. Princeton University Press.

Mayaux, P. L., & Rousseau, M. (2021). Extracting the resource, extracting from the conflict. Regulating the overexploitation of mines and groundwater in Morocco. *Revue internationale de politique comparée*, *28*(3), 125–153.

McCarthy, R. (2022). Transgressive protest after a democratic transition: The Kamour campaign in Tunisia. *Social Movement Studies*, *21*(6), 798–815.

Meddeb, H. (2021, February). Life on the edge: How protests in Tataouine forced Tunis to back down. *Carnegie Middle East Center*. Retrieved March 2, 2023.

Mills, R., & Alhashemi, F. (2018, April). Resource regionalism in the Middle East and North Africa: Rich lands, neglected people. *Brookings Doha Center*. Retrieved June 6, 2023.

Mitchell, T. (2013). *Carbon democracy: Political power in the age of oil*. Verso.

Naylor, P. C. (2000). *France and Algeria: A history of decolonization and transformation*. University Press of Florida.

OCP. (n.d.). *Partners and operations*. Retrieved March 2, 2023, from https://www.ocpgroup.ma/

OCPA. (2019). *Presence: Africa is our field of action*. Retrieved March 2, 2023, from https://www.ocpafrica.com/

Ostrowski, W. (2023). The twilight of resource nationalism: From cyclicality to singularity? *Resources Policy*, *83*, 103599.

Pistilli, M. (2022). 10 top phosphate countries by production. *Investing News Network*. Retrieved March 2, 2023.

Rignall, K. (2021, December 9). What can an old mine tell us about a just energy transition? *Transnational Institute*. Retrieved March 2, 2023.

Robert, D. (2021). Contestations croisées des nuisances environnementales des industries et des injustices territoriales à Gabès et Kerkennah (Tunisie). *Justice Spatiale/Spatial Justice, 16.*

Rousseau, M., & Harroud, T. (2021). Du "Maroc inutile" au Maroc en déclin. In V. Béal, N. Cauchi-Duval, & M. Rousseau (Eds.), *Déclin urbain: La France dans une perspective internationale* (pp. 253–287). Éditions du Croquant.

Salime, Z. (2022). A gendered counter-archive: Mining and resistance in Morocco. *Development and Change*, *53*(5), 1035–1058.

Saul, S. (2016). *Intérêts économiques français et décolonisation de l'Afrique du Nord (1945–1962)*. Droz.

Stora, B. (2003). Algeria/Morocco: The passions of the past: Representations of the nation that unite and divide. *The Journal of North African Studies*, *8*(1), 14–34.

United Nations. (1962, December 14). *General Assembly Resolution 1803 (XVII): Permanent sovereignty over natural resources*. https://www.ohchr.org/

White, N. (2015, December). Toxic shadow: Phosphate miners in Morocco fear they pay a high price. *The Guardian*. Retrieved June 5, 2023.

World Bank. (n.d.). *World Bank open data*. Retrieved March 27, 2024, from https://data.worldbank.org/

6 Extractivism, Rents, and the Middle-Class Pivot: Perspectives From Algeria

Salim Chena

Introduction

This chapter defends the idea that the Algerian middle class played a fundamental role in the mass mobilization in Algeria between 2019 and 2020, and particularly in the expression of the democratic expectations of the *hirak*. These unprecedented, twice-weekly, nationwide demonstrations, which were peaceful if not festive, illustrating a historical reconciliation and a sense of civic identity, had a profound political significance (Desrues & Gobe, 2019; Bensaâd & Rahal, 2020; Kadri, 2020; Allal et al., 2021; Alenius Boserup, 2021; Willis, 2022; Hemchi, 2023). Five years later, an authoritarian restoration process has taken control of the political and public spheres. Among the possible explanations, the social class approach has been the most neglected. This chapter remedies this shortcoming in the political sociology of contemporary Algeria, where the focus remains on elites and the political regime (Ghanem, 2022; Serres, 2019, 2023). Among the elements supporting Algerian authoritarianism, whatever adjective is applied to it (competitive, military, electoral, autocratic, etc.), social fragmentation appears fundamental. This fragmentation is a result of the history and political economy of the Algerian system, which should nevertheless be seen in the context of the pre-independence period. Despite the exhaustion of the traditional resources of legitimization (history, income, integration), the politico-military elites were able to capitalize on the internal divisions within the movement, and the *hirak* did not succeed in bringing about the emergence of sufficiently strong and coherent alternative political elites and organizations (Dris-Aït Hamadouche, 2024, p. 29).

Class divisions within Algerian society contributed greatly to this failure. More specifically, the middle class is a pivotal social group for protest in a context of rentier authoritarianism. So while its mobilization in 2019 gave the movement its power to exert political pressure, its gradual fading after the summer of 2019 and the spring of 2020 was one of the factors that weakened it. This argument is based on a historical analysis of the political role of the middle class in Algeria since independence in 1962. The middle class has alternated between solid support for the power elite, in the sense of Charles Wright Mills (2000), when it adheres to the foundations of its legitimization and believes in its competence to ensure its interests; but when this adherence and belief crumble, and the elites can no longer

DOI: 10.4324/9781003730750-6

satisfy its social, economic, and cultural expectations, it takes up opposition and can constitute a tipping point in the existing political order. To explain this pendulum effect of the middle class, which we will illustrate by looking back historically at the stages of its formation and its transformations, we postulate the existence of a *rentier mentality*. This is essentially defined by an internalization of the idea of rent. This rentier mentality is a disposition to define oneself and to act politically in relation to the idea of rents, according to the perceived usefulness of participation for one's own development or the maintenance of one's social position (material and symbolic). The rentier mentality tends to transform political participation into a rent of allegiance granted, or withdrawn, for the benefit of, or against, the ruling elite, depending on the perception of its interests and of the (material) rent itself. The concept applies a rentier logic to citizenship. This way of reacting to events, which Theodor Geiger called a "mentality" (Linz, 2000, pp. 162–163), and which is also a "generational" historical trait in the sense of Karl Mannheim (1972), makes the political attitude of the middle class a determining factor in the mechanisms of contention or consolidation of power in a rentier authoritarian situation. This definition adds to the classic conception of the rentier mentality as a reversal of the relationship between profit and production, and between the state and the economy (Beblawi & Luciani, 1987): in the first case, rents become the condition for production (salaried labor, productive capital investment); in the second, rents are the basis for economic intervention by the state rather than the product of public action. These socially internalized economic arrangements contribute to bureaucratization, aversion to innovation and economic initiative, ultra-specialization, external dependence, massive but unproductive investment, and corruption (Yates, 2015, pp. 83–90). Our definition is distinctive in that it politicizes the rentier mentality by applying the reasoning of classical liberal political economy to the political sociology of participation.

Class dynamics in the study of extractivist rentier systems is the second axis of our reading of Algerian history and current affairs. It is important, however, to return to the notions of extractivism and class in order to clarify how they are intertwined. Extractivism refers to a "development model" that structures all areas of society's life and activities around a political economy that exports natural resources, generating rents on which social reproduction depends, and the appropriation of which is a central political issue (Warnecke-Berger & Ickler, 2024, p. 7). In this way, extractivism establishes a logic of dependence. Extractivism constitutes a "mode of accumulation" essential to the development of capitalism and, particularly in colonial and neocolonial contexts, has fuelled the dynamics of growth and concentration of wealth in the industrialized countries of the North, and constituted the Global South as a periphery in its economic, social, and political dimensions around imports and exports centered on the unequal exchange of nature (Acosta, 2013, pp. 62–63). Extractivism is a "mode of appropriation" of nature and natural resources that, on the one hand, has its own historicity in its impact on the development dynamics of societies and, on the other, has multiple dimensions (ecological, territorial, technological, social, legal, political) (Gudynas, 2018, pp. 62–63, 2019, pp. 392–393). Linking accumulation and appropriation makes it possible to consider the importance of class dynamics in both the domestic and international domination that extractivism engenders, and in the resistance that it can provoke, and in the limits that class divisions impose on these contestations (Veltmeyer & Petras, 2014, pp. 28–30).

The notion of social class has had varying fortunes since the emergence of post-industrial societies. The disappearance of social class has been a staple of liberal social science, from Alexis de Tocqueville's emphasis on the equalization of conditions, through Robert Nisbet and Henri Mendras, to Anthony Giddens and Ulrich Beck, while others proclaim its "return" (Chauvel, 2001). The very idea of social class dates back to Antiquity, while the justification of inequalities in wealth and status is found in most beliefs and spiritualities. These characterizations presuppose an organic and naturalistic conception of human societies (Nederman, 2005, pp. 359–360). The emergence of modern sociology, with Karl Marx and Max Weber, transformed the conception of social classes from a simple perception, objective or subjective, of social position to a political and historical perspective linking it, first, to the idea of exploitation from which the members of a class must emancipate themselves and, second, to that of social differentiation where status, power, and income intersect (Olin Wright, 2005, pp. 720–722), making the state and politics the determinant, framework, and product of class struggle (Nederman, 2005, p. 361). The intersection of the class, race, and gender approaches has given new impetus to thinking about inequalities: On the one hand, the working classes are not homogeneous because they are often divided along racial lines, and are therefore not naturally inclined to unite and act politically in concert for a shared purpose; on the other hand, the attitude of the middle classes can range from allying themselves with the dominant classes to preserve or increase their position, to challenging class domination and playing a leading role in revolutionary processes—particularly in a colonial context (Bonacich, 2000, pp. 321–322).

When the notions of extractivism, rent, and class are linked, it becomes possible to refine our understanding of postcolonial authoritarianism in a situation of dependence on the export of natural resources, without neglecting the socio-anthropological impact of this political economy. This chapter is therefore organized around three points, which form the basis of a critical theory of the politics of extractivism. To begin with, following Marnia Lazreg and René Gallissot, it is necessary to return to the impact of the colonial context on the formation of social classes in Algeria, which did not follow the ideal-typical pattern leading to the existence of a class consciousness, carried by organizations founded on the basis of class membership. With Saïd Chikhi, Abdelkader Yefsah, and Djilali Liabes, the emergence of a genuine middle class can be linked essentially to the processes of industrialization, urbanization, and bureaucratization of the late 1960s and early 1970s, which also marked a tempering of the Algerian revolutionary project. I conclude that the cohesion and reproduction of the ruling class, closely linked to the availability of financial resources derived from rents, constitute the triggering factor for the middle-class pivot in terms of its symbolic and material redistributive capacities, following Rachid Ouaissa's model: in a situation of crisis of financing, legitimization, and co-optation, the middle class is led to change its allegiance and break away from participation in the political system. As a result of the deep divisions caused by the neoliberal turn of the elite, the shift of the Algerian middle class during the mobilization of 2019 and 2020 was not accompanied by that of the regime or part of its elites and, contrary to several academic, militant, and official analyses, it was neither the product of bourgeois domination, nor the absence of proletarian consciousness, nor the loyalty of the peripheries that were the main cause.

Against Institutionalism, Economism, and Culturalism

The few analyses that have addressed the issue of social classes in the political sociology of the Algerian regime suffer from a lack of historical depth or an economistic or culturalist reductionism. Indeed, these approaches to class struggle in Algeria require a critical review in order to highlight their conceptual and empirical limitations. Thus, three different discourses around the 2019–2020 *hirak*, each with a specific class analysis, seek to explain its failure at the cost of a broad distortion of the theories and history of social classes.

First, Mohammed Hachemaoui defended the idea of a permanent counter-revolution, initiated within the national movement by the ascendancy gained by "the petty bourgeois and right wing of the MTLD," consecrated by the accession to the leadership of the FLN of Ramdane Abane in March 1955, with the support of the Stalinists of the PCA, the conservatives of the Association of Ulemas, and the liberal supporters of Ferhat Abbas (2020, p. 10). The latter would thus have marginalized, excluded, or physically eliminated "Messali and his proletarian comrades," who were in favor of social progress, democracy, and the alliance between Europeans and Algerians (Hachemaoui, 2020, pp. 8–9). The mobilizations of 2019 and 2020 are the ultimate manifestation of the "omnipotence" of the neoliberal Algerian bourgeoisie, whose hegemony is produced and defended by the actions, diversions, and manipulations of the security services (Hachemaoui, 2020, pp. 7, 36, 40–41, 51). Second, Hocine Belalloufi (2020a), based on a strict Marxist sociology, considers that the absence of political and theoretical leadership of the Algerian working class during the *hirak* explains its inability to form an alternative organization (union or party). The absence of a "class vision" is linked to the retreat of "class formations" (Belalloufi, 2020b). The importance assumed by the intellectual petty bourgeoisie in the formulation of civic and democratic demands is said to have overshadowed the social demands of disadvantaged social groups, which he calls the proletariat, ranging from industrial and agricultural workers to the unemployed and pensioners. Belalloufi thus defends a binary vision of the Algerian class struggle, which pits liberal and authoritarian political, military, administrative, and economic elites against a socialist and democratic people, but not sufficiently revolutionary in a narrow Marxist sense. Finally, the official sociology of the *hirak* is that it is a movement that has deviated into a nihilistic and harmful radicalism—a view supported by the writings of Kamel Daoud and the declarations of Abdelmajid Tebboune and Emmanuel Macron. Urban social groups have rejected politics—advocating a boycott of the presidential election in December 2020—in contrast to provincial and rural Algeria, which is attached to stability and conservatism, and even religious fundamentalism, which it is essential to contain through elections in order to defend modernist and liberal conceptions of society, while protecting Algeria from widespread disorder brought about by the youth of working-class neighborhoods who are in favor of "dégagisme."[1] Here, the rural world is seen as politically apathetic and culturally passive, and the urban fringes as "quasi-anarchist and without alternative."[2] Only the urban middle class, educated, and westernized—the three terms of the equation being indissociable in this logic—would be civic-minded and could defend a democratization in line with the Tocquevillian model.

There are three theoretical and historical objections to these analyses of class relations in Algeria. First of all, although capitalism emerged in Algeria under the Second Empire, it would be wrong to deduce from this the beginning of a process of class formation similar to that which took place in European societies, from the point of view of both intellectual and political construction. Thus, the state—whether colonial or postcolonial—cannot be the locus of class struggle—that is to say, its outcome—between the colonized and the colonizers, just as it cannot be the product of relations between the colonized in the process of emancipation. These analyses postulate an antagonistic historical relationship between communism and nationalism in the South: on the one hand, the struggle for independence marks the beginning of a class struggle to come rather than the continuation of an old process in the process of change (Gallissot, 1995 p. 83) and, on the other hand, it is more in the encounter between the political socialization of workers and the feeling of relegation and socio-cultural contempt that the national movement was formed (Sayad, 2004, pp. 96–97). Similarly, it is ethnocentric to apply to colonial and postcolonial Algerian society the definitions and characterizations of social classes as they have historically manifested themselves in industrialized and post-industrial countries. Since the historical process of class formation—in other words, the transition from the pre-capitalist class structure to colonial influence and then to the emergence of social classes in an economy undergoing urbanization and industrialization—did not take place under the same conditions, the class relations that run through it and that derive from it cannot be the subject of political or theoretical reasoning by analogy (plastering one class structure on another) or by homology (duplicating class relations from one place to another: interests, representations, mobilization). Finally, what these analyses have in common is that they presuppose political attitudes and behavior on the basis of class membership; they exhibit a deterministic, objectivist tendency, the consequence of which is to deny the agency of individual or collective actors. For, on the one hand, social groups on the periphery are not naturally allies of the ruling elite, either during colonization (MacMaster, 2020) or at the time of the *hirak* (Bensaâd, 2021), and on the other, disadvantaged urban social groups are predisposed neither to formal politicization and participation (McAllister, 2016) nor to protest, as shown by the profile of Ali Mécili's assassin in 1987 or the *baltagia* [bullies, bandits] of the 2011 mobilization, all of which were triggered by processes of delinquent social disaffiliation.

The Formation of Social Classes in a Colonial Context

The pivotal nature of intermediate social groups in Algerian political history stems from the social history of politics and the process of class formation prior to 1962. Not only did social differentiation exist before colonization and industrialization, but it also had political and economic implications. During the Ottoman period, power was based on the domination of a Turkish aristocracy, on which a local aristocracy depended, both of whom drew the resources they needed from the countryside. In this sense, Algeria is a feudal system (Lazreg, 2018, p. 34). However, it already possesses particular characteristics linked to foreign political and administrative domination, which combines public and private forms of ownership in which family and community membership play the role of identity determinants and where collective interests do not necessarily coincide with class position (Lazreg, 2018, pp. 30, 34; Gallissot, 2019, pp. 200–201). The reproduction of communities cannot therefore be reduced to economic reproduction, or, in other words, political relations do not correspond either naturally or entirely to economic relations (Gallissot, 2019, p. 203). Thus, the Algerian aristocracy, whether religious or dominated by the Turks, did not support foreign power, while its counterpart, administratively and fiscally linked to Turkish power, was loyal only out of self-interest. Consequently, the *kouloughlis* and Arab tribes assimilated to Ottoman power transferred their allegiance to the new French conquerors as soon as the Regency of Algiers fell (Gallissot, 1965, p. 348). The same was true of the urban commercial bourgeoisie, who derived their wealth and status from the extraction of value from the countryside, all the more easily because they had been discredited and marginalized by the Turkish elites and were already seeking the support of another political guardian during social or political conflicts (Gallissot, 1965, pp. 345, 349). This differentiation explains the rapid political collapse of Ottoman domination after the conquest, just as much as the military balance of power and the violence of the conquest explain its material defeat (Lazreg, 2018, pp. 34–36). The entanglement of networks and scales of production, power, and identity drove social relations and stabilized (or destabilized) the coalitions in place (Gallissot, 1978, pp. 49–54).

The "colonial barrier" (Gallissot, 2007, p. 205) made it impossible to mechanically transpose a European class logic to French Algeria. There was a "dividing line" (Gallissot, 2007, p. 21) that separated workers in similar positions in production, first on the basis of their community affiliation, which determined their administrative status as natives or colonists, and second on the basis of their location, between the colony and metropolitan France, where the native became a North African and at the same time a "fully French citizen" (Gallissot, 2007, p. 32). The colonial context was over-determining in the formation of Algerian social classes, with the result that the formation of the workers' movement, through colonial socialism, preceded that of the Algerian working class as such. The Algerian experience of the Popular Front government, the trade union victories, and the positions of the PCA, each preserving inequalities despite the existence of common mobilization, reflect this contradiction between the objective interests of the two components of the working class. It should be noted that the dynamic of reproducing socioeconomic inequalities according to status in the colonial hierarchy was also found among non-French European immigrants (Spaniards, Italians, Maltese, etc.), who lacked the social, intellectual, or economic resources of the French, while at the same time having greater opportunities for social advancement than the non-Muslim minorities born in Algeria (Van Leeuwen & Maas, 2022, p. 262). The "colonial frontier" seemed impassable, constituting a shifting "front line" between social and national struggles (Gallissot, 2007, p. 33).

It was only during the interwar period that Algerians became significantly involved in collective action. The consequences of the 1929 crisis fueled communal polarization within the workers' movement, while at the same time dampening hopes of upward mobility, as a growing mass of the population found itself proletarianized in the countryside and the towns (Lazreg, 1976, pp. 48–52). The crisis constituted "a general rehearsal for the confrontations that would lead to what is known as decolonization" (Gallissot, 1976, p. 702). The result was a political division within the various tendencies of the social movement, which reinforced the identity-based logic of differentiation. In the end, socialism found itself constrained by nationalism, both among White populations, where anti-colonialism was in the minority, and among the colonized, where the struggle for independence was waged through a communitarian populism (Gallissot, 2009). However, it was indeed through the intermediary of communist organizations, won over to anti-colonialism by ideology as much as by interest, that the political current of anti-colonialism took hold, first in emigration (Stora, 1992), before penetrating the colonized populations in the towns and then the *douars* (see the personal account of Bennoune, 1986, pp. 131–138). Conscription and the war, followed by school and work, were sites of Algerians' politicization, as they fueled the experience of domination while simultaneously socializing collective action, at a time when modern forms of politics (parties, unions, citizenship, etc.) were being disseminated.

The colonial system resembled a positional rent captured by the colonists, to which the reformists and assimilationists tried to gain access at the cost of a wide gap between demands for equality and acceptance of the colonizer's values; the radicals, by demanding independence, intended to rebuild this rent by nationalizing its legitimization and distribution. The idea of independence took hold as attempts at reform and electoral participation tactics failed, especially after the events of the Second World War (Rey-Goldzeiguer, 2006). Nevertheless, regardless of party affiliation or political orientation, politicization mainly affects the most educated, not only through school but also through militancy and scouting. Among the natives, only the motivations differ, not the profile (Lazreg, 1976, pp. 65–66; for a monograph, see, e.g., Guennoun, 2021, pp. 51–90). This gives the impression that it was an "ascendant lower middle class" that launched the insurrection of November 1954 (Von Sivers, 1979), while its common peasant origins, and more specifically within the groups that were no longer peasants, those destructured, excluded, or immobilized by colonialism, are obscured (Sayad, 2004, pp. 28–62, 88–109; MacMaster, 2020). The transclassism of the FLN was above all linked to the erasing of the opposition between the cities and the countryside (Meynier,

1995, pp. 166–167); this was reflected in the politico-military sphere by the offensive of the summer of 1955. The pre-eminence of the national over the social was made possible by the cultural reaffirmation shared, albeit to varying degrees and with varying components, by all the political players. The FLN's ideological victory was indeed its lack of an elaborate ideology beyond the revolutionary incantation of independence (Meynier, 2004).

The FLN was not a tool for promoting the middle class in the game of hierarchization, reordering, and conversion that was the struggle for the national state: the colonial barrier meant that while these intermediate Algerian strata did invest in the organization, they did so as natives dominated by the colonial system as a whole, and therefore as "Muslim nationals" (Gallissot, 2007, pp. 265–268). Admittedly, the integration of sociopolitical groups between 1955 and 1957 under the impetus of Ramdane Abane, and in particular that of the centralists of the PPA-MTLD, constituted a form of averaging of the FLN (Harbi, 2001, pp. 134–135). However, the latter, like the supporters of F. Abbas, remained for a long time the object of distrust, rejection, and resentment on the part of the base of rural extraction who ran the party and the army in the service of the Liberation (Colonna, 2012; Rahal, 2017): they were excluded from the official history, dominated by plebeian populism and the myth of unity, marking the authenticity of the revolutionary people (Leca, 1970).

The Emergence and Decline of an Algerian Middle Class

If the FLN was not the organ of a real middle class, but of young colonized people who had been demoted and despised, and who were experiencing both a political and a generational break, then it was not the organ of the rise of a real middle class either. In fact, the political and military crisis of the summer of 1962 brought to a close a process of internal struggle between the political and military bodies, and inside and outside, of the national revolutionary movement, which had begun with the rejection by some of the founders of the FLN and the military chiefs of the provisions adopted at the Soummam Congress in August 1956 (Mohand-Amer, 2023). Independence marked the victory of the external military staff, which completed its political domination with the military *coup d'état* of 19 June 1965. However, it was not sociologically homogeneous and still represented the de facto alliance between educated rural people, descendants of colonial administrative or military families, and disadvantaged groups (Arezki, 2018, pp. 33–62). At the same time, these soldiers are subject to divisions linked to their training, their political trajectories, and their combat commitments, which fuel conflicts and interpersonal solidarity, and the segmentation of the leadership group (Harbi, 2001, pp. 280–282; Arezki, 2018, pp. 63–103). They did not constitute the social class that would be at the helm of the country, since it would split up as events unfolded (crisis of 1962; coup d'état of 1965; abortive coup d'état of 1967; succession of 1978–1979; crisis of 1988–1992), while certain segments would consolidate their positions through promotion and restructuring between the 1970s and 1980s, within an institution whose main concern was cohesion and loyalty (Arezki, 2018, pp. 23–24).

The emergence of the Algerian middle class was the result of a combination of the construction of the national state following political independence, the appropriation of income from the export of hydrocarbons, and the protective tutelage of the army, which had the means of coercion and control at its disposal. Previously, the self-management experiment had already helped to consolidate political power and influence around administrative and party cadres (Clegg, 1971, p. 177), who were ultimately subordinate to the military after 1965 (Raptis, 1967, p. 90). The latter were only very partially drawn from the privileged section of the colonized populations and depended more on the phenomenon of bureaucratization and the generalization of the wage-earning sector—the main route serving upward social mobility strategies—than on that of liberal entrepreneurship, which would be the route favored by their children (Étienne, 1977). The army's involvement in politics can be likened to Samuel Huntington's model (1968), which can be seen during the War of Independence, in 1965 and in 1992: "In the world of oligarchy, the soldier is a radical; in the middle-class world, he is a participant and arbiter; as the mass society looms on the horizon, he becomes the conservative guardian of the existing order" (221).

The FLN's sole aim was independence. It was led by young people from the rural gentry, in contact with the working classes but familiar with the urban and French-speaking bourgeoisie, whose legitimacy was assessed and acknowledged on both sides of the social arc. The formation of a bourgeoisie among the *indigènes*, within the colonial mode of production, began in the interwar period in the land sector rather than the commercial sector (Étienne, 1977, pp. 232–233). It was then formed through reciprocal transactions (clientelism, kinship) with the state apparatus (army, administration) and established itself as the dominant class in the second half of the 1970s by taking advantage of the economic and ideological shortcomings and flaws of socialism (Yefsah, 1990, pp. 226–234). It relies on the expansion of the domestic market, takes advantage of public policies and captures the profits of socialized resources (Liabès, 2006), and gradually asserts itself when it is recognized by the state, as long as it does not express political demands (Mokrani, 2012, p. 55). It did not take power directly in 1962: the decisive factor was the formation of the independent state, from which a new intermediate social class emerged, moving from a petty bourgeoisie of neo-functionaries to a genuine state bourgeoisie as state and bureaucratic control of the national economy intensified (Yefsah, 1990, pp. 222–223). The nationalization of hydrocarbons provided the financial basis for the over-developed post-colonial bureaucratic-military state, to use Hamza Alavi's (1972) expression, by ensuring the conditions for its relative strategic autonomy—the two mainsprings of the Algerian "revolution." The politico-administrative decision-making power, from the public sector to the army as a last resort, serves as a mediator between social groups, with a view to maintaining a balance that is necessarily precarious and unstable due to external dependence.

The emergence of the state bourgeoisie as a new social class and its complementarity with the private bourgeoisie is central to the class functioning of independent Algeria (Lazreg, 1976, pp. 182–183; Étienne, 1977, p. 116; Yefsah,

1990, pp. 215–222). However, the success of the private bourgeoisie's enterprise of domination was not conclusively achieved until the 1980s, with the gradual liberalization of the economy enabling it to put the state under its control (Liabès, 2006, p. 46), but at the cost of merging with the components of the state apparatus. The importance of segmentarity (family, tribal, regional), which is often emphasized, is in fact combined with other elements to form concentric circles between forms of legitimacy and organizations that enable the reproduction, including openness and partial renewal, of the power elite (Ouaissa, 2010; Werenfels, 2007). The oil counter-shock of 1986, the intensification of corruption at all levels, and the policy of economic openness, which strengthened the neo-patrimonial state, marked the first brake on the rise of the Algerian middle class, made up of occupations created by industrialization (civil servants, employees, intermediate professions, small traders, upper echelons of workers). The dual context of a younger population, now with access to secondary education and increasingly university education, and increasing difficulties in integrating graduates, has made it difficult to reproduce the upward social dynamic. The symbolic and material resources of legitimacy are at odds with each other. So-called "historical" legitimacy is no longer able to produce consensus and loyalty as the neoliberal order reaches hegemony, fueling both infra- and supranational challenges to identity. The political, financial, and socio-cultural crisis of the national state (Quandt, 1998) undermined the political and economic transition process launched by the reformers, who were opposed by private entrepreneurs for fear of competition, by public administrators for rentier reasons, and by the military aristocracy, which considered all questions of sovereignty to be its exclusive domain (Ouchichi, 2011, pp. 157–168). The political sociology of the 1980s saw a shift from the opposition between the "top" and the "bottom" of the social ladder, whose framework of expression was the factory and the workplace, to that of the "inside" and the "outside," where the exclusion of networks of clientele engendered "a process of fragmentation and dissolution of the social bond" which manifested itself in the emergence of urban riots (Chikhi, 1992, p. 82).

The construction of spaces of marginality that are difficult to mobilize for concerted and coordinated political action, but which are fueled by resentment, encourages the violent drift of protest from the urban margins, beyond the reach of the world of work and its organizations (Chikhi, 1994, 2001). The mobilization of religion as a resource for protest reveals the contradictions of identity in the modernization of Algeria, where the priority given to industrialization after 1971, which consolidated the middle class, was achieved through the ideological use of Islam to rally the religious bourgeoisie to the regime and marginalize communist intellectuals (Lazreg, 1976, p. 135). The middle class, whose material base was disappearing, divided along cultural lines, around the place of religion in society and the state, and political lines, rejecting the old single party and dividing itself between the currents of political Islam, the old opposition parties, and a new plethora of parties lacking any significant social base.

After the revolts of 1988, the new bourgeoisie, born of the merger of the public, private, and military sectors, used a distorted notion of democracy to defend its position against the mobilization of the masses around opposition parties. After 1990, a new political game began between social groups. The political system's ability to co-opt ensures its reproduction as long as it has the financial resources and political formulas to manage the unstable balances that sustain it, including through liberalization, but this type of social stratification does not allow the construction of democratic parties and movements with a chance of becoming hegemonic (Bennoune & Hayef, 1986). The civil war (Martinez, 2000) marked the second stage in the destructuring of the Algerian middle class, with the destruction of firms and factories by the conflict, a birth deficit, emigration, and the restructuring of the economy under the influence of the International Monetary Fund from 1994, which destabilized the established public sectors and the nascent private sector.

This accentuated the dynamics of the previous decade. Politically, a new authoritarian consensus was created under the patronage of the army around domesticated political parties, giving the image of a diverse political offer, with a precarious return to legitimizing electoral procedures in 1997 and 1999, completing the militarization of the political system begun under Houari Boumediène (Mahiou, 2001; Benchikh, 2003). From a sociological point of view, the ruling class, with its connections in the economic, media, and political worlds, has become internationalized, becoming part of the transnational dominant class with its financial circuits, communications, and intellectual networks. It is both the comprador class, relaying globalized capitalism in Algeria, following a strategy of omnibalancing (David, 1991), and a leisure class as identified by Thorstein Veblen,[3] spreading ostentation and enrichment through commerce as a societal model of achievement. On the economic front, entrepreneurship has taken various forms, from retraining former civil servants to the compulsion to create one's own job (Madoui, 2008). Above all, the accumulation of capital is based on a polarity between the formal and the informal, which is as much the result of the (lack of) regulation of the rentier state as it is of the clientelization and corruption of society, to the point of founding a mode of governance which is itself a source of inequality and legitimacy (Benabdallah, 2018, p. 118). The informalization of the economy, a product of structural adjustment and a consequence of neoliberalism in a context of weak institutionalization, continues the process of primitive accumulation launched by colonization (Liabès, 1984). Social classes are being recomposed and polarized by the new dynamics of rent appropriation and distribution, which determine dominant economic attitudes (Henni, 1994). These processes implement the three dimensions of neoliberalism in ideology (free market, consumer society, etc.), governance (glorification of entrepreneurship, new public management, etc.), and public policy (privatization, deregulation, etc.) (Steger & Roy, 2010, pp. 11–15), but break down the dominated classes, who lose their organizational capacities as their material and moral foundations are dismantled.

Conclusion: The Hirak of Social Classes

After the *Rahma*, the Concord, then the Reconciliation, thanks to the flourishing hydrocarbon market of the first 15 years of the 21st century, the middle classes were reconstituted, but were always dependent on the State: Revalued public jobs, massive infrastructure investment programs, new import channels for consumer goods and equipment, public subsidies for entrepreneurship. . . . The "reconciliation between the two elites," modernists and Islamists, refounded rentier allegiance around the neoliberal consensus in favor of authoritarianism (Ouaissa, 2014). The Islamo-nationalist commercial bourgeoisie has been consolidated through its integration into political representation and has grown through its conversion to neoliberalism and corrupt and predatory practices (Haenni, 2005). The liberal urban elites have created their own separate spaces for socialization and participation through the cultural and media worlds, without ever reaching a critical mass, which explains the failure of the protests against Abdelaziz Bouteflika's third and fourth terms in office. However, the resumption of the birth rate has clogged up the job market and public services, fuelled the rural exodus and uncontrolled urbanization, and thus strengthened marginalized urban groups. Society has become more individualized, weakening traditional and family solidarity and even promoting selfishness. What is more, the world of work remains segmented between the public and private sectors that support the government, and the informal sector (trade, construction, etc.), which is fragmented and designed for subsistence (Bellache, 2013). Maldevelopment has thus reclaimed its rights, unbalancing and distorting Algerian society at the same time (Tortosa, 2019). Demands for dignity refer to these processes of de-institutionalization of the sociopolitical bond, symbolized by the image of an ailing head of state, represented by a picture frame revered by his supporters, and which set off the hirak.

The failure of the *hirak*, its refusal to organize and structure itself, its difficulty in bringing out a consensual political program, and the absence of an alternative political elite, can largely be explained by polarized class relations. The fall in the price of hydrocarbons that began in 2014 fueled the segmentation of the class-state (Ouaissa, 2010) and the participation of the new middle class in the movement. Its withdrawal from the *hirak* was based on a fear of downgrading, linked first to a prospect of instability illustrated by the dynamics of its regional area and fed by the slow progress of the opposition, and second (and above all) by the economic impact of the pandemic, and then of imported inflation following the Russo-Ukrainian conflict. Nevertheless, it did not give it a new vote of allegiance because of its lack of a political project that would ensure its position beyond the maintenance of rent-based governance (Martinez, 2024). The *hirak* opened the way to post-extractivist demands: the role of local communities (neighborhoods, villages) in the mobilization, environmental demands that go beyond the sharing of rents, the defense of popular economic sovereignty (reasoned management of public finances, maintenance of collective solidarity), signs of citizenship and civic-mindedness that cut across classes, genders and opinions, and criticism of old (France, United States) and new (Gulf countries, Turkey, China, Russia) imperialism are an embryonic move beyond progress perceived as mere accumulation (Acosta, 2017).

Notes

1 "Dégagisme" refers to "Dégage!" which is the anti-regime slogan chanted during the Arab Spring manifestations and literally meaning "Leave/get away!".
2 Kamel Daoud, "Coupable de porter atteinte au moral . . . du *hirak*?", Maghreb émergent, 28 January 2020.
3 The idea was first suggested by Aissa Kadri in an interview with Algerian daily newspaper *El Watan* (30 juin 2018).

References

Acosta, A. (2013). Extractivism and neoextractivism: Two sides of the same curse. In M. Lang & D. Mokrani (Eds.), *Beyond development: Alternative visions from Latin America* (pp. 61–86). Fundación Rosa Luxemburg; Transnational Institute.

Acosta, A. (2017). Post-extractivism: From discourse to practice—Reflections for action. *International Development Policy*, *9*, 77–101.

Alavi, H. (1972). The state in post-colonial societies: Pakistan and Bangladesh. *New Left Review*, *74*, 59–81.

Alenius Boserup, R. (Ed.). (2021). *La nouvelle Algérie*. *Pouvoirs* (No. 176).

Allal, A., Baamara, L., Dakhli, L., & Fabbiano, G. (Eds.). (2021). *Cheminements révolutionnaires: Un an de mobilisations en Algérie (2019–2020)*. CNRS Éditions.

Arezki, S. (2018). *De l'ALN à l'ANP: La construction de l'armée algérienne, 1954–1991*. Barzakh.

Beblawi, H., & Luciani, G. (Eds.). (1987). *The rentier state*. Croom Helm.

Belalloufi, H. (2020a). *Algeria 2019–2020: Le peuple insurgé. Entre réforme et révolution*. Éditions du Croquant.

Belalloufi, H. (2020b, March 14). Algérie: Situation et tâches du Hirak (Interview). *Contretemps*. https://www.contretemps.eu/algerie-entretien-belalloufi-bloc-alternatif/

Bellache, Y. (2013). Le secteur informel en Algérie: Approches, acteurs et déterminants. *Les Cahiers du CREAD*, *105–106*, 159–185.

Benabdallah, Y. (2018). État développementiste vs État rentier: Qu'en est-il en Algérie? *Naqd*, *36*, 75–119.

Benchikh, M. (2003). *Algérie: Un système politique militarisé*. L'Harmattan.

Bennoune, M. (1986). *El Akbia: Un siècle d'histoire algérienne, 1857–1975*. Office des Publications Universitaires.

Bennoune, M., & Hayef, I. (1986). Class structuration and economic development in the Arab world. *Journal of Asian and African Studies*, *21*(1–2), 44–65.

Bensaâd, A. (2021). Prélude au soulèvement citoyen du 22 février: La montée des contestations dans les espaces de loyauté du régime. *Hérodote*, *180*, 7–31.

Bensaâd, A., & Rahal, M. (Eds.). (2020). *Les débuts du Hirak en Algérie*. *Maghreb–Machrek* (No. 244–245).

Bonacich, E. (2000). Class and race. In E. F. Borgatta & R. J. V. Montgomery (Eds.), *Encyclopedia of sociology* (Vol. 1, 2nd ed., pp. 319–323). Macmillan Reference USA.

Chauvel, L. (2001). Le retour des classes sociales? *Revue de l'OFCE*, *79*, 315–359.

Chikhi, S. (1992). L'exclu, l'intellectuel et l'État. *Naqd*, *2*, 80–89.

Chikhi, S. (1994). Question ouvrière et rapports sociaux en Algérie. *Naqd*, *6*. (Pages not provided).

Chikhi, S. (2001). Algérie du soulèvement populaire d'octobre 1988 aux contestations sociales des travailleurs. *Naqd*, Hors-série (1), 69–103.

Clegg, I. (1971). *Worker's self-management in Algeria*. Monthly Review Press.

Colonna, F. (2012). Les années 1950. Les Centralistes et les autres: L'indépendance, le bonheur, et plus si possible. In A. Kadri & O. Siari Tengour (Eds.), *Générations engagées et mouvements nationaux: Le XXème siècle au Maghreb* (pp. 153–173). Les ouvrages du CRASC.

David, S. R. (1991). Explaining third world alignment. *World Politics*, *43*(2), 233–246.

Desrues, T., & Gobe, E. (Eds.). (2019). *Quand l'Algérie proteste. L'Année du Maghreb* (Vol. 21).

Dris-Aït Hamadouche, L. (2024). Comment le Hirak questionne-t-il la résilience du système politique algérien? In S. Chena, A. Benantar, & L. Dris-Aït Hamadouche (Eds.), *Le Hirak algérien: Retour sur un mouvement contestataire inédit* (pp. 11–30). L'Harmattan.

Étienne, B. (1977). *L'Algérie: Cultures et révolution*. Seuil.

Gallissot, R. (1965). Abd el-Kader et la nationalité algérienne: Interprétation de la chute de la Régence d'Alger et des premières résistances à la conquête française (1830–1839). *Revue historique*, *263*(2), 339–368.

Gallissot, R. (1976). Rapport coloniaux, rapports sociaux et impérialisme. *Revue Française d'Histoire d'Outre-Mer*, *63*(232–233), 693–707.

Gallissot, R. (1978). Au Maghreb: Sociétés segmentaires et violence politique. Critique des interprétations par la segmentarité: Rapports d'exploitation et reproduction de classe. *Cahiers de la Méditerranée*, Hors-série (3), 33–59.

Gallissot, R. (1995). Lutte des classes et État national social. *L'Homme et la société*, *117–118*, 81–89.

Gallissot, R. (2007). *Algérie colonisée, Algérie algérienne (1870–1962): La République française et les indigènes*. Barzakh.

Gallissot, R. (2009). Socialisme colonial, socialisme national des pays dominés: Le socialisme contraint par le nationalisme. *Le Mouvement social*, *174*, 75–96.

Gallissot, R. (2019). Sur l'Algérie précoloniale: Communauté et mode de production. In K. Lindner (Ed.), *Le dernier Marx* (pp. 195–210). L'Asymétrie.

Ghanem, D. (2022). *Understanding the persistence of competitive authoritarianism in Algeria*. Palgrave Macmillan.

Gudynas, E. (2018). Extractivisms: Tendencies and consequences. In R. Munck & R. Delgado Wise (Eds.), *Reframing Latin American development* (pp. 61–76). Routledge.

Gudynas, E. (2019). Development and nature: Modes of appropriation and Latin American extractivisms. In J. Cupples, M. Palomino-Schalscha, & M. Prieto (Eds.), *The Routledge handbook of Latin American development* (pp. 389–399). Routledge.

Guennoun, A. (2021). *La question kabyle dans le nationalisme algérien, 1949–1962*. Éditions du Croquant.

Hachemaoui, M. (2020). Algeria: From one revolution to the other? The metamorphosis of the state-regime complex. *Sociétés politiques comparées*, *51*. http://www.fasopo.org/sites/default/files/varia2_n51.pdf

Haenni, P. (2005). *L'islam de marché: L'autre révolution conservatrice*. Seuil.

Harbi, M. (2001). *Une vie debout: Mémoires politiques, 1945–1962*. Casbah Éditions.

Hemchi, M. (Ed.). (2023). *Hirak du 22 février 2019 en Algérie: Un seul soulèvement, plusieurs approches* (in Arabic). Arab Center for Research and Policy Studies.

Henni, A. (1994). Ajustement, économie parallèle et contre-société. *Naqd*, *7*, 50–57.

Huntington, S. P. (1968). *Political order in changing societies*. Yale University Press.

Kadri, A. (Ed.). (2020). *Algérie décennie 2010–2020: Aux origines du mouvement populaire du 22 février*. Éditions du Croquant.

Lazreg, M. (2018). *The emergence of classes in Algeria: A study of colonialism and socio-political change* (Original work published 1976). Routledge.

Leca, J. (1970). Idéologie et politique en Algérie. *Études*, *5*, 672–693.

Liabès, D. (1984). Entreprises, entrepreneurs et bourgeoisies d'industrie en Algérie: Quelques éléments pour une sociologie de l'entreprendre. *Les Cahiers du CREAD*, *1*, 97–113.

Liabès, D. (2006). Sur la bourgeoisie privée. In D. Djerbal & M. Benguerna (Eds.), *Djilali Liabès: La quête de la rigueur* (pp. 17–47). Casbah Éditions.

Linz, J. J. (2000). *Totalitarian and authoritarian regimes*. Lynne Rienner Publishers.

MacMaster, N. (2020). *War in the mountains: Peasant society and counterinsurgency in Algeria, 1918–1958*. Oxford University Press.

Madoui, M. (2008). Les nouvelles figures de l'entrepreneuriat en Algérie: Un essai de typologie. *Les Cahiers du CREAD, 85–86*, 45–58.

Mahiou, A. (2001). Les contraintes et incertitudes du système politique. In A. Mahiou & J.-R. Henry (Eds.), *Où va l'Algérie?* (pp. 13–34). Karthala.

Mannheim, K. (1972). The problem of generations. In P. Kecskemeti (Ed.), *Karl Mannheim: Essays* (pp. 276–322). Routledge.

Martinez, L. (2000). *The Algerian civil war, 1990–1998*. Columbia University Press.

Martinez, L. (2024). Une nouvelle gouvernance pour en finir avec le clientélisme et les transferts sociaux? In S. Chena, A. Benantar, & L. Dris-Aït Hamadouche (Eds.), *Le Hirak algérien: Retour sur un mouvement contestataire inédit* (pp. 31–50). L'Harmattan.

McAllister, E. (2016). Youth, social justice and cynicism in Bab el Oued. In R. Alenius Boserup & L. Martinez (Eds.), *Algeria modern: From opacity to complexity*. Hurst. (Pages not provided).

Meynier, G. (1995). Profils sociaux et nationalisme algérien: L'exemple des neuf "Chefs historiques". *Arabica, 42*(2), 161–179.

Meynier, G. (2004). La "Révolution" du FLN (1954–1962). *Insaniyat, 25–26*, 7–25.

Mohand-Amer, A. (2023). *La crise du Front de libération nationale de l'été 1962: Indépendance et enjeux de pouvoirs*. Frantz Fanon Éditions.

Mokrani, A. (2012). Analyse sociologique de la crise du capital privé. In A. Mohand Amer & B. Benzenine (Eds.), *Les indépendances au Maghreb* (pp. 47–59). CRASC.

Mills, C. W. (2000). *The power elite*. Oxford University Press.

Nederman, C. J. (2005). Class. In M. Cline Horowitz (Ed.), *New dictionary of the history of ideas* (Vol. 1, pp. 359–362). Thomson Gale.

Ouaissa, R. (2010). *La classe-État algérienne, 1962–2000*. Publisud.

Ouaissa, R. (2014). Classe moyenne, rente et stagnation politique. *Naqd, 36*, 121–146.

Ouchichi, M. (2011). *L'obstacle politique aux réformes économiques en Algérie* (Doctoral dissertation, Université Lyon). (Repository/URL not provided).

Quandt, W. B. (1998). *Between ballots and bullets: Algeria's transition from authoritarianism*. Brookings Institution Press.

Rahal, M. (2017). *L'UDMA et les Udmistes: Contribution à l'histoire du nationalisme algérien*. Barzakh.

Raptis, M. (1967). Le dossier de l'autogestion en Algérie. *L'Autogestion, 3*, 1–168.

Rey-Goldzeiguer, A. (2006). *Aux origines de la guerre d'Algérie, 1940–1945: De Mers-el-Kébir aux massacres du Nord-Constantinois*. La Découverte.

Sayad, A. (2004). *The suffering of the immigrant*. Polity Press.

Serres, T. (2019). *L'Algérie face à la catastrophe suspendue: Gérer la crise et blâmer le peuple sous Bouteflika (1999–2014)*. Karthala.

Serres, T. (2023). *The suspended disaster: Governing by crisis in Bouteflika's Algeria*. Columbia University Press.

Steger, M. B., & Roy, R. K. (2010). *Neoliberalism: A very short introduction*. Oxford University Press.

Stora, B. (1992). *Ils venaient d'Algérie: L'immigration algérienne en France (1912–1992)*. Fayard.

Tortosa, J. M. (2019). Maldevelopment. In A. Kothari, A. Salleh, A. Escobar, F. Demaria, & A. Acosta (Eds.), *Pluriverse: A post-development dictionary* (pp. 9–12). Tulika Books.

Van Leeuwen, M. H. D., & Maas, I. (2022). Social mobility through migration to the colonies: The case of Algeria. *Journal of Interdisciplinary History, 53*(2), 225–265.

Veltmeyer, H., & Petras, J. (2014). *The new extractivism: A post-neoliberal development model or imperialism of the twenty-first century?* Zed Books.

Von Sivers, P. (1979). Colonial elites and nationalist politics: The analysis of Algerian political and social class structures. *European Journal of Sociology, 20*(1), 142–148.

Warnecke-Berger, H., & Ickler, J. (2024). The political economy of extractivism. In H. Warnecke-Berger & J. Ickler (Eds.), *The political economy of extractivism: Global perspectives on the seduction of rent* (pp. 1–13). Routledge.

Werenfels, I. (2007). *Managing instability in Algeria: Elites and political change since 1995*. Routledge.

Willis, M. J. (2022). *Algeria: Politics and society from the Dark Decade to the Hirak*. Oxford University Press.

Wright, E. O. (2005). Social class. In G. Ritzer (Ed.), *Encyclopedia of social theory* (Vol. 2, pp. 717–724). Sage.

Yates, D. A. (2015). *The scramble for African oil: Oppression, corruption and the war for the control of Africa's natural resources*. Pluto Press.

Yefsah, A. (1990). *La question du pouvoir en Algérie*. A.P. Éditions.

7 Ports and Railways, Tools for Extractivism in a Rentier Economy

The Case of the Gafsa Mining Basin

Anouar Hechmi

Introduction

After 2000, the international system shifted to a multipolar structure, and new powers from the South, represented by the BRICS countries (Brazil, Russia, Iran, China, and South Africa), emerged to compete with the traditional triad countries; it is "a trade unions confront a dynamic, dangerous world" (Bond, 2017, n.p.). The BRICS countries, a rising economic powerhouse, have relied on the issue of unfair sharing of the rents of extractive resources with Western countries, especially since most agreements to the benefit of these traditional powers at the expense of developing countries, thus the rising powers offer win-win economic cooperation, unlike the traditional rich countries that do not offer an alternative to their policy based on direct extractivism or unfair economic dependence (Bond, 2018).

The philosophy of the old colonial powers is still based on the logic of maximum exploitation to obtain as much profit as possible, without regard for the development and progress of peoples and their territories, in particular, the African and Latin American countries that were victims of extractivism (Bassey, 2020). Since the colonial period, these policies have led to an imbalance within the Tunisian territory between the coast and the interior regions, where all infrastructure, including railways and roads, concentrated on the coast, while the interior, especially the mining cities, have fallen into a crisis of poverty and lack of development, which has worsened particularly after the interruption of phosphate transportation from the port of Sfax, causing a sharp drop in production from 7.3 million tons in 2010 to 1.7 million tons in 2018, reaching zero in 2020. Tunisian politics failed to create an alternative to this colonial economic model even after independence in 1956.

In this chapter, we will adopt a historical approach to illustrate the evolution of the Tunisian rentier model from pure extractivism to absolute extroversion, and the opening of the national economy to imports, leading to a negative balance of trade and indebtedness. We will try to show how this extractivism operates and how its tools, such as ports and railways, have evolved within a dominant rentier economy. We will also study its negative effects on the mining cities in particular and the national economy in general.

DOI: 10.4324/9781003730750-7

Tunisian Ports: From Capture Rent to Negotiation Rent

This chapter presents a geographical reading of the trajectories of natural resource extraction in Tunisia. The study concerns the Gafsa phosphate basin in southwestern Tunisia, specifically the mining towns of Redeyef, Moulares, Metlaoui, and Mdhilla. This chapter outlines the territorial dimension of rents. The chapter explains the methodological framework of the approach taken in this work and clarifies the relations between the rentier system and the development of exploited territories. It questions the forms and variables of rent conjugation in Tunisian territory and argues for reconciling resources and local territories. The trajectories of Tunisian trade reflect a deep-rooted colonial heritage that reveals the infinite tutelage of the French colonial power, influencing the disarticulation between a developed and an underdeveloped country, between a colonist and a colonized.

The development of the Tunisian port system reflects the evolution of extractivist models: the first generation of ports embodied colonial extractivism, while the second and third (Table 7.1) express modern extractivism based on exchange and economic dependency. Thus, the first generation of ports was designed to facilitate the capture of rents from looting, military conflicts, and other means of controlling natural resources. On the other hand, second- and third-generation ports are better suited to negotiating rents, which are linked to bargaining power and the ability of certain groups to benefit from these resources.

Theoretical Frame

My primary concern in this chapter is to examine and present theoretical and conceptual discussions, define the main terms used to address the problematic, and clarify the main elements of interest. Among them, we mention:

Extractivism: The term extractivism is used in the broad sense to describe activities that remove great quantities of natural resources that are not then processed (or done so in a limited fashion) and that leave a country as exports (Gudynas,

Table 7.1 Diachronic Typology of the Tunisian Port System

First Generation				
Port	Tunis	Bizerte	Sfax	Sousse
Creation date	1893	1893	1897	1899
Second Generation				
Port	La Goulette		Gabes	
Creation date	1968		1971	
Third Generation				
Port	Rades		Zarzis	
Creation date	1986		1990	

2020). Due to the multiplicity of literature that attempts to provide a definition of the term and apply it to a variety of situations and regions, a large number of studies have emerged that talk about different types of extractivism and its applicability to different geographical scales The concept of extractivism has shifted and expanded and is no longer limited to sectoral analysis based on the analysis of natural resource extraction, both theoretically and geographically, and the concept of "global extractivism" has emerged (Chagnon et al., 2022, p. 667). Our work will build on the classical concept of extractivism related to the intensive exploitation of phosphate and then consider the evolution of the model of extractivism as a process based on the intensive exploitation of natural resources for export, and try to identify a series of relationships, often historical and linked to colonization, in the Gafsa mining basin in Tunisia.

The difference between classical extractivism and neo-extractivism: Classical extractivism is based on the appropriation of natural and human resource wealth, leading to its depletion or the depletion of its source in a way that may be irreparable (Chagnon et al., 2021). In fact, the colonial powers did not hesitate to use military force to seize natural resources, as happened with France in 1881 when it took control of Tunisian lands, where the phosphate mines were owned by its settlers under a concession to companies based in Paris, which expected the entire quantities extracted to their lands in a framework of inferiority treaties for the colonized countries. Extractivism also represents a development model that contributed to the rise of northern countries at the expense of peripheral countries. This model was developed especially during the colonial period, characterized by the theft and exploitation of rare natural resources, particularly in Africa and Latin America. There is considerable debate about the concept of neo-extractivism and whether the implementation of development projects using some extractive revenues in Latin American countries should be understood as neo-extractivism, a concept that refers to the increasing use of resource rents resulting from rising commodity prices for social purposes (Andrade, 2022; Acosta, 2013; Veltmeyer & Xiaoguo Lau, 2020). In our work on this definition, we will focus on what we consider a very important aspect, which is increasing the profit margin for countries exporting extracted materials, by allowing them to convert a small part of the resources after the colonial period and establishing many conversion units (the SIAPE plant in Sfax in 1947, the phosphoric acid plant in Gabes in 1971, the DAP factory in 1979, the ammonitrate factory in 1983, the TSB factory in Medila in 1985, the phosphoric acid factory in Skhira in 1988). However, this development took place while raw-material exports remained important.

The relationship between extractivism and rent: Extractivism remains a key element in the structure of the globally dominant capitalist system, in which power rests with those who own capital and control the extractive industry.

Extractivism is based on the accumulation of capital and the centralization of power. It can be caused by relational inequalities in power (inequality). Attrition, associated with extractivism, can be analyzed as flows of financial

> resources, profits, and wealth in time and space (at and across different and overlapping levels, including local, state, regional, and global levels). It is a rent that is often in the hands of the state and sometimes corrupt, monopolists and speculators at different levels. Extractivism is thus a mode of capital accumulation in current global capitalist development that adapts, constrains, and pressurizes the lives of almost all human and non-human beings. However, it is not subordinate to or synonymous with global capitalism, but rather an integral part of it.
>
> (Chagnon et al., 2022, p. 763)

All extractive underground wealth is a source of rent. "Oil is a source of energy that underpins the material conditions of contemporary economies, global trade, population growth and rural-urban migration, and a source of wealth that constitutes state power between states and oil companies" (Vázquez Lezama et al., 2023, p. 10).

As for the situation in Tunisia, rent has been closely linked to extractive resources since the colonial period, raising many questions about who owns the rent and how it is distributed. We will also focus on the side effects of the unfair distribution of wealth in Tunisia and its role in creating an inequitable regional balance and social crises, especially in the mining areas of the Gafsa Basin. Our reading of the Tunisian case is to identify the reasons for the country's economic underdevelopment, even after the colonial period, in its inability to escape total dependence on the extractive model for development and to break the link between rents and extractivism. In our view, the country should diversify its sources of rents and diversify its partners to achieve real development based on production.

The relationship between extraversion and rent: After independence, rents in Tunisia were in the hands of the central authorities, who drew regular, more or less separate revenues from processing, value-adding, and production activities. The extraversion that has characterized industrial–commercial systems since the 1970s is based on the capture of various rents to integrate into a global exchange system shaped by these relationships with the exterior (Bayart, 2006, p. 8). "Land is a natural resource, and rents derive from its rarity. The owner is an idler who benefits from unjust enrichment" (Magrin, 2011, p. 10). Indeed, the creation of port infrastructures such as La Goulette in 1968 and Gabés in 1971, and of new industrial parks such as the Manzel Bourguiba free zone and the Gabes industrial zone, has not been accompanied by an expansion in production. The structures of the economy have remained surprisingly stable: Tunisia exports raw products (phosphate, salt, oil, olive oil) and imports manufactured or semi-manufactured goods under subcontracting agreements. However, since at least the 1990s, Tunisia has been experiencing a variety of ongoing crises (ecological, economic, and political). These difficulties are part of a historical trajectory dominated by extraversion. As a result, the country's political parties were quick to emphasize control over relations with the outside world, rather than production for the domestic market.

This failure is due to conflicts and popular uprisings (the Gafsa mining basin in 2008, Sidi Bouzid in 2010), and to cities too dependent on imports (those of the Sahel and Sfax) to encourage their hinterlands and accumulate rents. The paradigm of the extraversion strategy insists on the creation and capture of a veritable rent from dependence as the historical matrix of inequality, political centralization, and social struggles (Bayart, 2006, p. 11). The permanence of extraversion as the primary modality of Tunisia's relationship with the world is not really different from the model of extractivism, even if it does not exclude a large part of autonomy by giving Tunisian players a marginal share of on-site processing, as in the case of Gabes and the transformation of phosphates into DIAP, which is a highly polluting operation reminiscent of the concept of the malediction of natural resources. A curse is created by the unjust sharing of rents resulting from resource extraction, which benefits global players to the detriment of vulnerable local groups.

Ports as Pawns in the Game of Capture Rent: Classic Extractivism

This type of extractivism is classic in that it relies on a series of activities involving the extraction of massive quantities of raw or rare natural resources under the supervision of the colonizer, who often discovers the natural resources and then builds infrastructure such as ports, railways, and roads to exploit them and satisfy the needs of his local market. This is exactly what has happened to Tunisia's resources since the discovery of phosphates in 1885. This type of extraction differs from neo-extractivism, which not only implicates colonization but also indirectly creates economic dependence on colonial markets. Four criteria distinguish classic extractivism from other forms of natural resource exploitation. These are the form of the resource (raw, unprocessed), its destination after extraction (mainly exported to international markets), and the volume and intensity of extraction, which reflect the extent of environmental degradation. The quest for raw materials prompted the French colonists to build infrastructure in a rentier logic, both on land and at sea (ports, railroads, roads, and airports), which served to transport natural resources to the colonial metropolises to fuel equally unlimited economic growth. The profitable use of extractivism implies the use of ever more cumbersome technologies to access deeper resources, in terms of both health and the environment, and for the benefit of a few players. Rent comes from the commercial process of exporting primary products in bulk, without transformation within the colonies, guaranteeing maximum profit and inevitable gains by depriving all colonies of any profit (even marginal), imposing dependency in "primary export" (Bebbington, 2012), presenting the "risks" associated with neoliberalism, and the primary export industry is poorly integrated into the national economy, forming an enclave economy with little knock-on effect on other sectors (Frenoux, 2018, p. 8).

The port represents a fulcrum of domination, a starting point for penetration, and a link with the foreland between the dominated and the dominant. At this stage, the colonizer is authorized to export the phosphate he has extracted, and directing natural resources abroad makes the port a pivotal point in the economic and social process. The port is a breaking point between land and sea traffic, and a collection and storage point for local products destined for export. Ports were also decision-making centers and key points for colonial equipment, often controlled by port cities. Thus, extractivism has succeeded in creating economic dynamism in Tunisia, especially around ports and coastal areas, at the expense of the interior regions, which remain a source of raw materials with little profitability or economic dynamism. In the wake of the protectorate, France decided to build four ports along the coast to ensure the permanent and active drainage of natural resources, giving Tunis primacy and making it the master city of the regency, supporting its role as capital with the colonial fact. The colonial order gave the area an outward-looking structure that had the potential to be repeated and to guide certain choices. The structure comprises three parts: the hinterland, the (western) mining sites, the network providing connections and drainage, and, finally, the port: a place for processing, upgrading, exporting, and redistribution.

The port was crucial for the colonialists, serving as their starting point for penetration into Tunisian territory and as a link between the port's hinterland (the source of cargo movement) and the foreland (where cargo was delivered). During this phase, the colonies were allowed to export large quantities of phosphate, thereby fueling the flow of natural resources into French territory, given the necessity of the rentier economy linked to land ownership. The sharing (shaping) of rents and their distribution are at the heart of shaping the politico-economic system of the colonies. The existence of rents was based on monopolistic forms of ownership and dominance, which made it possible to impose phosphate prices higher than those justified by the cost of extraction and production, thanks in particular to institutional arrangements (royalties to the Tunisian state of 1 franc per ton, equivalent to at least 150,000 francs per year) (Direction générale des travaux publics, 1900, pp. 11–12).

In a system of colonial exploitation (Figure 7.1), there are, first of all, the colonies, which are conquered territories occupied and, above all, exploited by a foreign power called the metropolis, which is the power that runs the colony. In these exploited colonies, the colonists' main aim is to exploit resources. This is evidenced by the administrative headquarters of most mining companies being outside Tunisian territory, especially in Paris. For example, the Tunisian Phosphate Company (Société des Phosphates Tunisiens, 1904) was a limited liability company with headquarters in Kalaa Jerda and administrative headquarters in Paris. He will have to create a port, since the sources are generally far from the metropolis, and these ports will enable the riches of the exploited territory to be transported very quickly, thanks to numerous roads or railroads. These resources are then transported to the metropolises, where they are processed. The port's openness to the outside world makes it the axis of the extractive economy. This extractive process concentrated economic and industrial dynamism along the coast, particularly near the ports. In the wake of the protectorate, the colonial authorities decided to focus on developing just four ports capable of efficiently and sustainably facilitating the extraction of natural resources. As a result, Tunis assumed a leading role as the city controlling the regency, consolidating its position as the colony's capital.

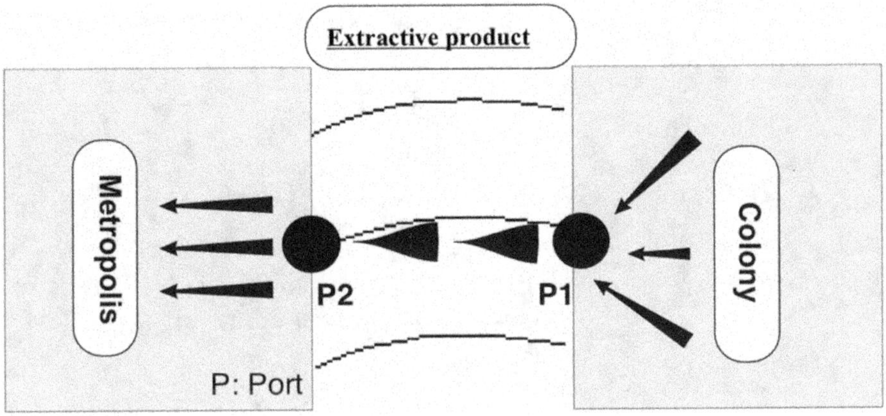

Figure 7.1 The colonial mining system.

Source: Own elaboration

The first generation of ports had their heyday after 1925 and after the Second World War, with the rise of industrialization linked to phosphate traffic; Sfax and Sousse, these two ports have played the role of outlets for phosphate traffic for the French colonists since 1899, and the port of Sfax has retained this function to this day. The area of influence of the port of Sfax depends on the phosphate-producing area west of the Gafsa governorate. The ports of Tunis, Sfax, Sousse, and Bizerte were built in the early years of the French occupation, and their creation was the result of the export of specific regions.

Bizerte has never been an important city, and Nabeur Minerais and Nefza are undoubtedly behind the port's creation. Sousse, the outlet for the Sahel region, was rich in oil, crafts, and trade, but during the 19th and 20th centuries, these three activities gradually declined. For a time, the port of Sousse pushed its hinterland as far as Henchir Souatir, that is, as far as the phosphates in the Gafsa region. In reality, the territory was divided into four hinterlands, with each port having its zone of influence reserved for its operations (Belhedi, 1980) (Figure 7.2):

- Nabeur and Nefza ores for Bizerte
- Moularès phosphate for Sousse
- Gabès phosphate for Sfax
- Kalaat Snan phosphate, Jrissa iron, Tell cereals for Tunis.

Ports as Transit Points for Extraversion Rents: Neo-Extractivism

The form of resource appropriation in classical extractivism is absent. It is to be distinguished from neo-extractivism as a process by which the state exploits resources on nationalized or privatized sites (Acosta, 2017). This exploitation is asserted by

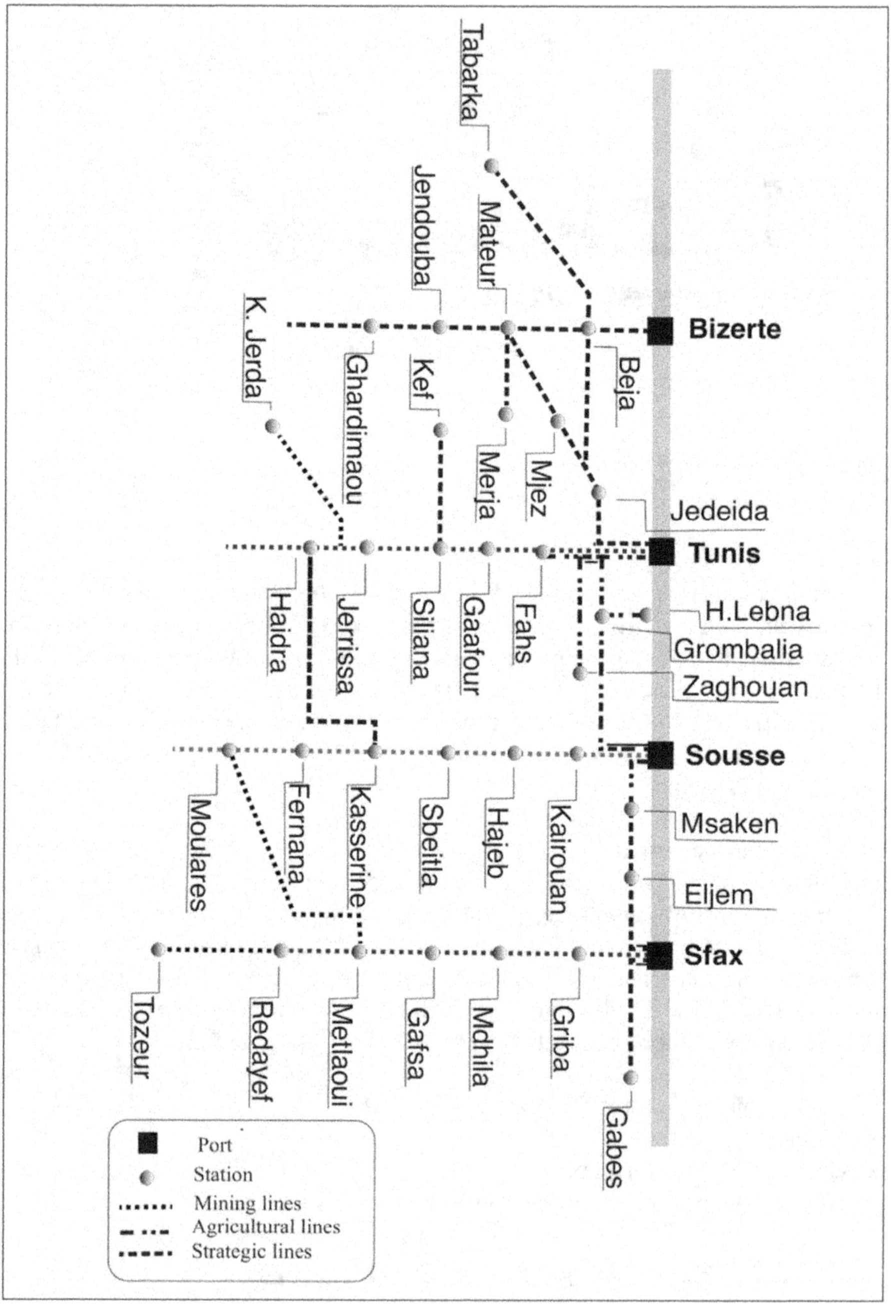

Figure 7.2 Typology of railroad lines according to their extraverted products.

Source: Own elaboration

private companies mobilized by the state in situations of nationalizing the economy, or by "concession" (Frenoux, 2018, p. 12) on behalf of foreign companies. As part of the global neoliberal reform, multinational corporations encouraged investment in the South to extract rents and impose regulations (Emel & Huber, 2008). As tools of extractivism, ports have become carriers of extraversion (Figure 7.3), manifested in the dominance of export activities in a logic of neoliberalism where has been the restoration of the primacy of export-led development, and have undergone the changes that the national economy has undergone since independence, when they were used as military barracks or platforms for the transportation of raw materials (Amin, 1973).

One aspect of neo-extractivism is the exploitation of all the natural resources of a country, such as phosphates, salt, hydrocarbons, and their export at low tariffs as stipulated in treaties and agreements between the newly independent states and the colonial powers. After the country gained independence, the Tunisian government sought to change its economic status but accepted the fait accompli and helped defend French interests as a privileged partner. The port thus played an important role in supporting the various stages of French colonialism, from direct exploitation to disguised exploitation through the introduction of new operating systems, by soliciting the support of political parties committed to safeguarding French interests.

The genesis of a second generation of ports, daughters of political independence, which brings together the two ports of La Goulette, redeveloped in 1968 to boost the docking capacity of the port of Tunis, which was unable to keep pace with changes in maritime shipping, and Gabes, built in 1971, while the latter was preparing for the establishment of an industrial port zone as part of a policy to rebalance

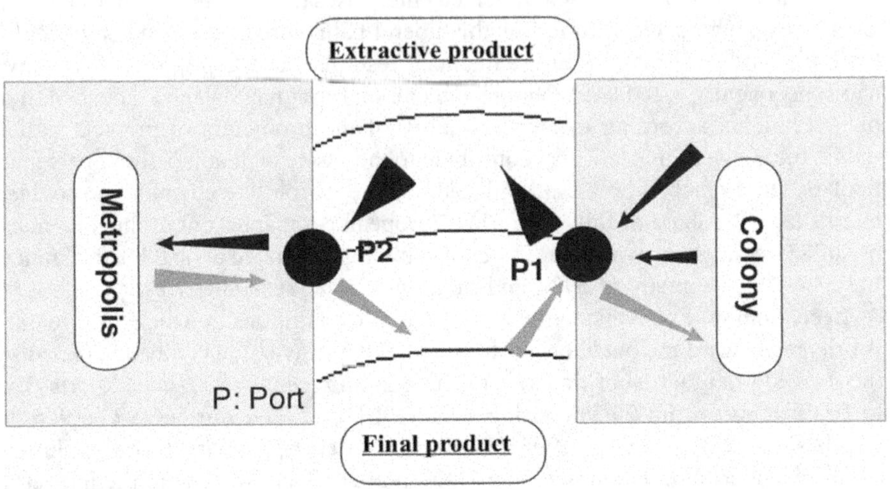

Figure 7.3 The evolution of the colonial mining system.

Source: Own elaboration

the region and strengthen the weak points of the coastline (Salem, 2005). This was followed by the third-generation ports, represented by Rades, which opened in 1986, and Zarzis, which began operating in 1990. This generation is rather the expression of an anticipatory port strategy, amply justified in the case of the Ro-Ro and container port of Rades, but which proved unsuitable, if not ill-timed, in the case of the port of Zarzis. The last two generations of Tunisian ports reflect the transition from a colonial economy to an economy of extraversion, whose needs are constantly being met from abroad. This reversal, which occurred across the entire chain in 1974, occurred earlier in Tunis-Goulette (1967) and the historic ports of Bizerte and Sousse (1973). On the other hand, it is very recent in the case of Gabes, where the beginnings of a slight diversification of traffic quickly resulted in a dominant import movement. This increasingly frequent recourse to imports is not unrelated to the country's exploding need for capital goods, industrial inputs, especially raw materials and intermediate consumer goods, and food and other consumer products.

As for La Goulette, which represents the second generation, today it is by far the main port for drivers and passengers, despite the mediocrity of the site, the facilities, and their accessibility by land. The opening of the port of Gabes, however, fed nascent traffic closely linked to the industrial choices made. An artificial port was opened in 1973, in response to the State's desire to kick start economic (industrial) growth in the south and to embark on a rentier economy of extraversion (Salem, 2005). Industrialization began in 1973 with the enactment of laws designed to promote export-oriented industries (Law 72–38 and Decree-Law 85–14 of 11 October 1985, establishing export enterprises), marking a decisive turning point in the country's industrialization policy (Chkir, 1984). After the failure of the cooperative experiment in 1969, a succession of laws furthered the clear orientation toward the development of small- and medium-sized enterprises (SMEs), that is, private initiatives. Those who decided to follow this liberal path were aware and convinced of the limits and inadequacies of the financial resources available to local investors and consequently opted to encourage and call on foreign assistance. The evolution of investments according to the nationality of the promoters of projects falling within the scope of this law may contribute to the assertion that it is foreigners, particularly the French, who are best placed to benefit from the advantages provided by this law (the share of fully exporting European companies out of the total number of 833 companies with 100% foreign capital is estimated at 46.34% for France, Italy 30.77%, Germany 11.37%, and Belgium 5.98%, see Table 7.2).

In economics, extraversion refers to economic conditions in which the structure is oriented toward the outside world. The rate of extraversion can be measured by the ratio of emigrant labor transfers (TT), tourism receipts (RT), and exports (Ex) to GDP: it rose from 20.2% during 1957–1961 to 29.6% during 1973–1976, to 43.4% since 1982 (Belhedi, 1994). In the past, after the January 14th Revolution, the Tunisian economy contracted by 8.8% in 2020. This was due to the impact of COVID-19 on global markets, the decline in passenger traffic (tourists) and freight traffic (imports and exports), as well as the revolution difficulties and political chaos the country experienced. In terms of phosphate crude exports, due to the lack of extractive products, post-revolutionary social problems, and the impact of

COVID-19, the proportion of phosphate exports decreased from 100% in 1990 to 32% in 1980, then to 8.59% in 2010, reaching zero in 2022. (Table 7.3). However, salt exports remain high, accounting for 78.3% of salt production in 2020, as Tunisia does not have an industry to value sea salt. The same applies to exports of converted phosphate production. The export ratios for 2022 are 100% heavy superphosphate, 70.05% ammonium superphosphate, and 37.65% phosphoric acid (Ministry of Industry, Mines and Energy, 2023) (Tables 7.3 and 7.4).

The main aspects of the current state of the Tunisian port system are the redeployment of the port of Tunis, the dynamism of the port of Rades, the decline of the ports of Bizerte and Sousse, and the vulnerability of the overly specialized port of Sfax, which competes with Gabes (Salem, 2005). The decline in the export rate of raw phosphate reflects the boom in industries linked to phosphate processing,

Table 7.2 Mixed-Use Companies by Country and Sector

Sectors	*France*	*Italy*	*Germany*	*Belgium*	*Others*
IAA	2	5	0	0	23
IMCCV	1	13	2	1	8
IMM	73	34	3	1	21
IEE	58	46	28	1	32
ICH	50	25	9	1	16
ITH	157	93	43	41	62
IB	7	2	0	0	2
ICC	22	29	7	1	9
ID	17	10	3	4	14
Total	**387**	**257**	**95**	**50**	**187**

Source: Tunisian Industry Portal (2023)

Table 7.3 Development of Phosphate Rock Mining Between 1990 and 2022

	Phosphate Production (thousand tons)	*Phosphate Export (thousand tons)*	*% Export*
1900	0.2	0.2	100
1910	1.35	1.29	95.55
1920	1.482	1.482	100
1930	3.4	2.643	77.73
1940	1.2	0.975	81.25
1950	1.6	1.572	98.25
1960	2.1	1.639	78.04
1970	3	2.109	70.3
1980	4.5	1.449	32.2
1990	6.3	0.593	9.41
2000	8.3	1.07	12.89
2010	8.131	0.699	8.59
2020	3.144	0	0
2022	3.563	0	0

Source: Ministry of Industry, Mines and Energy (2023)

Table 7.4 Extraversion Rate of Processed Phosphate Extractives

	Production (thousand tons)	*Exportation (thousand tons)*	*% Export*
Phosphoric acid 54% P2O5 (PA 54%)	521	196,197	37,65
Triple super phosphate 45% (T.S.P.)	173	173	100
Dicalcium phosphate (D.C.P.)	32	10,4	32,5
Diammonium phosphate (D.A.P)	482	337,675	70,05

Source: National Institute of Statistics (2023)

driven by Law 72's inducement effect. This extraversion explains the concentration of spatial dynamics on the coast to the detriment of the Tunisian interior, and the post-independence North–South divide was replaced by a clearer coastal–inland division, as manufacturing was largely concentrated in coastal port cities. Herein lies the dilemma of clinging to the foreign-oriented model: to achieve economic growth, exports must far exceed production to achieve a positive trade balance. To export, you must take on debt to import more and more. This is the inevitability that developing countries are experiencing today.

Railroads as Phosphate Extractive Lines

Railways are the preferred means of transportation, as they provide connectivity between the transit port and the remote phosphate mining area. In fact, the main role of the railway network is to connect remote areas to ports, enabling phosphates to be extracted and transported abroad cost-effectively. Indeed, the main role of the railroad network is to link the hinterland to the port. The mission of the railroads as a means of connecting with the port determined the layout of the rail network in Tunisia. However, the rail network linked to the port has become the driving force behind spatial dynamics, reflecting a strong concentration of population and activities toward the coast.

Railroads: Tracing the Path of Phosphate Penetration–Extraction and Transport

In 1881, the year Tunisia was colonized and the golden age of railroads, establishing a rail network facilitated the penetration of settlers and capital into Tunisian territory. The rail network's connectivity to multiple ports defined the functioning of the Tunisian space in accordance with the classic colonial coastal layout.

> The network is loose and rudimentary, faithfully reflecting the imperative of its constructive origins: The route taken is subordinate only to considerations

> of a mining nature. We look for the shortest route, the least steep slope, and the least prominent ramp to allow long, heavy convoys. We go straight to the final goal without worrying too much about the areas we cross.
>
> (Miossec & Signoles, 1976, p. 153)

The military authorities supported the construction of several stretches of railroad of purely strategic interest to facilitate troop movement between Algeria and Tunisia. To achieve this, the colonists wanted to build on the direct Tunis-Gadimau line, 6 km from the border, linked to the Algerian network in several sections between 1878 and 1880. Between 1894 and 1899, the northern section Jedada-Bizerta and the central section Tunis-Zagoouan-Fahes were created, as well as the section Tunis-Cap-Bon-Nabeul-Enfidha-Sousse-Moknine on the coast ending at Kairouan, and following the discovery of phosphates in the Gafsa basin, the colonists set about creating the Sfax-Moularès line. Then, between 1901 and 1912, the railway network was expanded, with the creation of the Mateur-Béja section and, at the same time, the discovery of iron ore in the extension of the Nabeur line was a pretext for covering the costs borne by the Tunisians. The Fahes-Kalaa-Jerda section was built at the urgent request of the military authorities. The middle line runs from Sousse to Redayef-Moulares-Tozeur, crossing Henchir Souatir and joining the Sfax-Gafsa line. Another Sousse-Sfax line was strategically important, ensuring the convergence of the Bône-Guelma network (to the north and center) with the Sfax-Gafsa network (to the south). The final phase, 1912–1942, was characterized by the extension of the Nefza line, imposed by the military authorities for strategic purposes, offering two solutions as invasion routes, namely via Nefza or via Jedaida, demonstrating the importance of Bizerte for the French colonial consideration as the key to the defense of the Maghreb possessions and presenting superiority over the capitals (Tunis and Algiers). The second extension was the Cap-Bon line: Menzel Bou Zelfa-Kélibia to supply the regency. The Haidra-Kasserine line was built during the Second World War to ensure a rapid connection between Algeria's Bizerte region and the South, to control the population and territory of the South, and to allow troops to be moved easily from north to south and to Algeria.

The railway network at that time was built mainly to meet military strategic needs, and on the other hand, to meet economic needs based on intensive wealth extraction, which determined the layout of the railway network. Thus, "the railway was a tool of penetration and an auxiliary of diplomacy, transformed into a means of extraction after the protectorate. Ultimately, the network is a mosaic of sections that respond to diverse demands and express financial objectives" (Belhedi, 1980, p. 39). "This network can be likened to a comb, the essential function of which is to pour agricultural and mining products from the interior to the coast" (Miossec & Signoles, 1976, p. 153).

In 1906, the Slatat and Hameina concession led to the continuation of the Jerissa to Slata section. The ore export port was La Goulette, and the Bir Kassaa-La Goulette section was leased in 1908. Under the 20 March 1906 agreement, the company was to build the Moularès-Henchir Souatir section. The Jebel M'dilla deposit was conceded on 15 October 1913, to the Company of Mines and Chemical Products of Châlons/Saône, with a minimum production of 250,000 t/year. The rest of the Nebeur, Tamera, and Nefza deposits were connected by sections of railroad. All limited liability companies are controlled by leading French banks and subsidiaries, often operate under different names or remain anonymous, usually act under unconditional authority, and are headquartered in France or Italy. For example, the Bône-Guelma company, based in the ports of Bizerte, Tunis, Sousse, Sfax, etc., is a subsidiary of "the Batignolles" and has close links with the Banque de Paris and the Banque des Pays-Bas. The close links between the financial and banking worlds and the political sphere reinforce this financial oligarchy. The state built the network, financed by local taxpayers and managed by private companies.

In fact, the colonists deployed numerous mining laws to exploit the mines in their favor (Public Works of the French Protectorate in Tunisia: Chapter III, Mining Services, Mining Legislation in the Regency). The legislation confirms that the bidding process for mines was devolved to prospectors authorized by the Director of Public Works to search for phosphate. The auction was based on royalties the leaseholder paid to the State of 0.50 Fr per ton of phosphate exported from Tunisia. Once the inventor's privilege has been granted, the right does not cease until 30 years after the date of the decision recognizing this status. In effect, the rent is linked to ownership through the concession and, moreover, financially generated by a dominant monopoly position that has enabled the new owner (the concessionaire) to determine the rents and their distribution for 30 years, and through institutional arrangements. So, we have private appropriation of mines justified by laws and regulations.

Mining Lines: The Gafsa-Sfax Phosphate Corridor

In 1885, the French geologist Philippe Thomas discovered phosphate in the Selja valley (between Metllaoui and Moularès), turning the railway network upside down (see Figure 7.4). Following this discovery, the number of applications for exploration permits rose from fewer than 50 in 1895 to over 1,800 in 1903. Exploration work intensified between 1899 and 1906, and numerous deposits were discovered, including Aïn Moularès, Zbeuss, Mdhilla, Kalaa Jerda, Jerissa, Tamera, Nefza, Douaria, Nebeur, and Slata. In 1901, the Kalaat Senam and Rebiba deposits, discovered in 1900, were leased to the Compagnie de phosphates du Dyr, with production of 100,000t/year. In 1904, the Kalaa Jerda deposit was discovered, which became the terminus due to its importance. The Moulares deposit was recognized in 1902 and leased to the Sfax-Gafsa Company. The export port is Sousse, and the minimum tonnage is 250,000 tons per year. The railroads, initially an instrument of penetration, were transformed after colonization into a means of taxation and levy (Belhedi, 1980, p. 37).

Mines were successively opened at Métlaoui (1899), Moularès (1902), Redeyef (1903), and Moularès (1904). The railroad line linking these deposits to the port of Sfax, which relied solely on the mines for its operations, depended on those of the deposits. Construction of the line began on 1 December 1897, and was completed in April 1899. The success of the Metlaoui-Gafsa line encouraged mining,

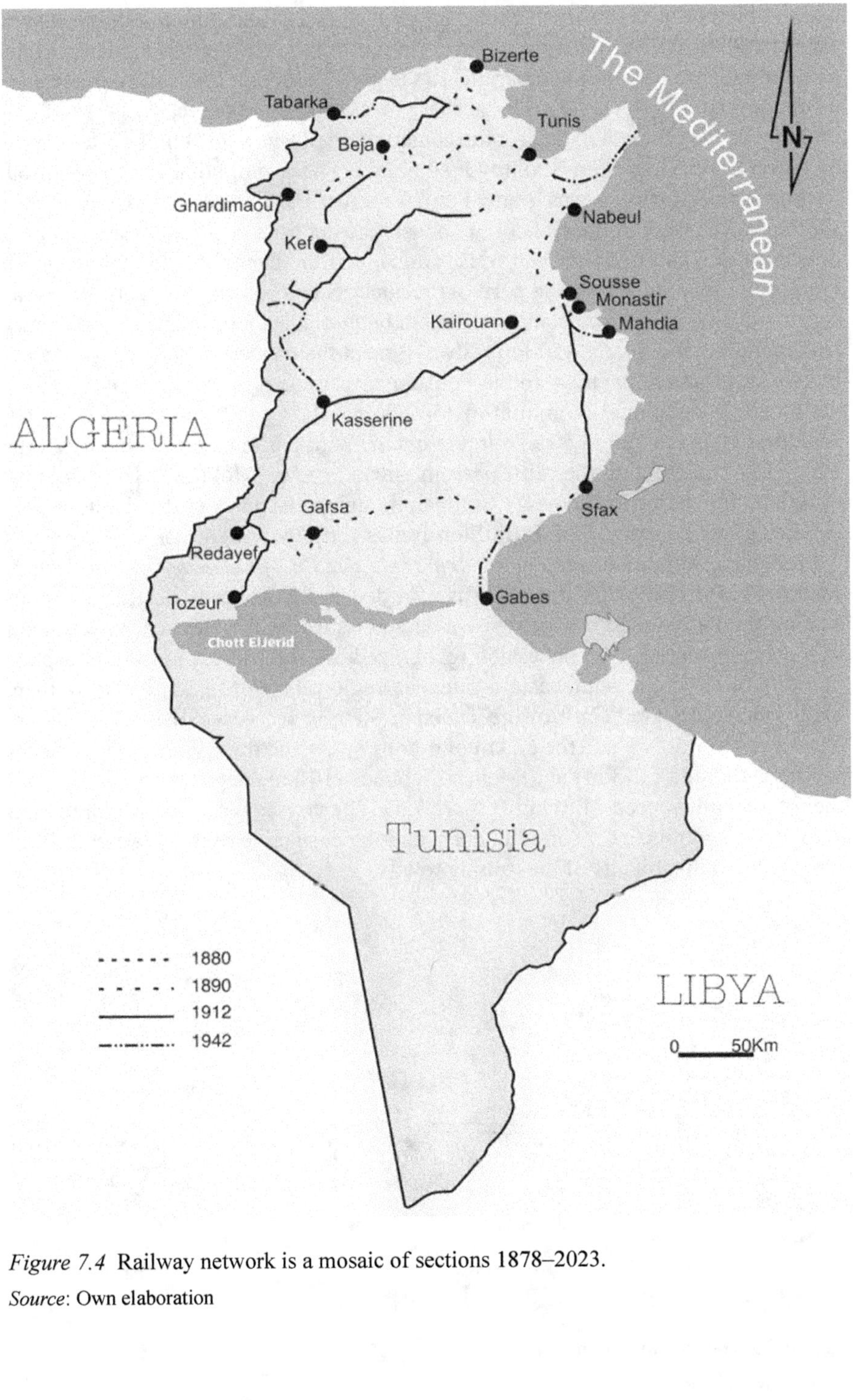

Figure 7.4 Railway network is a mosaic of sections 1878–2023.

Source: Own elaboration

and the history of the railroad became linked to that of the mines. The success of the Gafsa-Sfax line provided the best formula for the creation of new lateral lines perpendicular to the coast and parallel to the great mountain folds and connected to a commercial port to capture a large share of the mining revenue.

The Tunisian State will pay for the construction of a new 250-km line, to be built by private initiative, from Sfax to Oued Seldja. The exploitation of the enormous lime phosphate deposits was granted on 24 August 1896, to M. Maurice de Robert for the exploitation of the Gafsa lime phosphate deposits and the construction and operation of a railroad between Sfax, Gafsa, and the deposits. The concession is granted entirely at the risk and peril of the concessionaire, with no guarantee whatsoever payable by the Tunisian government budget. It provides for the construction and operation of a nearly 250-km railway line at the concessionaire's expense and includes the latter's payment to the Tunisian government of a royalty of 0.5 francs per ton, with an annual minimum of 150,000 francs. On 4 October 1896, Société Mokta-el-Hadid acquired a stake in the company to participate in phosphate mining and in constructing the railway from Gafsa to Sfax. Mokta-el-Hadid held 1/5 or 4,000,000 shares in the new "Compagnie des phosphates et du chemin de fer de Gafsa," with a capital of 18 million francs (http://www.entreprises-coloniales.fr/(Tunisia)), which was renamed *Compagnie des Phosphates de Gafsa*—CPG in January 1976. The entire deposit was awarded to Mr Maurice de Robert, representing the Paris-based company, by a decree issued by the Beylical government. The decree granting the concession recognized the right to exploit the phosphate deposits of the entire southeastern Tunisian region. From Metlaoui, the company extended the line on behalf of the Tunisian State to the oases of El Oudiane and Tozeur (54 km). If we add the 62 km of mining spurs and the special spurs connecting the M'Dhilla (13 km) and Meheri-Zebbeus (10 km) deposits to the network, the total length exceeds 400 km (Figure 7.5). The consequences of which were of great concern to the extraverted country and the extractive region, particularly for the exploited inhabitants of the mining towns.

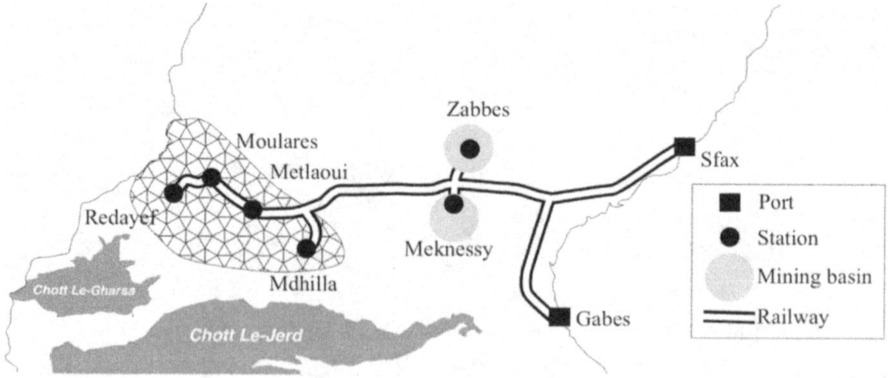

Figure 7.5 Gafsa-Sfax mining corridor.

Source: Own elaboration

Phosphate: A Treasure Turned Into a Curse for Mining Territories

The production of phosphates led to the organization of local territories and populations according to the colonists' way of life. Moreover, the evolution of independent Tunisia is far from breaking with the past; on the contrary, it has further intensified the main features that have characterized the spatial organization of the Tunisian territory. Indeed, the economy's extraversion has been further reinforced since 1970 with the coastalization of the spatial structure (Belhedi, 1994). This outward-oriented economic system integrated inland mining areas into a global system based on a hierarchy of nations. The mining system has a highly discontinuous spatial effect, and the phosphate deposits introduce a degree of spatial heterogeneity, marked by a patchy, uneven landscape. These deposits are marked out by physical and symbolic barriers against the local population, representing, on the one hand, points of connection to globalization and, on the other hand, plunging the rest of the territories into the shadow of marginality (Ferguson, 2006). These local territories do not survive on these rents any more than they suffer from them.

The idea is to see if the concept of extractivism in its broadest sense, including the plundering of natural, human, and financial resources, can explain the rise in socioeconomic inequalities and the ever-increasing entry into credit.

At the Regional Scale: The Gafsa Basin: An Extraction Hinterland in Cumulative Crisis

Extractivism and openness are a pair that cannot, on their own, create a balanced economy because they do not foster a sustainable industry that respects the rights of future generations. As a result, the socioeconomic spin-offs—notably job creation and export earnings for local territories—are sometimes minimal compared to the price to be paid (exodus of the Indigenous population, outbreak of new dangerous diseases caused by chemicals, overexploitation of water, etc.). Some resource-rich territories are experiencing what researchers such as Southcott (2016) have termed "natural resource curse." This expression describes the inability of these territories to raise their level of economic growth despite their high natural potential. The system of extractivism has a huge potential for territorial fragmentation, which refers to the tension between mining towns and port cities, thus expressing a territorialization imposed by the settler, which in turn exports the crisis to the source region of extractive activities.

The focus has now shifted to the coast, specifically Tunis and the Sahel, leading to the domination of the coast (in this case, the port cities) over the rest of the territory. These exogenous infrastructures quickly left their mark on the country as outward-looking structures that guided how the space functioned. This logic produced an unbalanced territory, poorly designed in favor of the coast, which monopolized the main industrial area stretching from Tunis to Sfax, from the eve of independence. Even the industrialization policies that followed (1962–1970) focused on rebalancing the coast by creating units in Bizerte and Menzel Bourguiba, the Sahel, Sfax, and Gabes. After 1970, the liberalization of the economy contributed to the densification of industrial space limited to the coast. Even with decentralization, the inland regions have not succeeded in monopolizing companies, and the concentration on the coast is only slightly altered, with a diversified industrial fabric on the coast. The dominance of the coastal zone is not limited to the industrial areas; more than 70% of economic activity is concentrated here, and 90% of the tourist hotel capacity is located in the coastal area, which represents the vital hub of the Tunisian country, while the interior remains mainly a transit area (APAL, 2022). It plays a significant role in redistribution (ports, import–export, wholesalers, etc.), making it the backbone of the country's spatial dynamics; however, in terms of volume, the west–east axes remain important due to the preponderance of heavy goods and drainage. It symbolizes a destabilizing national integration that proceeds through extraversion.

Exporting local natural resources (such as phosphate ore) for the purpose of extracting rents does not create any local added value or tangible positive impact on the national economy, other than creating jobs, and, in most cases, these rents are negligible. They are not reinvested in productive activities or diversification of income sources. At the same time, rivalries over their capture or redistribution make them factors in the weakening of institutions and the economy, as well as in social and political tension. The disparity in rent distribution also created an imbalance between the north or south and east or west regions within Tunisian territory, which justifies maintaining extraterritorial dependency in exchange for further internal marginalization. This imbalance is evident in excessive political centralization in favor of the coastal regions, while the northern, central, and southwestern regions are more marginalized and impoverished, leading to tensions since 2008 between the residents of mining cities and successive regimes during independence. The rents associated with phosphate extractivism have so far structured Tunisia's political, economic, and spatial system, revealing several damning truths through the existence of two gradients of inequality: first, east–west, then northwest–south. The organization and dynamics of Tunisia's territory reflect the measures taken to create these rents and redistribute them in favor of major coastal cities at the expense of other inland areas. This has led to an open logic of rentierism and clientelism that has constrained the country's politics and economy even after independence.

The Tunisian Institute of Competitiveness and Quantitative Studies (TICQS) has developed a synthetic index combining several variables across different areas of economic and social development (see Table 7.5). This index classifies the variables according to areas focused on regional development and the main causes or sources of regional disparities in Tunisia: living amenities, the social aspect, the size of the labor market, and human capital (basic infrastructure and equipment, access to health services, access to leisure services, the social aspect, human capital, the absorption capacity and understanding of the labor market, and finally the tension and profile of the labor market). The breakdown of agglomerations into four groups or zones, which differ by level of development, reveals disparities within regions, especially in the governorates of Sfax and Bizerte. Indeed, the first two least-developed zones contain delegations belonging to the fourth group. The relatively developed areas are essentially made up of delegations from the first group. The distribution of delegations by group reveals an almost symmetrical picture

Table 7.5 Distribution of Delegations by Development Zone and Governorate

	Group 1		*Group 2*		*Group 3*		*Group 4*	
	nbr	*%*	*nbr*	*%*	*nbr*	*%*	*nbr*	*%*
Port cities	50	75.79	34	64.14	21	29	8	9.8
Tunis	19	28.79	1	1.89	1	1.5	0	0
Ariana	2	3.03	4	7.55	1	1.5	0	0
Manouba	1	1.52	6	11.32	1	1.5	0	0
Ben Arous	9	13.64	2	3.77	1	1.5	0	0
Bizerte	3	4.55	6	11.32	1	1.5	4	4.9
Sousse	9	13.64	5	9.43	2	2.9	0	0
Gabes	1	1.52	3	5.66	5	7.4	1	1.2
Sfax	5	7.58	2	3.77	6	8.8	3	3.7
Médenine	1	1.52	5	9.43	3	4.4	0	0
Mining cities	**1**	**1.52**	**2**	**3.78**	**25**	**36.7**	**36**	**44.3**
Gafsa	0	0	0	0	7	10.3	4	4.9
Kef	1	1.52	1	1.89	7	10.3	2	2.42
Béja	0	0	1	1.89	3	4.4	5	6.12
Kasserine	0	0	0	0	0	0	13	16.05
Siliana	0	0	0	0	6	8.8	5	6.17
Jendouba	0	0	0	0	2	2.9	7	8.64

Source: Own elaboration based on TICQS (2021)

between coastal and inland governorates. Indeed, 94% of the first group (the most developed) are coastal delegations, and 76.5% of the fourth group are inland cities (ITCEQ, 2021).

The disparity between the Eastern and Western regions is also highlighted by the poverty index, as shown in Figure 7.6, which reflects the depth of the imbalance between the coastal port cities of Sfax, for example, with a rate that does not exceed 2%, and the inland mining cities of Moulares et M'Dhilla (16.5% and 21 %), Redeyef (21% and 26%), and Metlaoui (12.5% and 16.5%). It should also be noted that the disparities can be found within the coastal cities, as not all cities are fortunate. For example, the poverty rates in the rest of the cities are very large, between 34% and 54% in the cities of Cherbane and Oulad Chamakh in the central East of Tunisia.

At the National Scale: A Mining Treasure Crumpled Under Sustainable Debts

This part of the work explains the profound effects of the determinism that governs the economy that the Tunisian country envisaged at independence, which is an economic model inherited from colonial period and in which it does not differ from its counterparts in the African colonies, since most of them are still subject to classic extractivism, such as oil in Niger and Uganda, natural gas in Mozambique and Tanzania, and iron ore in Guinea and Sierra Leone. The lucky ones are those who have moved to the stage of extraversion, especially in the Maghreb countries. This is a debt dumping model, a kind of disguised extractivism that, in the search

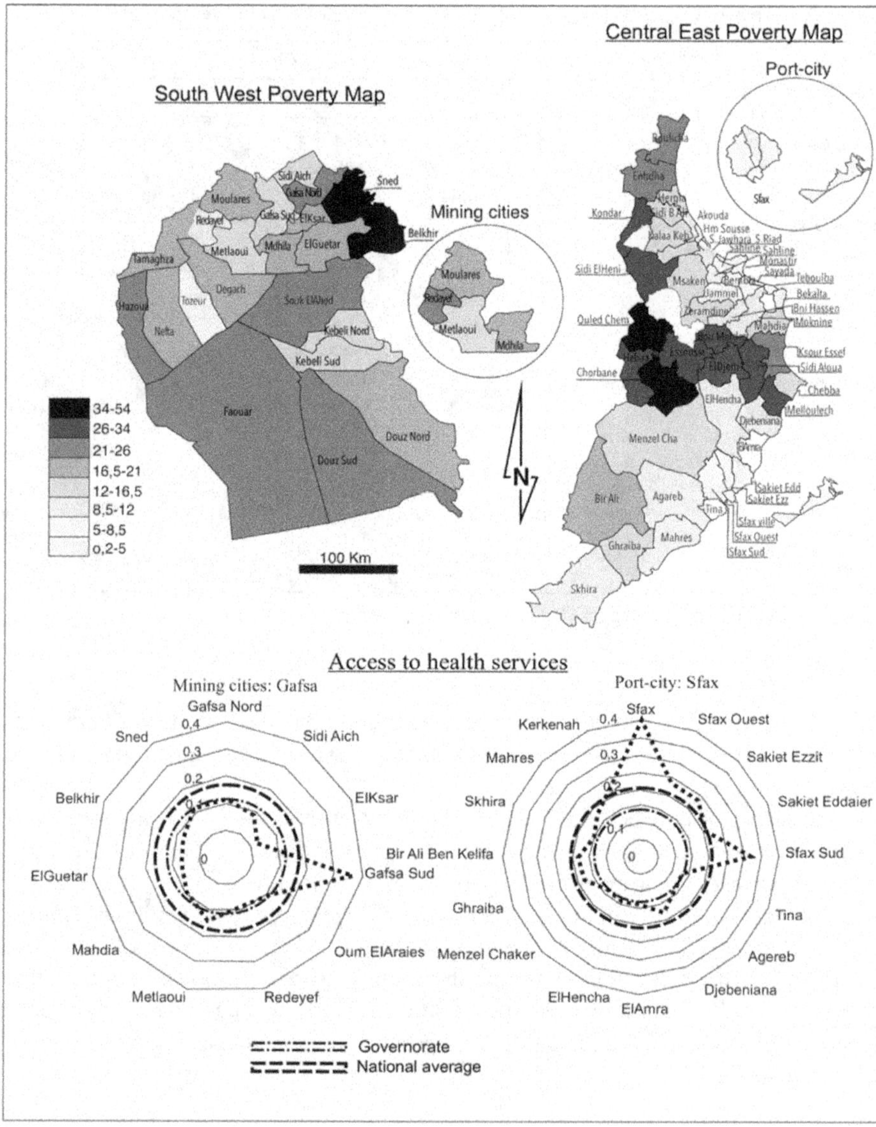

Figure 7.6 Comparison map between the mining towns of the Gafsa basin and the port city of Sfax.

Source: Own elaboration based on data provided by the National Statistics Institute (INS) (2015)

for more supplies, pushes countries into debt in exchange for continuing to export natural resources. This debt is not given for free, but because of the need to follow the dictates of the financiers, the World Bank and the IMF, in order to draw the outlines of the imposed development model. This explains the failure of any proposed model in most Third World countries. The analysis of the destructive duo of debt and extractivism (Sersiron, 2018) and their interdependence can be explained by the shift from extractivism to extraversion, which imposes a permanent cycle of debt. The evolution of capitalism since the Second World War has been characterized in the North by Fordism and the 30 glorious years, and in the South by nationalism–clientelism development based on increasing the volume of mining rents, industrialization through import substitution, investment in infrastructure, and clientelist redistribution of part of the rents. Since 1970, economic liberalization through Law 72–38 has encouraged exports by supporting the development of foreign private industry, enabling wider distribution, and helping to create an industrial space truly confined to the coast. By 2023, 84% of industrial potential (employment, added value, sales, investment, and industrial projects) will be concentrated in coastal areas (API, 2023).

This explains the trade deficit Tunisia faces. It is represented by the inability of exports to cover imports. This deficit is neither new nor accidental; it is a persistent problem. Certainly, at the end of 2020, the deficit reached an unprecedented level: −12,830.3 MD, compared with −64.6 MD in 1970 before the revolution and –8209 MD in 2010. But in terms of import and export coverage, Tunisia is again in a situation similar to the last years of the Protectorate, with 77.3% in 1950 versus 75.1% in 2020 (Table 7.6).

Looking at the relationship between total exports and imports of goods, this is an allometric relationship that negatively affects GDP. This is the dilemma that accompanies adopting an extroverted model. If you want to develop, you have to export, but if you want to meet your daily needs, you have to import more and more goods, using debt, and that is where the system gets stuck.

Table 7.6 Tunisia's Foreign Trade in 1,000 dinars

Years	*Export*	*CAF Import*	*FOB Balance*	*Coverage Rate = Exp/Imp*
1950	39.826	51.533	−11.707	77.3
1955	37.388	63.276	−25.888	59.1
1960	50.267	80.092	−29.825	62.8
1965	62.9	129.1	−66.2	48.7
1970	95.8	160.4	−64.6	59.7
1975	345.6	572.8	−227.2	60.3
1980	904.8	1428.4	−523.6	63.3
1985	1443	2287	−844	63.1
1990	3087.4	4826.8	−1739.4	64
1995	5172.9	7464.1	−2291.2	69.3
2000	8004.8	11738	−3733.2	68.2
2005	13793.6	17291.5	−3497.9	79.8
2010	23519	31817.1	−8298.1	73.9
2015	27607.2	39609.7	−12002.5	69.7
2020	38705.9	51536.2	−12830.3	75.1

Source: BCT

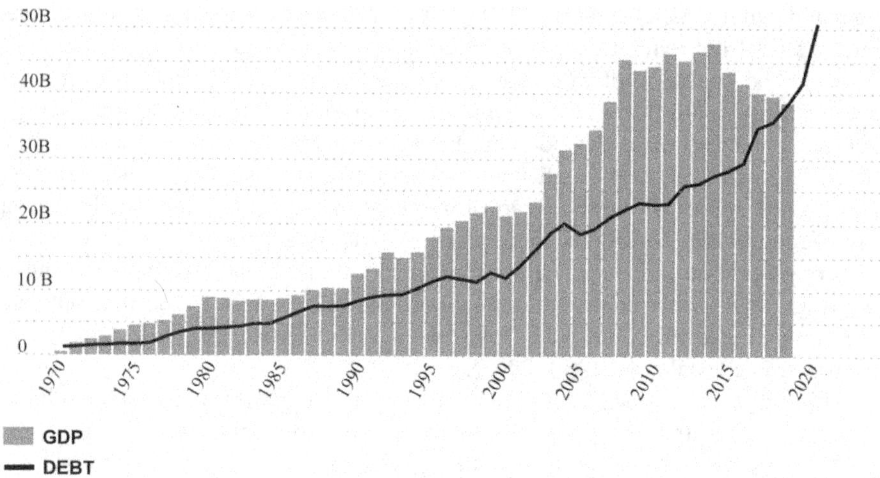

Figure 7.7 A comparison between the growth of external debt and GDP.
Source: World Bank (2023)

On the one hand, extractivism is a competition among the strongest nations to monopolize the earth's resources to ensure the continued functioning of their economies. However, the expropriation of resources for the benefit of the most powerful is being accentuated through the implementation of illegitimate and odious debt systems that will enable the economies of weak countries to be rapidly subjected to the injunctions of the World Bank and IMF. As a result, the economies of weak states will always be controlled by the countries of the North, albeit less visibly, for the greater benefit of its multinational corporations. Colonial exploitation, therefore, hides behind the mask of independence, which is often no more than an illusion.

Debt, on the other hand, is a nexus of power relations that imposes the South on creditors able to transform their wealth into influence and then, in return, allows their political influence to become the source of their wealth. The plundering of natural resources is at the root of a capitalist, clientelist global economy in which there is a dominant center and a dominated, enslaved periphery. Debt was a determinism imposed on the new political decision-makers of colonial states by the West after independence, replacing the constraints imposed by occupying forces to ensure the continuity of plundered resources. Integration into the capitalist system implied increased exports of raw materials, which reinforced external dependence and the development effort, requiring enormous financial resources, hence the need to increase recourse to borrowing through easy credit (see Table 7.7). Over-indebtedness is a tool used by capital owners to impose ultraliberal policies on developing countries through IMF and World Bank conditions and directives and is always linked to access to new financing. They will impose these programs on numerous neoliberal structural adjustment programs imposed without the consent of the people. All these impositions have resolutely anchored the economy in its extraverted vocation, linked to Tunisia's enslavement to the neocolonial domination of the global market, which has served the interests of corrupt[1] politicians so well, in collusion with the interests of foreign multinationals, that they do not want to change.

The IMF is trying to plunge Tunisia, like all developing countries, into debt, in exchange for demanding responses to conditions imposed by experts without reference to the people, since their reports are far from the desired development. Instead, its effect has been to grant unfair loans to those who meet the reform requirements. In many cases, these reforms contradict the country's reality, as was the case in Tunisia in March 2022, when the IMF called for lower wages. Tunisia rejected these directives, considering them a danger to social peace.

The work of these financial structures is limited to providing loans to those who do the bidding of the IMF and World Bank and then programming loans for years to come. The projected payment to the IMF for Tunisia is 2,157,019,759 from 2023 to 2043, and therefore, to provide sustainable loans (Table 7.7 and Figure 7.8).

Table 7.7 Outstanding Obligations and Scheduled Payments: Millions of Special Drawing Rights (SDRs[2])

	2023	*2024*	*2025*	*2026*	*2027*
Principal	150,23	466,22	329,92	174,68	136,8
Interest	55,69	85,88	61,16	49,18	40,77
Total	205,92	552,1	391,08	223,86	177,57

Source: IMF (2024)

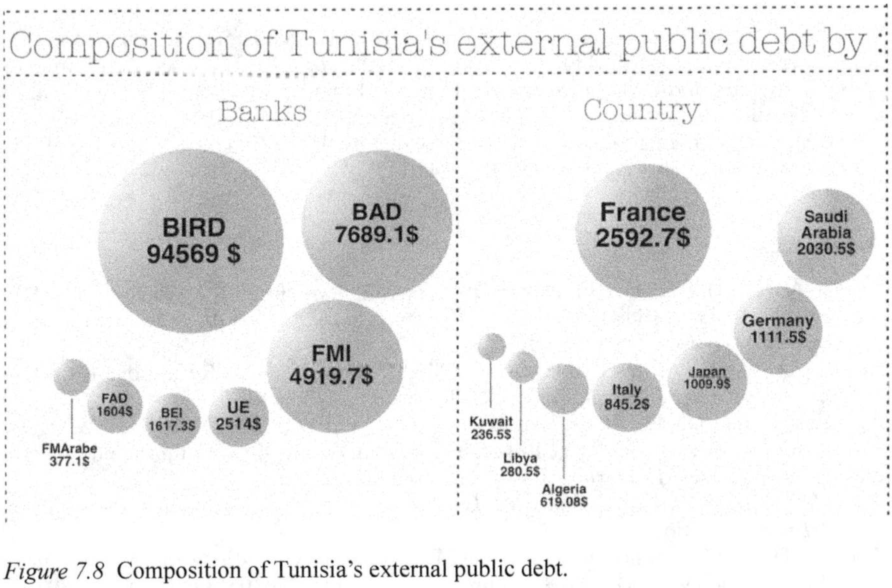

Figure 7.8 Composition of Tunisia's external public debt.

Source: Tunisian Ministry of Finance (2023)

Conclusion

The continuation of the same colonial-era economic policies has led to the mismanagement of Tunisia's natural resources (phosphate, oil, and salt). The Tunisian country must abandon colonial paternalism, diversify its partners, and develop a progressive development model aligned with global economic changes, sustainable, and that respects the rights of future generations, especially in extractive activities. Tunisia needs to get out from under France's thumb. We need to rethink development models and support more public–private partnerships (PPP) over time. We need to broaden the sharing of mining rents, with a positive differentiation, to achieve the integration of mining towns into the national territory and enable the valorization of more endogenous dynamics.

We need to get away from the rent-seeking and fragility of dependency by diversifying rents and broadening their base. We need to find another way to build a post-extractivist world before natural resources become scarce. Catching up is possible, but we need to respect the ecosystem and achieve resilient, green mining by changing lifestyles based on conso-waste, and establishing a new post-extractivist, post-consumerist, just, and ecologically sustainable model because it enables a better life by refusing to be enslaved to the material economy. This exploitation must be framed by a relational rent that doesn't operate according to the alliance-type market mechanism but stems from privileged relationships nurtured by at least two parties who choose to cooperate rather than clash, and exploit this synergy to control the development of power stakes and power relations within the coalition, even if they are inevitable.

Notes

1 The Natural Resources Governance Index (RGI) in Tunisia is 50% for bulk solids and 53% for bulk liquids (Worldwide Governance Indicators, 2023) is used as a diagnostic tool to measure the governance of the oil, gas, and mining sectors in selected countries, assessing the resource sector through the policies and practices used.

2 The SDR is an international reserve asset created by the IMF to supplement the official reserves of its member countries (IMF, 2024).

References

Acosta, A. (2013). Extractivism and neoextractivism: Two sides of the same curse. In M. Lang & D. Mokrani (Eds.), *Beyond development: Alternative visions from Latin America* (pp. 61–86). Transnational Institute.

Acosta, A. (2017). Post-extractivism: From discourse to practice—Reflections for action. *Revue internationale de politique de développement*, *9*, 78–101.

Agence de Promotion de l'Industrie et de l'Innovation (API). (2023). *Monographies régionales*. Ministère de l'Industrie, de l'Énergie et des Mines. https://www.tunisieindustrie.nat.tn/fr/doc.asp?mcat=13&mrub=105

Amin, S. (1973). *Le développement inégal: Essai sur les formations sociales du capitalisme périphérique*. Éditions de Minuit.

Andrade, D. (2022). Neoliberal extractivism: Brazil in the twenty-first century. *The Journal of Peasant Studies*, *49*(4), 793–816. https://doi.org/10.1080/03066150.2021.1911893

APAL. (2022, November 11). Un littoral résilient intégré dans la transition écologique. *Leaders*. https://www.leaders.com.tn/article/34051-apal-un-littoral-resilient-integre-dans-la-transition-ecologique

Bassey, N. (2020). Les populations africaines victimes de l'extractivisme. *EcoRev'*, *49*(2), 73–86. https://doi.org/10.3917/ecorev.049.0073

Bayart, J.-F. (2006). Comme vous en Afrique, ou l'hégémonie dans l'extraversion. In *Préface à la nouvelle édition de L'État en Afrique: La politique du ventre* (pp. III–LXVIII). Fayard.

Bebbington, A. (2012). Underground political ecologies. *Geoforum*, *43*(6), 1152–1162. https://doi.org/10.1016/j.geoforum.2012.05.011

Belhedi, A. (1980). *Le chemin de fer et l'espace en Tunisie: Transport et organisation de l'espace*. Université de Tunis.

Belhedi, A. (1994). L'inégal développement régional en Tunisie: Accumulation spatiale et littorisation. *Cahiers de la Méditerranée*, *49*(1), 133–156.

Bond, P. (2017). *BRICS trade unions confront a dynamic, dangerous world*. Friedrich Ebert Stiftung.

Bond, P. (2018, April 25). The BRICS, global governance, accumulation, class struggle and resource extractivism. *CADTM*. https://www.cadtm.org/The-BRICS-global-governance-accumulation-class-struggle-and-resource

Chagnon, C. W., Durante, F., Gills, B. K., Hagolani-Albov, S. E., Hokkanen, S., Kangasluoma, S. M. J., Konttinen, H., Kröger, M., LaFleur, W., Ollinaho, O., & Vuola, M. P. S. (2022). From extractivism to global extractivism. *The Journal of Peasant Studies*, *49*(4), 760–792. https://doi.org/10.1080/03066150.2022.2069015

Chagnon, C. W., Hagolani-Albov, S. E., & Hokkanen, S. (2021). Extractivism at your fingertips. In J. Shapiro & J. A. McNeish (Eds.), *Our extractive age* (pp. 176–188). Taylor & Francis.

Chkir, A. (1984). L'extraversion de l'économie tunisienne à travers les textes de loi. *Cahiers du CREAD*, *3*(3), 99–107.

Direction générale des travaux publics. (1900). *Les travaux publics du protectorat français en Tunisie* (Tome 3). Protectorat français.

Emel, J., & Huber, M. T. (2008). A risky business: Mining, rent and the neoliberalization of "risk". *Geoforum*, *39*(3), 1393–1407. https://doi.org/10.1016/j.geoforum.2008.01.010

Ferguson, J. (2006). *Global shadows: Africa in the neoliberal world order*. Duke University Press.

Frenoux, D. (2018). Mozambique: Une économie de "concessions". *Afrique contemporaine*, *266*(2), 115–129. https://doi.org/10.3917/afco.266.0115

Gudynas, E. (2020). *Extractivisms: Politics, economy and ecology*. Fernwood Publishing.

Institut national de la statistique (INS). (2015). *Enquête nationale sur le budget, la consommation et le niveau de vie des ménages 2015*. INS Tunisie.

International Monetary Fund (IMF). (2024). *Tunisia*. https://www.imf.org/fr/Countries/ResRep/TUN

Magrin, G. (2011). *Des rentes au territoire* (HDR dissertation, Université Paris 1 Panthéon-Sorbonne).

Ministry of Industry, Mines and Energy. (2023). *Development of monthly export sales of phosphate derivatives (tons)*. Government of Tunisia.

Miossec, J., & Signoles, P. (1976). Les réseaux de transport en Tunisie. *Cahiers d'outre-mer*, *29*(114), 151–194.

National Institute of Statistics. (2023). *Principal export products: Mines, phosphate and derivatives*. https://www.ins.tn

Salem, A. (2005). *L'espace des ports de commerce tunisiens*. Rapport de synthèse.

Sersiron, N. (2018). *Dette et extractivisme*. Éditions Utopia.

Southcott, C. (2016). Y a-t-il possible d'échapper à la malédiction des ressources dans l'Arctique? In M.-J. Fortin et al. (Eds.), *Ressources naturelles, gouvernance et collectivités* (pp. 9–27). Éditions du GRIDEQ.

Tunisian Industry Portal. (2023). *Companies with 100% foreign capital.* https://www.tunisieindustrie.nat.tn/en/etrangere.asp
Tunisian Institute of Competitiveness and Qauntitative Studies (TICQS). (2021). The 2021 regional development index. http://www.itceq.tn/en/
Vázquez Lezama, P., Talahite, F., Rousset Yépez, B., & Laourari, I. (2023). Introduction: Pétropolitiques, rente et extractivisme dans les pays des Suds. *Revue internationale des études du développement*, *251*, 7–31.
Veltmeyer, H., & Lau, E. (Eds.). (2020). *Buen vivir and the challenges to capitalism in Latin America.* Routledge.
World Bank. (2023). *International debt statistics.* https://datatopics.worldbank.org/debt/ids/countryanalytical/TUN?utm_source=chatgpt.com
World Bank. (2023). *Worldwide Governance Indicators.* Washington DC: World Bank, accessible at: https://www.worldbank.org/en/publication/worldwide-governance-indicators

8 Rentier State, State Class, and Social Movements in Algeria

Mourad Ouchichi

Introduction

This chapter explores the link between the recurrent crises of the rentier State (1986–2014) and the two most significant popular uprisings in the history of independent Algeria, namely the popular revolt of October 1988 and that of the *hirak* in February 2019. According to our hypothesis, the simultaneity of these two uprisings, which began during periods of crisis for the rentier State, is no coincidence. We argue that the socioeconomic and political conditions that prevailed strongly influenced their outbreak and scale.

After more than a decade of exceptional opulence, Algeria faced a financial crisis in the mid-1980s that was without precedent in its independent history. The sudden and lasting fall in international hydrocarbon prices called into question the country's entire macroeconomic balance. The government responded with drastic austerity measures, triggering a social crisis across all sections of society, marked by soaring unemployment, worsening food shortages, and falling purchasing power. Within the government, dissent emerged over the means to tackle the crisis. Two years later, the popular uprising of October 1988 broke out, marking a radical turning point in the history of independent Algeria.

At the end of the 1990s, international hydrocarbon prices rose sharply and remained high for a long time, enabling Algeria not only to re-establish its macrofinancial equilibrium and pay off its foreign debt ahead of schedule but also to build up a substantial financial cushion in the form of foreign exchange reserves. In addition, the government embarked on generous, albeit unequal, social policies through massive job-creation and housing-construction programs. At the same time, the government implemented a number of investment programs, notably in infrastructure, agriculture, and services.

However, in 2014, a major event occurred, namely the turnaround in the international hydrocarbon market, and the Algerian rentier State once again found itself facing a financial crisis. Faced with this situation, the reaction of the authorities was, as usual, very similar to that of the mid-1980s, marked by austerity, reduced imports of capital goods, a halt to civil service recruitment, and so on. As a result, social unrest set in, and once again, dissension emerged within the various clans of power. Every day, through the media, Algerians were stunned to discover

DOI: 10.4324/9781003730750-8

corruption scandals involving several dignitaries of the regime, the extent to which public money had been wasted on infrastructure projects that had previously been heralded as the project of the century, such as the East–West motorway, capital flight, and money laundering—in short, a total breakdown of State institutions. It is against this backdrop that, on 22 February 2019, Algeria will witness the largest and most original popular uprising since its independence, known as the *hirak*.

In order to decipher the workings of the Algerian political and economic arena since the late 1980s, we have chosen to structure our analysis as follows. First, we will review the main political and economic events leading up to the 1988 revolt. We will then look at the background to the long period of financial prosperity (1999–2014). Finally, we will analyze the economic, political, and social developments that followed the sudden downturn in the global oil market from 2014 to 2015 and ultimately led to the popular *hirak* uprising in February 2019.

Our aim will be to highlight the *similarities* and *differences* between the popular uprising of 1988 and that of 2019, while taking account of our starting hypothesis, namely the link between the crisis of the rentier State and its consequences for the constituent segments of the State class and the emergence of social movements.

The Theoretical and Conceptual Framework of the Study

Given the multiple aspects of our theme, we feel that some introductory remarks are in order.

It is quite clear that the main concept underlying our subject is that of rents. In this case, we are talking about the decline in oil revenues in the mid-1980s and from 2014 onward, in addition to the two movements that followed, namely the popular uprising of October 1988 and the popular *hirak of* 2019.

In our case, the rent corresponds to the income the State receives from the sale of hydrocarbons on the international market. This income is therefore of external origin, totally independent of the local mode of production and accumulation. This State monopoly of rents and its strangeness from productive investment gives the social groups that control State power an autonomy that enables them to assert their dominance over society (Beblawi, 1987). This brings us to another concept, that of the rentier State. Without wishing to go into detail on the numerous works on the Rentier State, we will briefly recall its main characteristics.

A rentier State is one whose economy is essentially based on revenues from the export of raw materials (Beblawi & Luciani, 1987)—in Algeria's case, hydrocarbons. Drawing on Beblawi (1990), we will briefly outline the key characteristics of a rentier State. In a rentier economy, only a minority is involved in controlling the rents, while the majority is involved in consumption and distribution. A rentier economy is also doubly dependent: on rents for its foreign exchange inflows and on the international market for its supplies. Furthermore, because of the concentration of revenues in a single export sector and the monopoly exercised over the distribution of these revenues, the rentier State is often prone to poor governance, lack of transparency, corruption, and permanent political and social tensions.[1]

Another question posed by the rentier State relates to the social groups that gain access to the power to control and distribute rents. On this point, it seems appropriate to refer to the theoretical model constructed by R. Ouaissa (Ouaissa, 2010) and the evolution of the State class in Algeria. Far from being fortuitous, this choice is the result of consulting practically all the theses on the subject, first, in the context of a doctoral thesis that I defended at the *Institut d'Études Politiques de Lyon* in 2011 on the political obstacle to economic reform in Algeria and several studies, then with reference to articles produced since then.

Drawing on Hartmut Elsenhans' concept of the State class, Ouaissa's model provides us with the keys to some stimulating reflections, not only on the sociological component of this class in Algeria but also—and above all—on its development as a function of variations in the State's main source of income, namely oil revenues. With regard to the structure of this class—not to be confused with the Marxist sense of the term—Ouaissa's model offers many original avenues; we will mention a few by way of illustration.

First, the model has the advantage of revealing both the political and economic aspects of this class. It links issues of power to issues of control and distribution of an external source of income, namely oil revenues.

Second, Ouaissa's model reveals, contrary to many theses, that the State class is not made up of clans. The clan in Ouaissa's model is a small entity, and therefore not a determining factor in the recomposition of the State class. For the author, the State class is made up of segments that are sometimes united and sometimes rivalrous, and these segments are made up of clans and groups that move according to the political situation, but above all the economic situation, in relation to the financial "health" of the rentier State.

Third, with regard to the mechanisms of recruitment and, more broadly, of the renewal of the personnel of the State class, the author has had the ingenuity to supplement the economic aspect of Hartmut's Elsenhans' concept with the teachings of the Bourdieusian theory of social space. In addition to material capital, which is rent, the author adds social, cultural, and symbolic capital as factors of ascent within the State class.

Finally, on the question of changes or evolution of the State class, the author points to the volume of rent as an explanatory factor. In his view, the State class undergoes two main phases of development: a consolidation phase, which itself goes through several stages (when the rent increases), and a segmentation phase (when the rent decreases). These two phases or cycles are interspersed by a buffer phase that the author calls the "zero moment," in which an "inter-segment consensus" is reached between rival segments (Ouaissa, 2010, p. 71).

Ouaissa divides the consolidation phase into several stages. First, the unification of segments around a segment in power. Second, the segment in power attempts to broaden its legitimacy base. Third, the stage involves constitutional and institutional changes. Finally, there are two phases, characterized, respectively, by the sidelining of political opponents and the organization of elections that confirm the total reign of the segment in power.

Ultimately, the present work will be based simultaneously on the *theory of the Rentier State* (Beblawi & Luciani, 1987) and on the *concept of the State class*, as formalized initially by Hartmut Elsenhans (1996), based principally on the observation of Algeria's economic and political development, and subsequently enriched by Rachid Ouaissa (2010) by integrating Algeria's contemporary developments.

The Revolt of October 1988 as a Consequence of the Crisis of the 1980s

The aim of this section is to provide a retrospective of the most significant political and economic events leading up to the revolt of October 1988.

Long hidden from national and international public opinion, thanks to oil revenues, the contradictions of the Algerian political and economic model were brutally exposed during the bloody events of October 1988. For several days, even weeks, the country was in a state of widespread insurrection. Young and not-so-young alike poured into practically every town in the country and ransacked everything that symbolized the "FLN State,"[2] from party offices to ministry headquarters, including State-run distribution outlets (Souk-El Fellah, Monoprix, etc.).

It was an outright rejection of anything reminiscent of the party State (the FLN). Panic set in at the top, and the President called in the army to restore order. The military intervened—a first in the country's history—and fired live ammunition at the demonstrators, causing 159 deaths according to the official toll and more than 600 according to other hospital sources, thousands of detainees and, above all, torture on a massive scale. The "tacit contract"—maintained at a cost of billions of dollars—linking the population to the regime had broken down, and the image of the so-called People's Army had seriously deteriorated.

The following section examines some of the facts behind these events. In this sense, it seems that they are, above all, the expression of an acute political and socioeconomic crisis accelerated by the oil shock of 1986. Indeed, it is difficult to understand the scale of the bloody events of October without recalling the crisis generated by the reduction in State resources following the oil shock, which affected the population's access to essential goods and services.

The 1986 Crisis and Its Management

It is important to stress that until the mid-1980s, Algeria never experienced any financial constraints. On the contrary, the State's financial comfort grew steadily throughout the 1970s and early 1980s. Indeed, the share of oil taxation in the State's fiscal resources rose steadily from 31.5% in the period 1970–1973 to 63.3% in 1980, after having been only 12% between 1963 and 1966. The nationalization of hydrocarbons in 1971 and the two oil shocks of 1974 and 1979 led to a steady increase in the State's foreign exchange earnings. In the minds of most Algerian leaders, the rise in prices and the oil windfall were virtually irreversible (Ouchichi, 2014, p. 122).

However, two phenomena occurred simultaneously in 1986, which had a profound impact on the Algerian economy: the fall in hydrocarbon prices and the devaluation of the dollar. During the winter of 1985, crude oil prices had fallen to 30 dollars, but within a few months this trend accelerated, reaching a low of 10 dollars a barrel in July 1986, before finally stabilizing around the last quarter of the year at 15 dollars, a drop of 45% compared with 1985. At the same time, the Algerian economy was affected by another phenomenon: the devaluation of the dollar. In 1986, the dollar lost value against several currencies: 18% against the German mark and 21% against the yen.

The first consequences of this reduction in external means of payment were seen in the sharp fall in investment volumes and imports. The 1985–1989 five-year plan was abandoned and its investment program reduced: in 1985–1986 alone, the volume of investment was reduced by 9% per year. On the other hand, productive investment fell by an average of 13% a year between 1987 and 1989, and overall investment was reduced by 7% in real terms over the same period. Imports in turn experienced a negative growth rate of −7.8% on average between 1985 and 1989 (−0.5 in 1985, −16.4 in 1986, −6.7 in 1988, and −2.2 in 1988). In addition, between 1986 and 1987, household and business supplies fell by 32.6% (Dahmani, 1999, p. 83). The consequences of these simultaneous falls in investment and imports—mainly of equipment—were particularly felt by the national production system.

The deficit of public enterprises, which was already substantial, was worsening due to a lack of supplies of raw materials and other necessary equipment; their bank overdraft amounted to DA 42 billion on 31 December 1988. For the sake of maintaining social peace and concealing the extent of the crisis from public opinion, the government resorted to a number of practices whose consequences were more serious than the evil they were supposed to curb. It cut back on imports of equipment rather than consumption, resorted to short-term borrowing, and even went so far as to "offer suppliers oil in exchange for semolina" (Gouméziane, 2004, p. 176). The result was a slowdown in investment programs and an increase in financial costs, further penalizing already fragile businesses and having a negative impact on economic growth. To make up the budget deficit, the authorities also resorted to printing money, which had the mechanical effect of fuelling inflation, deepening deficits, and eroding the purchasing power of fixed incomes.

Between government action aimed at "hiding" the effects of the crisis, and that of the various networks and interest groups, the crisis was constantly feeding on its own consequences, leading to the total paralysis of the system. This was manifested in the breakdown of macroeconomic balances, the worsening of the budget deficit and that of the public sector, a dangerous increase in indebtedness, shortages, the development of the informal market, and so on. The combination of all these phenomena has led to a rise in unemployment and a fall in purchasing power. In short, the accelerated deterioration in the social situation of the population has led to an increase in social discontent, which has been expressed through a proliferation of urban riots and workers' strikes.

The Economic Origins of the Scale of Social Protest: Shortages and the Development of the Informal Market

From 1985 onward, social discontent worsened as a result of the oil crisis. Two phenomena directly linked to the administrative management of the economy developed: shortages and, as a corollary, the development of the parallel market.

In this respect, it should be noted that prior to 1984, the informal market in Algeria occupied a relatively marginal position, due to the State's almost unlimited capacity to meet the population's demand for goods and services through imports and price subsidies. However, with the currency crisis (1985–1986), the State found itself unable to bridge the gap between supply and demand. Rather than formulating an alternative economic policy, the government settled for administrative measures that further complicated the situation. These measures contributed to the development of an informal market that now invaded all trading spaces. The lack of means of payment was added to the rigidity of import procedures (quota system, prior authorizations, etc.), causing recurring shortages that now affect all sectors of activity.

Faced with the sharp fall in means of payment, the government led by A. Brahimi took action that had consequences all the more harmful than the others: the strengthening of State control over the distribution channels for imported products allowed State-owned companies, under pressure from the trade union, to set up a "State" network for the distribution of subsidized products, especially for public-sector employees, and also gave them the possibility of importing without declaring the origin of the currency used.

The first measure, initially aimed at controlling the distribution of products in short supply, accentuated the monopoly over the import and distribution of sensitive products held by a few State-owned companies. This administrative monopoly turned the threat of shortages into an effective means of exerting pressure on the government by the managers of State-owned companies. Some managers of large State-owned companies took advantage of this situation to impose their "import quotas." The result was a significant increase in imports. This was possible because the government responded to the tightening of financial and commercial credit by encouraging short-term credit to finance current supplies. However, the population continued to suffer from shortages. Products passed through parallel-market channels before reaching the final consumer, who had close links with distribution managers in the administered market.

At the same time, the official trade union, the General Union of Algerian Workers (UGTA), demanded and obtained privileged access for public-sector workers to limited consumer goods, via a national network of subsidized consumer cooperatives. This led to the development of a "parallel" administered market from which the unemployed and private sector employees were excluded. With the complicity of the union's social work leaders and even public-sector employees, a "permanent shortage" was organized within these cooperatives. In reality, scarce goods and services, at subsidized prices, were immediately bought and resold eight to ten times more expensively on the parallel market. Employees spent more time "queuing" for these products than working in the workshops, resulting in a general relaxation of factory discipline and contributing to an even more pronounced fall in the profitability of the public sector.

Faced with the scale of the shortages and the scarcity of foreign currency, the government decided to authorize private companies—and individuals—to pay for foreign transactions without going through the official foreign exchange channels (declaration of imports without payments). The result was the development of an informal foreign exchange market. The combined effect of the immediate interests of the government, the managers of public import and distribution companies, the official trade union, and private entrepreneurs, encouraged the emergence and development upstream and downstream of a parallel market—a real parallel economy, one might say—which invaded all sectors of activity, from the consumer goods market to the foreign exchange market, via the property and building materials markets.

Clearly, the additional costs generated by these rents were ultimately borne by the final consumer, whether unemployed or on a fixed income. The resulting shortages and social frustrations were all the more difficult for the population to bear because they followed a period of prosperity, under the official slogan "For a Better Life."

This economic and financial crisis, which has given rise to an acute social crisis, is not without impact on the political system and the centrifugal and centripetal forces that make it up.

The Political Consequences of the Oil Shock: Political Divisions and Segmentation of the State Class

The effects of the 1986 oil shock were not only felt in economic and social terms. Politically, the unanimity around the President began to crack, particularly in terms of the solutions to be found to the crisis. Faced with a worsening economic situation and social discontent, the different segments of government were divided, each seeking to neutralize its opponents by any means possible, including economic sabotage. A look back at the positions and motivations of the various components of the coalition around President Chadli Bendjedid is crucial to understanding the extent of the crisis of the rentier State in the mid-1980s and the outbreak of the October 1988 uprising.

To understand the logic of the multiple subdivisions that the Algerian political system underwent under the pressure of the 1986 counter-oil shock, we refer to Ouaissa's explanatory model (Ouaissa, 2010), presented earlier.

Since the coup d'état of 19 June 1965, President Houari Boumediene reigned as absolute master for 13 years. With his death in 1978, independent Algeria was confronted for the first time in its young history with the problem of succession to the summit of power without a military coup.

Faced with the danger of the system as a whole disintegrating, and in the event of a public outbreak of conflict between the many factions that overlapped but opposed each other within the same political regime, the army intervened and imposed the succession. The compromise between the different clans, under the aegis of the intelligence services (Military Security), concerned the appointment of Chadli Bendjedid.

Chosen by his peers but President nonetheless, Chadli Bendjedid inherited several of his predecessor's prerogatives, which he did not hesitate to use in order to strengthen his position within the system. He reactivated the FLN, which at the time of Boumediene resembled, to use M. Harbi's metaphor, "a ship at berth which should neither move nor sink" (Harbi, 1994, p. 196). He reorganized the old system of power by restructuring the dreaded Military Security and widening the circles for the distribution of rents. These "changes in continuity" were carried out against a backdrop of economic "reforms," "for a better life," to use the slogans of the single party (the FLN) in the early 1980s.

Our earlier analysis of the first years of the reign of the new team led by President Chadli Bendjedid shows that it took several years for the new configuration of the regime to stabilize.[3] These were years during which relentless struggles for power were waged, combining economic reorganization and political dividends against a backdrop of reorganization of the centers of State power. The result was an all-out reorganization that gave rise to a multipolar system under the direct control of the security services.

It is therefore quite clear that what Ouaissa calls the "moment Zero" corresponds to the period of the "consensual" choice of Chadli Bendjedid. The State class entered a phase of consolidation, all the more propitious as the first half of the 1980s coincided with a particularly high level of financial comfort for the State following the second oil crisis at the end of the 1970s. However, this stability did not last long. The financial crisis of 1986 revealed the existence of at least three poles, or segments, at the top of the State: the now rehabilitated FLN, the Presidency under the control of the presidential cabinet, and finally the Government. Thus began the phase of segmentation of the State class.

On the one hand, there was the FLN. Long marginalized, the single party was rehabilitated by President Chadli Bendjedid in the 1980s. It made a dazzling comeback on the Algerian political scene. It monopolized the official discourse and took charge of controlling society through mass organizations, and the productive apparatus through the official trade union, the UGTA. From then on, the FLN was the refuge for all those who had been excluded from the direct management of affairs and who were waiting for the right moment to return to center stage. It brought together what is usually described as the conservative wing of the regime. The FLN's political line was based on strict compliance with the constitution, which instituted political monolithism and socialism, considered to be an achievement of the Algerian revolution.

On the other side was the presidential cabinet, headed by General Larbi Belkheir. He represented the real power within the Presidency. He was particularly responsible for the so-called areas of sovereignty. A discreet man, he played a major role in the choice of President Chadli Bendjedid as the successor to President H. General Belkheir was considered to be the "real boss" within the Presidency, having played a major role in the choice of President Chadli as the successor to President

H. Boumediene, and forging numerous links with business circles both inside and outside the country. The clan represented by Belkheir was described as "privatist," because it expressed the wish of business circles to steer State action toward total privatization of the public economic sector. However, the privatization advocated by the Cabinet should not be confused with liberalization. The "privatist" clan, like its competitors, remained committed to political control of the company. The "privatization" advocated by the Cabinet was part of a "sham liberalism" approach, aimed more at transferring State ownership to the private sector than at establishing a market economy with its political implications.

Last came the Government led by Abdelhamid Brahimi. It was Brahimi's task to manage current affairs after the—unconfessed—failure of his plan to restructure the financial and organizational structure of State enterprises. Moreover, he had not proposed any alternative project as part of the second five-year plan for 1985–1989.

While the three poles mentioned earlier rallied around the new President in the early 1980s, the financial crisis revealed their differences on the economic role of the State and the future of the public sector. Put another way, a sort of "political" division of labor between these three poles was established during the period from 1979 to 1985. But it was called into question by the worsening socioeconomic and political situation generated by the oil shock of 1986. While the FLN clung to the eternal line that socialism was an irreversible choice, the President's Cabinet acted through the press by attacking the "socialism of the teat." The government, for its part, tried to play down the seriousness of the crisis. A careful reading of the articles in the public press at the time perfectly illustrates the positions of the various parties. For example, the influential weekly *Algérie actualité* conveyed the positions of the "privatists," while the magazine *Révolution africaine* echoed the positions of the party. Faced with these two positions, the government tried as best it could to manage the consequences of the crisis. Meanwhile, the contradictions were sharpening, provoking an unprecedented social crisis. This was the third factor, as important as the first, in analyzing this revolt, the most significant the country had ever seen.

It was against this backdrop that the reformers emerged and, once in power, led the structural reforms that put an end to the centralized planning system and the one-party system. This experiment was quickly aborted in September 1991.

At the end of this section, which examines the conduct of economic policy in Algeria after the oil crisis of 1986 and the ensuing crisis of the rentier State, it is clear that the many contradictions in the management of this financial crisis led to a political and social crisis, which in turn triggered the popular uprising of October 1988.

Will the February 2019 *hirak* Be History Repeating Itself?

In February 2019, Algeria experienced one of the largest popular uprisings in its post-independence history. Millions of citizens took to the streets across the country every Friday at 2 p.m. sharp. Since then, every Friday and every Tuesday (for students), millions of Algerians have marched for more than two years. These weekly demonstrations emerged in a fragile political and economic climate, with a president who has been ill since at least 2013. This crisis had also been brewing for several years, fueled by internal divisions exacerbated by the end of the financial boom that maintained consensus at the top of the State. Between 2015 and 2018, a period covering almost the entire duration of the fourth mandate, hydrocarbon export revenues fell by an average of 14% a year.[4]

This movement, which began by contesting a possible fifth term for President Abdelaziz Bouteflika, quickly became radicalized and demanded the departure of the "system." This system had taken to extremes the logic of predation of national wealth and submission to imperialism. A section of civil society, previously disengaged from "politics" through weariness and fatalism, once again mobilized to denounce this prebend, erected as a mode of governance.

Following the example of our analysis of the events of October 1988, we shall seek to answer—from the privileged angle of political economy—the question of the economic factors generated by the crisis of the rentier State at the revolutionary moment of the *hirak*.

Chronicle of a Period of Financial Opulence (1999–2014)

Since 1998, international oil and commodity prices have soared, leading Algeria into a period of unprecedented financial prosperity. Between 2003 and 2013, oil revenues brought in between 800 billion and 1,000 billion dollars. Taking advantage of this windfall, President Bouteflika's regime launched a vast program to restructure the economy. On the one hand, it centralized public-sector management and called into question the independence of the Central Bank. On the other hand, he decided to open up to the international market by ratifying the association agreement with the EU in 2002 and by joining the Arab Free Trade Area in 2009, thus completely opening up the national economy to international competition without it being really prepared for it (Ouchichi, 2011). In addition, as part of its economic recovery plans, the government embarked on a policy of massive investment in infrastructure (construction of motorways, housing, dams, etc.). This massive injection of money into an economy with little local supply led to an explosion in imports.

According to Algerian customs figures, the period 2001–2014 was marked by a surge in imports. This explosion is notable from 2001 onward, with growth peaking in 2004 (+46.7%), 2008 (+33.0%), and 2011 (+16.7%). Average annual growth in imports between 2001 and 2012 was around 33.7%. The total value of imports rose from 9.9 billion dollars to 58.33 billion dollars. Non-food consumer goods recorded the highest growth rate at +579%, rising from 1.5 billion dollars in 2001 to almost 10 billion dollars in 2012 (Ouchichi, 2011).

Despite the facilities and advantages granted to the private sector, such as advantageous taxation, bank loans, and the introduction of the 51/49 law[5] on foreign investment by private nationals, Algeria has not seen the emergence of a major industrial sector or a significant increase in the number of large economic enterprises. Indeed, according to figures from the Ministry of Small- and Medium-sized Enterprises (SMEs), at the end of 2019, 97% of the overall SME population consisted of Very Small Enterprises (VSEs) (with fewer than ten employees), with this model remaining strongly dominant in the national economic fabric, followed by Small Enterprises (SEs) with 2.6% and Medium-sized Enterprises (MEs) with 0.4% (Ministère de l'Industrie et des Mines, 2019).

Paradoxically, despite the State's financial ease, thanks to the increase in revenues from hydrocarbon exports, the real economy has remained in a State of virtual stagnation, with a marked decline in the industrial sector in particular. In 2012, the hydrocarbon sector still accounted for more than a third of GDP (37%), more than two-thirds of budget revenues (70%), and virtually all of the country's foreign currency earnings (97%).

As in 1986, it was against a backdrop of structural weakness in the real economy and total dependence on oil and gas revenues that the financial crisis of 2014 occurred, following the fall in international oil and gas prices. This crisis gave rise to a social crisis, which in turn fueled political dissension within the ruling class.

Austerity Sets in for the Long Haul

At the end of 2014, a major event occurred with the upheaval of the international oil markets. The price per barrel fell from 96.29 dollars in 2014 to 49.26 dollars in 2015, then to 40.60 dollars and 52.51 dollars in 2016 and 2017, respectively, before rising slightly in 2018. Faced with falling revenues, the Government panicked and took measures that were as ineffective as they were harmful.

In fact, the government's only solution was to resort to internal debt in an attempt to cushion the deficit by means of a national bond issue. All the bonds were worth 50,000 dinars and had maturities ranging from three to five years, with interest rates ranging from 5% to 5.75%. Far from attracting informal funds, subscriptions were limited to public bodies and private individuals involved in the system (Forum des Chefs d'Entreprises).

Faced with the rapid erosion of foreign exchange reserves and the depletion of the Revenue Regulation Fund, the authorities decided to resort to direct monetary financing of the public treasury by the Bank of Algeria from 2017, by printing money as part of the so-called non-conventional financing for the period 2017–2019. This arrangement resulted in an outstanding amount of 6,556.2 billion dinars, representing around 32.3% of GDP at the end of 2019.

Furthermore, in order to curb spending, the State has taken measures such as halting infrastructure projects and reducing the budgets allocated to equipment and operations. The 2016 and 2017 Finance Acts reduced the investment budget by 19% and 28%, respectively, giving a total budget reduction of 41% compared with 2015.

In parallel with the stagnation in wages and the apparent deterioration in public services, the government has resorted to a recruitment freeze in the civil service. While the public sector used to account for up to 40% of employment in the country, by 2019 it accounted for just 38%. In the process, thousands of jobs were cut in the civil service. After early retirement was abolished, thousands of workers rushed to take advantage of this provision before it was abolished; only some of these workers were eventually replaced by new recruits.

The multiplication of protests in the world of work, in the towns and countryside, is indicative of the social stagnation that reigns in the country. Social protest has even spread to the south of the country, where the population is reputed to be rather "calm," to the point where its inhabitants have ended up joining these national protests.

The social movement that best expresses this widespread social stagnation and protest is certainly that of the unemployed in the Algerian Sahara. It is an interesting illustration of this phenomenon of social unrest and ambivalent relations between the state and society (Belakhdar, 2015). More broadly, the protests that took place in the south of the country between 2004 and 2017 may be a representative sample of the experience of the majority of the Algerian population. These movements, which initially focused on the issue of employment raised by the movement of the unemployed in the South, gradually extended to the issue of local development, the environment (shale gas), and national sovereignty (Belakhdar, 2015). We believe that this case alone embodies the denunciation of the structural marginality suffered by whole sections of society, whether in urban or rural areas, in the North or the South. The movement's flagship slogans, such as "Oppressed and dispossessed citizens in a country of gas and oil" and "Poor people in a rich country," still ring in the ears of the millions of "left behind" in Algeria. The slogan *Mahgourin fi bled el pétrole*,[6] literally "Marginalised in the land of oil," shows that this movement has a real desire to represent all those left behind on a national scale.

Rise and Fall of the "Bouteflika system": From Consolidation to Segmentation of the State Class

After a decade of civil war and four years under the dictates of Structural Adjustment, Algeria embarked on a distinctive journey in the 2000s. Politically, the decade was marked by the accession to power of President Abdelaziz Bouteflika following the early and controversial presidential elections of April 1999. On the economic front, the country returned to significant financial prosperity. Following the stabilization of macroeconomic indicators, thanks to the SAP, the country's financial situation improved considerably as a result of the substantial and lasting increase in hydrocarbon prices on the international market.

To analyze the main political and economic events of this decade, we rely on the theoretical model developed by Ouaissa (2010), similar to our analysis of the crisis of the rentier State in the mid-1980s. According to Ouaissa, the State class goes through two phases depending on the volume of rents: a phase of consolidation and a phase of segmentation. Between these two phases, there is a period of consensus, which the author describes as "moment zero" (Ouaissa, 2010, p. 71). Between the resignation of President Liamine Zeroual in 1998 and the first years of Bouteflika's reign, it seems that the Algerian State class experienced this situation. A consensus seems to have developed between the different segments, allowing Bouteflika to work methodically on consolidating the State class around the presidency.

Ouaissa divides the consolidation phase into several stages. The first consists of the unification of segments around a dominant segment, in this case, President Bouteflika's clan during this period. Second, the segment in power sought to broaden its legitimacy base. The Civil Concord Act of 2002 and the National Reconciliation Act of 2005 appear to be aimed, among other things, at compensating for Bouteflika's lack of legitimacy at the time of his election in 1999. The third stage involves constitutional and institutional changes. In April 2002, President Bouteflika revised the constitution. The importance of this revision lay above all in the referendum, which legitimized it.

The next two phases were characterized by the marginalization of political opponents and the organization of elections, which confirmed the total domination of the segment in power. One example is the dissension between the segments when Bouteflika was re-elected for a second term, which led to the dismissal of the army's powerful Chief of Staff, General Mohamed Lamari, in 2004.

This phase of consolidation of the State class around the presidential circle was characterized by two phenomena during the 2000s. The first was the strengthening of the influence of the presidency at the expense of the other two poles of Algerian power, namely the General Staff and the security services. The second was the rapid rise of influential businessmen grouped within the powerful *Fédération des Chefs d'Entreprises* (FCE), chaired by Ali Haddad, currently in prison for corruption and influence peddling.

The consolidation phase is followed by segmentation. According to Ouaissa's theoretical model, this segmentation is caused by the decline in rents. With the fall in hydrocarbon prices in 2014, the consensus around Bouteflika became more fragile. In 2015, a media "war" broke out between the DRS and the presidency, allied with the army general staff. The latter two succeeded in getting General Toufik sacked. This short-term pact was shattered with the emergence of the *hirak* in February 2019, leading to a new segmentation of the State class. After Bouteflika's resignation, the General Staff proceeded to dismantle the network of influence led by the President's brother, Saïd Bouteflika, and to marginalize the loyalists of the powerful General Toufik. The ensuing purge illustrated the incestuous relationship between the groups at the top of the power structure around the sharing of revenue.

In conclusion, these dysfunctions of the rentier State and its rentier growth model are at the root of the popular *hirak* uprising. Although this movement expresses political demands, denouncing corruption and the mismanagement of the State and demanding the departure of the "system," it also represents, and more than ever, the expression of a profound economic and social malaise.

Conclusion

At the end of this study, it is appropriate to offer a brief comparative analysis of these two periods, which gave rise to two major social movements in Algerian political and economic history. As the previous analysis has shown, the similarities between the factors that led to the outbreak of the events of October 1988 and the *hirak* of February 2019 are striking. They can be summarized as follows: Whenever the international oil and gas market turns downward, the rentier State faces violent financial crises. The reduction in financial resources is simultaneously causing a deterioration in living conditions for large sections of society and dissension within the political system over the solutions to be adopted to overcome the crisis. This dissension reflected the segmentation of the State class and the emergence of rivalries over the control and distribution of a now-restricted income. New political and social alliances were formed to dominate or maintain power. Over time, the crisis of the rentier State, initially financial, became multidimensional (political, economic, and social). It was against this backdrop that the revolt of October 1988 and the popular movement of February 2019 broke out. At first sight, there's nothing paradoxical about this if we consider that the same causes produce the same effects. However, how can we explain this similarity, given that the two periods preceding these social movements are radically different? Let's look at a few examples.

Algeria in the 1980s operated under a system of centralized socialist planning and a single-party regime. The economy was entirely administered by the State, and economic policies were decided by the party's central committee, and the government was appointed by the president. The 2000s present an entirely different context. Since the early 1990s, the Algerian economy has been undergoing a process of "liberalization," marked by a four-year SAP under the aegis of the International Monetary Fund (IMF). Politically, Algeria is officially under a democratic regime, despite the realities on the ground.

Another difference lies in the weight of the public and private sectors in the economy. In the 1980s, the public sector monopolized all economic activities. The Algerian private sector was subject to investment ceilings and administrative authorizations from the State, thus operating under a "provisional freedom." In the 2000s, the public sector occupied a marginal position, while the private sector held an almost total monopoly over the country's economic activity.

With the deepening of the financial crisis in 1986, the public sector, which was mainly in deficit, became a burden for the State. The severe reduction in public investment and the de-industrialization of the economy were accompanied by privatization imposed by the IMF as part of the SAP, thus considerably reducing Algeria's public sector. Meanwhile, the private sector experienced a rapid rise, marked by the emergence of billionaires who ostentatiously flaunted their wealth and openly flaunted their links with politicians. They are also setting up media outlets and venturing into the political arena.

At the same time, there has been a proliferation of foreign multinationals dominating major public projects, such as housing construction and the East–West motorway. They are even penetrating traditionally regulated sectors, such as the manufacture and marketing of tobacco, or the granting of mobile phone and internet licenses.

Since the 2000s, Algeria has gradually opened up to the international market, ratifying the Association Agreement with the EU in 2002 and joining the Arab Free Trade Area in 2009, thereby exposing its production base to foreign competition without adequate preparation.

These examples, and many others, clearly demonstrate the differences between the two periods preceding the social movements studied (1988/2019). However, the similarities in the political and economic consequences of the financial crises of 1986 and 2014 on the Algerian politico-economic system are striking: segmentation of the State class, economic and social crisis, and the triggering of major social movements.

The reasons for this continuity in change, to paraphrase a key slogan of the single party in the early 1980s ("change in continuity"), lie in the nature of the Algerian State and the relationship between politics and economics in this country.

Algeria is a rentier State dominated by an authoritarian regime since its independence in 1962. This neo-patrimonial regime uses economic resources to maintain power and reconfigure society. By distributing part of the rents in a discretionary manner, it creates a clientelist social base in place of electoral support. The size of this base fluctuates with the abundance or scarcity of financial resources: it expands in times of opulence and shrinks in times of crisis. This discretionary distribution, for clientelist purposes, in turn gives rise to widespread corruption.

This mode of operation of the rentier State remains the same under the so-called socialist economy and after the 1990s liberalization. An analysis of Algeria's economic history during the crisis phases of the rentier State provides a better understanding of the nature of the political system in Algeria through the composition of its ruling class. This system follows an overall logic, the continuity of which is not called into question by the many changes at the head of the State, nor by the economic reforms undertaken since the 1980s. The integration of the economy into the political sphere and the use of economic resources to maintain power symbolize the system's continuity, despite the many changes it has undergone since the 1980s. This sums up the ambiguity of the Algerian political system, which, on the one hand, seeks to eliminate the deficits that sterilize oil revenues but, on the other, refuses to abandon the use of the economy to dominate society.

Notes

1 For further analysis of the contingent effects of rent on political regimes, see Dunning (2008), Karl (1997), and Ross (2001).
2 Front de Libération National, Algeria's single party from 1962 to 1989.
3 Chadli Bendjedid is co-opted by the 5th FLN Congress as the sole candidate for the presidency. Chosen for a second term from 12 January 1983.
4 Average calculated from Banque d'Algérie annual reports.
5 This rule sets the threshold for foreign investor participation at 49% of the capital of companies governed by Algerian law.
6 "Mahgourin" actually comes from the word "Hogra," which in Algerian and North African dialectal Arabic designates any form of injustice, contempt, or abuse of power.

References

Beblawi, H. (1987). The rentier state in the Arab world. *Arab Studies Quarterly*, *9*(4), 383–398.

Beblawi, H. (1990). The rentier state in the Arab world. In G. Luciani (Ed.), *The Arab state* (pp. 85–98). University of California Press.

Beblawi, H., & Luciani, G. (Eds.). (1987). *The rentier state*. Croom Helm.

Belakhdar, N. (2015). "L'éveil du Sud" ou quand la contestation vient de la marge: Une analyse du mouvement des chômeurs algériens. *Politique africaine*, *137*, 27–48. https://doi.org/10.3917/polaf.137.0027

Dahmani, A. (1999). *L'Algérie à l'épreuve: Économie politique des réformes 1980–1997*. L'Harmattan.

Dunning, T. (2008). *Crude democracy: Natural resource wealth and political regimes*. Cambridge University Press.

Elsenhans, H. (1996). *State, class and development*. Sangam Books.

Gouméziane, S. (2004). *Le fils de Novembre*. Paris-Méditerranée.

Harbi, M. (1994). *L'Algérie et son destin: Croyants ou citoyens*. Médias Associés.

Karl, T. L. (1997). *The paradox of plenty: Oil booms and petro-states*. University of California Press.

Ministère de l'Industrie et des Mines. (2019). *Bulletin d'information statistique de la PME* (No. 35, 1er semestre 2019). https://www.mipmepi.gov.dz/IMG/pdf/Bulletin_PME_N_35_vf.pdf

Ouaissa, R. (2010). *La classe-État algérienne 1962–2000: Une histoire du pouvoir algérien entre sous-développement, rente pétrolière et terrorisme*. Publisud.

Ouchichi, M. (2011). *L'obstacle politique aux réformes économiques en Algérie* (Doctoral dissertation, Université Lyon 2). http://theses.univ-lyon2.fr/documents/lyon2/2011/ouchichi_m

Ouchichi, M. (2014). *Les fondements politiques de l'économie rentière en Algérie*. Déclic Éditions.

Ross, M. L. (2001). Does oil hinder democracy? *World Politics*, *53*(3), 325–361. https://doi.org/10.1353/wp.2001.0011

9 Post-Extractivism, Rent, and Political Participation

The Struggle for Power in Jerada, Morocco

Mustapha Majidi

Introduction

During the 2000s, the map of protests in Morocco changed completely. The "peripheral Morocco" has seen a proliferation of local protest movements, "all politically managed by actions that oscillate between sanctions and concessions" (Bennafla & Badimon, 2010, p. 84). The list is long and includes mobilizations around mines and other natural resources.[1] The scale and outcome of these conflicts vary from one region to another, depending on the specific features and complexity of the territory. In the case of Jerada, for example, the protests sparked by the death of two young people in one of the town's illicit wells in 2017 are calling into question the state's policy of reconverting a mining town after extractivist activity came to a halt at the end of the 1990s.

Jerada is representative of a rent-based economic model, characterized by a historical dependence on coal mining, which began in the 1930s under French colonial rule and continued after Moroccan independence. This single extractivist industry has shaped the local economy around this single resource, with little diversification or investment in other areas. The state and companies profited above all from mining revenues, while the region's inhabitants, especially the miners, lived in difficult conditions, with modest wages and low levels of social protection. The accumulation of profits in the hands of an elite and the absence of fair redistribution intensified disparities, exposing Jerada to market fluctuations and resource depletion.

The town was structured around coal mining, and found itself without a viable economic alternative as soon as the mines began to close. The 2017 protests reflect the failure of an extractivist economic model and a state policy that relies on rentier notables. Triggered at the same time as the *Hirak* du Rif,[2] the Jerada protests were to gain new momentum following the royal pardon of the *Hirak* activists and their adhesion to the *Parti du Progrès et Socialisme* (PPS). At the end of the 2021 municipal elections, militants representing the protest movement won the majority of seats on the Jerada municipal council (the movement won 27 of the 30 seats).

The electoral participation of young protesters in 2021 thus reflects major political stakes, in a context marked by post-2017 tensions and the difficulties of post-extractivist transition in Jerada. It is in this sense that this chapter explores the role of the extractivist rentier model in the crisis, detecting the links between

DOI: 10.4324/9781003730750-9

extractivism, the rentier economy, and political power. This will enable us to fully understand the stakes involved in the political participation of actors from the protest movement in the management of local affairs, and apprehend the dynamics of their transition between social mobilization, electoral commitment, and public management. It also examines the implications of this transition for the activists themselves, in a context marked by the end of the local extractivist economy, the domination of notables who profited from a rentier resource economy, and the search for a new development model in Jerada.

Our qualitative approach combines a documentary analysis of extractivism and the Jerada movement,[3] with interviews with local elected officials, activists, and militants. The survey explores the origins of the crisis, the challenges of youth participation, and the economic and political constraints.

Our analysis is structured around two major axes. The first focuses on issues of power and the transformative potential of political engagement in an environment of crisis brought about by a rent-based economic system. This model, based on mining, has benefited a small fringe of the population while relegating the majority to the margins, generating considerable socioeconomic disparities. We study the contexts in which political commitment can play a dual role as an engine for pacification and an instrument for changing perspectives, by dissecting the motivations of those involved and the ways in which this commitment is applied. The second will focus on the internal and external dynamics that result from this political involvement. This includes the study of tensions and alliances within the local council, as well as relations between the newly elected representatives and other local players.

From Extractivist Rents to Political Commitment: What Are the Dynamics of Change in Jerada?

Drawing on the literature relating to the aims of political participation,[4] we can affirm that two motivations, closely linked to the extractivist rent (1), pushed the young people of the *Hirak* to take part in the elections and contribute in effect to the management of local affairs. The main impetus for the newly elected is political and moral; (2) their intention is to put an end to the domination of the notables whose corrupt and clientelist management of public affairs has marginalized many of them. Motivated by a sense of civic duty, they are committed to transparent and inclusive governance, and to breaking with the extractivist dynamic. The second motivation, of a practical nature, aims to stimulate Jerada's development and meet the challenge of its socioeconomic transformation, by putting a decisive end to the cash economy that has kept the town dependent on coal extractivism, and the rentiers who benefit from it (3).

At the Root of the Crisis, an Extractivist Rentier Economic Model

Jerada is a mining town at heart; in other words, it is not a town that used to have a mine but one that has been entirely shaped by it. This is due to the central role played by the mine in the town's economic and urban development. Indeed, all the town's economic activities were closely dependent on the existence of the mine, which structured local life at every level.

Charbonnages du Maroc (CDM) not only managed mining operations but also provided essential services such as drinking water, electricity, street lighting, and liquid waste disposal. In addition, CDM owned a considerable real-estate portfolio, estimated at 3,358 residences—half of the city's real-estate stock—as well as commercial premises. This control over infrastructure and housing gave CDM a dominant role in the organization and development of the town, making the mine the beating heart of Jerada (Iraki & Zabadi, 2021, p. 85).

As Aziz Iraki points out, it was the existence of the mine that imposed the town's location outside the spatial practices of rural populations. The town was not a crossroads for exchange and trade, hence the absence of a commercial elite; and all its land had a domanial status, that is, it was state-owned, which gave advanced power to the central administration and prevented the emergence of a dynamic elite competing for land (Iraki, 2021, pp. 326–327). This is why the political and economic elite were closely linked to the extractivist industry. Before the mine closed, executives from the company that ran the mine (CDM) were at the head of the Jerada commune and on its council.[5] In fact, the boundaries between the commune and the mine were blurred, with some municipal employees also working for CDM. Senior government officials enjoyed privileges such as water, electricity, free accommodation, and catering at the Company's Engineers' Club, reflecting the CDM's stranglehold on the town's management (Iraki, 2021, p. 329).

Controlled by the CDM, this system represents a rentier economy based on extractivist activity. By regulating mining, urban services, and a large proportion of real estate, and even the management of the local council, the CDMs have created a dependency on extractivist rents. This restricts the distribution of profits and hampers economic diversification. This extractivist approach has made Jerada sensitive to economic shocks, amplifying the socioeconomic crisis following the closure of the mines after the failure of the 1988 modernization and expansion plan. Financed by the World Bank to the amount of 27 million dollars, the project proved to be financially unreliable after the fall in the price of coal and the geological difficulties encountered (Iraki & Zabadi, 2021, p. 54). Mine closure was the most appropriate outcome. The mono-industrial model based on extractivist rents had shown its limits and led to the town's collapse.

The final shutdown of the mine on 17 July 2000, and the dismissal of over 5,500 employees were factors that generated a major socioeconomic crisis, marked by accelerated decline.[6] The CDM company, which managed the mine, was the largest employer in Jerada, and its closure in 1998 after 70 years of activity (Berrada, 2018, p. 10) had a considerable impact on the whole region, transforming it into one of the poorest towns in Morocco, with an unemployment rate of over 30% (compared with the national average of around 10%) and a poverty rate of 11%, six points above the national average (Berrada, 2018, p. 6).

To address this situation, the public authorities set up a reconversion plan, comprising several measures, including compensation for the miners and economic reconversion of the town. However, although compensation has been paid out,[7] the reconversion project has not achieved the expected results. This dynamic raises questions about the reasons for the failure of public intervention between 2000 and 2017, from the closure of the mine to the outbreak of the Jerada *Hirak*.

In fact, state action has been deployed in two ways: the first is formal, consisting of equipping the town with major facilities (hospital, bus station, stadium, swimming pool, etc.) through Jerada's territorial upgrading program (2008–2011),[8] while the second is informal, characterized by increased tolerance of informal activities, reflecting a pragmatic adaptation to the post-mining crisis. Indeed, it is through the informal sector that the State transfers resources to local notables in charge of redistributing them to the population.[9] Following the closure of the mine and the withdrawal of CDM, four coal mining licenses were issued to companies by the supervisory ministry.[10] The new owners were former CDM employees, an engineer, and three former trade unionists who managed to obtain these permits, thanks to their relationship with the local and central authorities.[11] They were authorized to operate and distribute coal legally. But, at the same time, other, informal entrepreneurs appeared who had dug their own extraction pits or restored abandoned ones.

Extractive activity was thus relaunched according to two parallel systems: the first of these, a formal one, benefited from a rent granted by the state, while the second, an informal system, emerged out of economic and social necessity. Throughout this period, informal mining was commonplace, tolerated and even tacitly accepted by local authorities. Between 800 and 1,000 miners worked in extremely difficult conditions, exposed to high health and safety risks (Berrada, 2018, p. 7). Unemployed young people had no economic alternatives or prospects other than venturing into clandestine[12] shafts, and even the little-used construction sector was owned by these rentier notables[13] known to the local population as *barons*. These notables drew their legitimacy from the resources granted by the center rather than from their local roots.

In this system of exploitation, the relationship between the two types of enterprise was profoundly unequal and unfair. The informal enterprises, often made up of precarious miners, were forced to sell their coal at low prices to the middlemen of the formal enterprises owned by these barons, who resold it at double the price. This dynamic was a kind of unjust subcontracting, where the rent barons exploited the vulnerability of needy workers, perpetuating a relationship of economic servitude.

This dynamic established a new form of rent around clandestine coal mining, where control of informal resources strengthened the power of these new rentiers while maintaining the population's economic and social dependence on them. This "laissez-faire" management of the State by the informal sector has regenerated a rentier elite that has profited from the closure without providing a real economic solution for the town. The gamble of cushioning the crisis through the informal sector failed and only slowed the onset of the crisis.

In December 2017, the death of two young people in a clandestine well-triggered weeks of protests in Jerada. The population denounced their socioeconomic marginalization and demanded dignity and employment. Negotiations between the local authorities and the protest movement failed. The *Hirak* was put down by the arrest and conviction of dozens of young activists, who received sentences ranging from 3 to 20 years' imprisonment. In June 2019, on the occasion of Eîd El Fitr, the King pardoned the 47 detainees of the Jerada *Hirak*, putting an end to their imprisonment. Two years later, *Hirak* activists decided to run for office, marking a strategic shift toward change through political participation. Their landslide victory for Jerada city council in the 2021 elections embodies both the hope of transformative change and the fear of potential failure, reflecting the ambivalence inherent in any process of social transformation.

The Power of Political Participation: A Democratic Dynamic of Elite Renewal

Far from expectations, the victory of the anti-establishment electorate and the "general orientation"[14] candidates marks the arrival of a new generation of young people in the management of local affairs.[15] The participation of young people who had been boycotting elections put an end to the domination of notables during the two previous communal mandates.[16] The new candidates are mostly young graduates of Oujda University who have never stood for election before.[17] These young figures of the protest movement have been pushed to the forefront of the local political scene by the economic, social, and political crisis. Participation was encouraged by the protesting electorate and popular support from neighborhood committees, resulting in a landslide victory that surprised both *Hirak* activists and the *Makhzen*.[18]

The transition from unconventional to conventional political participation marks a shift from protest logic (strikes, marches, sit-ins . . .) to a logic of institutional and legal participation. The people interviewed affirm that their collective action is part of this continuum between protest and participation in elections. In other words, it is a "continuum of political participation," to use the concept developed by Olivier Fillieule (1997). The latter proposes a non-dichotomous vision of participatory practices, suggesting that the different forms of political participation (conventional and non-conventional) are not distinct and opposed but rather form part of a continuous spectrum. Conventional forms (such as voting, joining political parties) and non-conventional forms (such as demonstrations, strikes, activism) are not mutually exclusive; there is a kind of interconnection between forms of participation. Individuals can engage in several types of political action simultaneously, or at different times in their lives.[19] In the context of the Jerada protest movement, the continuum allows us to understand how young activists moved from one form of participation to another according to local political and social- economic contexts. Participation in the 2021 elections was the result of a long, "democratic" process of deliberation that lasted four months. This was divided into three stages: popular deliberation, meetings with political players, and candidate selection.

The first phase, dedicated to popular deliberation, was decisive, with the aim of choosing between taking part in the elections and boycotting them.[20] To decide, lengthy consultations and in-depth debates were held between supporters of electoral participation and boycott advocates. These deliberations led to the necessity of participation in the elections, as the non-participation of young people would inevitably result in the same notables who had governed the town for over two decades continuing to head the municipal council. However, "it was inconceivable, after so many sacrifices and gestures, to leave the field empty and boycott the elections," in the words of the council president,[21] and it was the residents who decided in favor of the participation of a youth group born of the protest movement.[22]

In fact, since 2003, Jerada's town council has been chaired by notables. These are people who wield both political and economic powers (see axis 1), and who are seen by the young protesters as responsible for the town's "catastrophic" situation. Fueled by a clientelist system, the notables possessed symbolic resources through which they granted advantages to their electorate. This so-called asymmetrical clientelism (a client beholden to a patron) was dominant in the granting of scholarships, jobs, and even communal services, without any quid pro quo (Iraki, 2021, p. 348).

It is in this sense that the newly elected members of the communal council emerging from the protest movement are attempting to put an end to this corrupt system, which uses the commune's resources for political ends by strengthening their position within their electorate. By protesting or voting, the supporters of "L'orientation générale" are fighting against this corrupt system and for change both in the elites in place and in the city's socioeconomic conditions. It is in this sense that one of the major concerns of the new council is to put an end to this clientelist system of entitlement by removing it from positions of political responsibility.

But if the militants have won the elections, do they really have the means to develop the town and achieve the reconversion so hoped for by the local population?

The Development Challenge in Jerada: What Alternatives Are There in the Face of Local Resistance and the Extractivist Rentier Legacy?

With insufficient financial and human resources,[23] the first measures taken by the President of the Communal Council and his office were twofold: a return to normativity to put an end to clientelism, and economic and social development through the Communal Action Plan (PAC).

Cleaning up and rationalizing the commune's expenditure, and putting an end to the illegal favors granted to certain individuals, was a priority for the newly elected officials. These illegal favors include "phantom" or seconded civil servants, seasonal workers, "ephemeral" telephone lines, excessive diesel consumption by the commune's vehicle fleet, "La promotion nationale" cards, communal premises for which rent has never been collected, and other benefits for citizens. In other cases, this translates into tolerance toward certain transgressions of the law, or the illegal granting of tax exemptions on communal taxes. These illicit maneuvers enabled former elected notables to win the allegiance, loyalty, and support of beneficiaries during elections. However, they also had a negative impact on the town's budget revenues, compromising its ability to finance its projects and meet the needs of the population. Rationalization of the commune's budget and the fight against "passe-droit" have enabled it to achieve a budget surplus for 2023.[24] Applying the law upsets those who enjoy certain privileges outside the law and brings the new council members face to face with the population. And yet, "to progress, one must obey the law and contribute as a citizen to the development of the town, both by respecting the rules and by paying the sums owed to the commune."[25] However, these measures are a double-edged sword. On the one hand, they help to strengthen the commune's budget by increasing revenue and also rationalize financial and human resources, thereby improving the financing capacity of local projects and the quality of public services. On the other hand, they give rise to tensions and confrontations with the beneficiaries concerned, who see themselves deprived of certain advantages perceived as acquired, albeit unjustified or undeserved. These tensions can engender a climate of mistrust, making the implementation of reforms more complex and sometimes conflictual.

The Commune's Action Plan is considerably behind schedule. Scheduled to run from 2022 to 2027,[26] it will not be operational until 2024, for a number of reasons. According to the Vice-Chairman of the Communal Council,

> the newly elected officials have no experience in managing the commune, so we had to learn and take our time to get to grips with the legal texts, procedures and administrative and financial organization of the commune. It took us a long time to act and be effective.[27]

An assertion echoed by several other members of the Communal Council, and which explains the delay in the Council's action. The newly elected activists have the skills needed to assume power, but they are insufficiently prepared to do so. Lack of management, legal, technical, and managerial skills, and the absence of the requisite experience, hamper their ability to effectively administer communal affairs.

Opposition from former notables is also present, albeit hidden but real. The notables have shown resistance to change since the success of the new council. Some of the newly elected officials implicitly or explicitly denounce the blocking effect of local interest networks, which hinder the implementation of their projects. Through informal networks or influence, they have succeeded in slowing down or diverting certain investment projects. As things stand, it seems difficult to counteract the economic influence of the notables, who wield considerable power. They are even called upon by the authorities to intervene and unblock certain situations deemed delicate and problematic, thus reinforcing their hold and role in the local economy.

The Practice of Power: Exploring Internal and External Dynamics

While the question of power is a classic theme in the political and social sciences, the concerns associated with its exercise reveal a particular complexity. In the case of Jerada, the integration of the new Council into the political system, as well as its interactions with other institutions and the internal dynamics it must manage, present themselves as major challenges. Interviewees expressed doubts as to the willingness of other deconcentrated and decentralized institutions to cooperate with the new Council. What is more, the political tensions aroused by certain councilors or militants of the protest movement risk weakening, or even splintering, the majority within the Council.

The Local Council and Local Players: Cooperation or Repulsion?

Let us start by recalling that the authorities had a more or less strained relationship with the leaders of the protest movement, a relationship that eased slightly after the release of the prisoners.[28] However, *Hirak* youth meetings were held far from the authorities, for fear of further demonstrations. That said, the authorities were in favor of participation rather than a boycott and even warned activists to call on citizens to boycott the elections.[29] Aware of the limited powers of local authorities, the communal council favored participation and cooperation with other centers of power, including decentralized government departments. Those interviewed agreed that the central authorities, through their representatives, notably the Governor, are cooperative and do their best to unblock certain problematic situations.

> Generally, there are moments of agreement and others of disagreement with the governor or other officials, but it seems unfair to claim that they are trying to derail the experiment. On the contrary, it's in the Makhzen's interest for the experiment to succeed, for the simple reason that if it fails, there's no alternative but to return to protest and confrontation with the state.[30]

The participants' responses testify to their awareness of the governor's place in the Moroccan political system and his supremacy over local authorities. For this reason, the newly elected officials show a certain pragmatism in their relationship with the representative of central power, in this case, the governor.

> The Makhzen is stronger than we are, and we don't have the means or the power to confront it, so it's wiser to cooperate with it and not regard it as an enemy. He's a player we can't ignore, and nothing can move forward without the approval of the Makhzen's representatives.

confided one of the interviewees.

The actions of the Communal Council office reflect a pragmatic approach to managing relations with representatives of central government. Instead of confrontation, pressure from the street and militant action, the new approach is one of persuasion, argumentation, and mutual understanding of each other's constraints.[31] A position that some *Hirak* activists criticize, accusing the new council of aligning itself with the positions of the *Makhzen* and distancing itself from the concerns of the marginalized local population who elected them. Here, we might consider the more recent work of Luc Boltanski (2009), who points out that the trials of our society often reinforce the state of power relations far more than they change them. Participation tends to reinforce adherence to institutions and the world as it is, without contributing sufficiently to the will and ability to change it (Cantelli et al., 2013, p. 7).

While relations with central government can be described as "normal," this is not the case with decentralized administrations. Cooperation with the Oriental Regional Council in particular is less fruitful, as evidenced by the distribution of projects programmed in the Regional Development Project covering the period (2022/2027), which has allocated only 11% of the overall budget to the provinces of Berkane and Jerada.[32] A situation that council members describe as "normal," given the political affiliation of the members of the regional council, in this case the party of the former leaders of the local council belonging respectively to the Authenticity and Modernity Party (PAM),[33] deemed responsible for the economic and social crisis ravaging the town. During the term of office of the new regional council, a promise was given to deliver refuse collection trucks for the collection and transport of waste, which was formulated by the president of the council, but he was incarcerated following a case of international drug trafficking.[34]

In the process of institutional integration, the local council has lost its main support, the protest movement. Internal divergences and criticism from activists on social networks risk splintering the majority within the local council.

Participation Between the Risk of Splintering and the Amplification of Commitment

The division between the young people of the protest movement is today the main threat to the unity of the majority within the local council and its supporters of the "general orientation." Opposition to the choices made by the president of the council and his team is becoming increasingly apparent as the city's affairs are put to the test, whether within the council or among activists, supporters, and former *Hirak* detainees. In 2023, a year and a half after their election, the majority of the members of the Communal Council published a communiqué in which they denounced the "unilateral decisions" and lack of competence and communication on the part of the President of the Communal Council, and called on him to resign from his position of responsibility. A break-up that required the intervention of the central office of the PPS, to which the majority of the Council belong, to reconcile the members and avoid division.

Having said that, there are generally two major points of disagreement that persist to this day: the first is the project to build a brick-making factory, described by the President as harmful to neighboring residents. The second is the slow pace of the town's economic conversion, which has yet to materialize on the ground.

It seems that the exercise of power has revealed the diversity of orientations, commitments, and interests among Council members. It has also called into question certain elements that were supposed to serve as unifiers, such as partisan commitment, political culture, and the primacy of the general interest, as expressed by some Council members. Gathered around the Party of Progress and Socialism, the members embody neither the party's principles nor its political culture. The lack of political guidance due to recent membership in this party (PPS) taints the discipline of these supporters. Some members remain supporters of another political party, the Federation of United Socialism (FSU), and their membership of the PPS is only formal.[35]

In the same vein, a press release from the local PPS office, published on 2 December 2023, criticizes the irresponsibility and indiscipline of its one and only representative on the Provincial Council, who also holds the position of Council President. The press release deplored the latter's disengagement from the interests of the people of Jerada, despite his status as a candidate from the protest movement.[36] In the same vein, the attitude of Jerada's representative on the Regional Council was also criticized, to the extent that some members of the Council felt that "he no longer defends the interests of the town, and should rather be considered as an opponent."[37] How, then, can we explain the change in attitude observed among certain activists who have become elected representatives, between the ideals of activism and the demands of exercising power?

Another explanation lies in the logic of benefit sharing, whether material or symbolic. Public choice theory, developed by Dennis C. Mueller (2000) and the seminal work of Buchanan and Gordon Tullock (1962), provides a relevant analytical framework for understanding certain political attitudes. Indeed, these newly elected officials seem to orient their behavior toward maximizing their benefits, both symbolic and material, in their interactions with other political actors within the Regional Council and the Province. These two entities, with greater material and symbolic resources than the local council, become a strategic space for strengthening their position and influence.

The exercise of power is a tough test for young activists, and the advantages that power can provide, whether symbolic (being a member of a committee, being close to the local decision-making circle, or others) or material (allowances, position of responsibility, etc.) explode the divergences within the Council.

However, despite the problems experienced, those questioned agree on the need for participation. When asked: "Will you participate again, whatever the outcome of the current experience?", all expressed their intention to get involved again, either as candidates or through voting. Boycotting or abstaining does not seem to be on these respondents' minds. "Participation taught us a lot of things we didn't know. Now we know the reality and the current situation of our city, and how matters were managed during a given period."[38] In this respect, it can be said that participation promotes the commitment and political inclusion of young protesters and social movement activists. The refusal to disengage from electoral processes testifies to a desire to continue investing in political spaces. In short, even in the face of political, cultural, and economic uncertainties and obstacles, the struggle continues to transform local reality.

Conclusion

The analysis of the situation in the mining town of Jerada shows the complexity of the political and economic transition in a post-extractivist context, marked by structural imbalances related to the dominance of extractivist rent. The social tensions caused by the exclusion of a large vulnerable population and the fragility of the local economy, primarily mining and rentier, are major challenges. In this context, the analysis of the dynamics of political participation in Jerada, following the arrival of elected activists at the head of the municipality, reveals complex issues marked by a mix of hope, challenge, and disenchantment. On the one hand, the newly elected officials represent the aspirations of the protest movement, which is a bearer of change and social transformation. On the other hand, the exercise of power highlights structural, organizational, and relational challenges that hinder the emergence of just and equitable governance, particularly in the context of a transition toward a post-extractivist, diversified, and productive economy. Far from being a mere democratic formality, political participation in Jerada seems to be confronted with issues intrinsic to the Moroccan political system. These challenges include the influence of notables and the old power structures, which sometimes hinder the actions of the new council by mobilizing their economic and political influence. That is why the success of this transition is conditioned by the ability of the elected activists to overcome these structural barriers, dismantle the rentier economy, while stimulating citizen participation and diversifying the local economy. Through close collaboration between local actors, the State, and civil society, could set up sustainable resolutions, allowing Jerada to go beyond its extractivist past, overcome challenges, and establish a just and sustainable future.

Notes

1 Examples include the following towns and cities: Tamassint (2004), Al Hoceima (2005), Bouarfa (2006), Sefrou (2007), Sidi Ifni (2008), Beni Mellal (2009), Sidi Bouafif (2010), Imider (2011), Youssoufia (2011), Khourigba (2011), Taza (2012), Al Hoceïma (2016), and Jerada (2018) (quoted in Mayaux & Rousseau, 2021, p. 135).

2 *Hirak* is an Arabic term meaning "movement," and refers to the protest movements in certain Arab countries in the early 2000s. The "*Hirak* du Rif" is a protest movement that began in the town of Al Hoceima, located in the Rif region of northern Morocco, following the death of a fishmonger (Mouhcine Fikri) in 2016. The story began on October 26 of that year, when police confiscated his merchandise and threw it into a dumpster. When the fishmonger tried to retrieve his merchandise, the police officer ordered the machine to be turned on, resulting in his immediate crushing and death. This led to demonstrations against contempt and humiliation, and to calls for dignity. The Rif *hirak* shares many similarities with the Jerada *Hirak*, notably the struggle for a fair distribution of wealth and against the notables who are strengthened by the rents granted by central government.

3 It is also a synoptic reading of writings on protest movements in Morocco, especially after the popular uprisings of 2011, notably the Rif *Hirak*, which bears elements of convergence and divergence with the Jerada protest movement.

4 For more on this subject, see Verba et al. (1995).

5 CDM executives ran the city until 1992.

6 Despite a number of positive indicators relating to the rate of electrification and access to drinking water, which are largely due to the achievements of the mining period and the compensatory equipment policies that followed, other indicators are below the national average and have been deteriorating over time since the early 2000s. Examples include emigration to other towns, which has accelerated since the mine was shut down,

the unemployment rate, the decline in the working population and access to the Internet or ownership of a laptop computer (see, e.g., Goeury, 2019).

7 A total of 4,168 people received compensation between 1998 and 2000.

8 Only a few income-generating projects have been carried out, as well as other unregulated housing interventions. Other economic and social facilities have not been built.

9 Three areas reflect this informal management: unregulated housing, illegal extraction, and smuggling. In this chapter, we focus on informal extractive activity.

10 Each licensee has set up one or two companies: Société Darhou Charbo, Best Charbon et Société Minière TOP (SOMITOP), Sorexmine and Société Charbonnière de l'Oriental (see Iraki, 2021, p. 67).

11 They include Mohamed Daghou, former miner, initially a simple merchant of melons and watermelons, he served two terms as mayor of the town of Jerada (2003/2009 and 2010/2015), with a son who has been a deputy of the Istiqlal party since 2016; also, Mustapha Toutou, son of a miner, current influential member of the Authenticity and Modernity Party (PAM), deputy and whose sister has been president of the communal council since 2015; finally, Amnoun Bachir Oubaha, son of a merchant, wholesaler of food products throughout the region, influential member of the Oriental Chamber of Commerce, elected council member and first vice-president of the city council during the 2015/2021 term (quoted in Iraki, 2021, p. 346).

12 Ahmad's (2020) study of the relationship between protest movements and population growth shows that the imbalance between the age categories of jobseekers (19–25) and employers (35–45) was flagrant. In the regions that saw protests such as Jerada, in the absence of economic opportunities and prospects, the accumulation of unemployment among the first and second categories undoubtedly contributed to the demographic formation of the protesting crowds.

13 Literally "Abateraa أباطرة " in Arabic.

14 In Arabic "التوجه العام" is the name that *Hirak* activists have given to candidates from the protest movement.

15 50% of the newly elected are under 35, compared with just 6.9% in the 2015 communal elections.

16 When asked about their reasons for taking part in the elections, those questioned said first and foremost that they wanted to put an end to the domination of notables.

17 All those questioned, including members of the communal council, said they had never taken part in elections, either by voting or by standing as a candidate.

18 In reality, no one foresaw this landslide victory for the protest movement in the 2021 communal elections. The most optimistic were hoping for a few seats on the communal council.

19 Several sociologists and political scientists share perspectives similar to those of Olivier Fillieule (1997) on the varied forms of political participation and civic engagement, see, for example, Tarrow (2011) and Tilly (2004).

20 The second stage was devoted to choosing the right political party, the third to nominating candidates.

21 Statement by the current President of the Communal Council to the newspaper "Ennass," dated 08/10/2021, visited on 10/04/2024. Available via link: https://urlz.fr/qRgR

22 The protest movement has appointed coordinators in each district to lead debates and draw out the population's opinion.

23 This was in deficit, given the low level of local taxation and the dominance of the operating budget, which makes up almost the entire budget, not to mention the outstanding balance of 15 million dirhams.

24 This surplus, valued at over one million MDH, is allocated to social and cultural projects. See more details on the official page of the Jerada City Council available at the following link: https://vu.fr/AcnGK. Accessed 04/04/2024.

25 The comments are made by H.A., member of the Communal Council office.

26 As part of the preparation of the Jerada commune's action plan for 2022–2027, the Jerada communal council held consultative sessions and meetings with the population of Jerada's districts over a three-day period, from Monday, 14 November 2022, to Wednesday, 16 November 2022. In its updated version, the Communal Action Plan was adopted in the extraordinary session of July 2023.

27 Statement by one of the vice-presidents, confirmed by the other interviewees, concerning problems in the management of the city.

28 Since the deaths of two young people in late December 2017, the authorities had favored "open dialogue" to calm the situation, in order to ease tensions. However, a climate of mistrust persisted between protesters and state representatives. Despite several meetings and promises of reform, the discussions failed to produce a concrete agreement (Quoted in Ǧālī 2018, p. 6).

29 Statement by one of the *Hirak* activists to the newspaper on 16/09/2021, available via the link: https://urlz.fr/tM2O. Accessed 01/06/2024.

30 Statement by Mr A.B, member of the Communal Council.

31 Statement by Mr H.A, member of the Communal Council.

32 The overall budget is 12.8 billion dirhams (MMDH), spread over the region's eight prefectures and provinces.

33 The Authenticity and Modernity Party (PAM) is a centrist or center-right party created in 2008 by the King's advisor Fouad Ali El Hima, which is why it is often accused of being an administrative party, created "out of thin air" to counter the historical parties born of the national movement.

34 In December 2023, Abdenbi Bioui, President of the Oriental Regional Council, was jailed along with other officials and elected representatives, for international drug trafficking in the so-called Le Malien case.

35 Press release from the Provincial Secretariat of the Party for Progress and Socialism in Jerada dated 02/12/2023.

36 This concerns one of the "General Orientation" candidates who took part in the communal elections on behalf of the "Parti du Progrès et Socialisme" (PPS), and who was elected to the Communal Council and held the position of first vice-president of the Council before his election by the "grand electors" to the Provincial Council and his appointment as President of the latter.

37 Statement by Mr H.A, member of the Communal Council Bureau (H.A).

38 Statement by Mr Y.B, a member of the Communal Council who belonged to the majority before becoming an opponent of the new Communal Council's policies.

References

Bennafla, K., & Emperador Badimon, M. (2010). Le "Maroc inutile" redécouvert par l'action publique: Les cas de Sidi Ifni et Bouarfa. *Politique africaine*, *120*, 67–86. https://doi.org/10.3917/polaf.120.0067

Berrada, K. (2018). *Beyond the Jerada mines: The need for a sustainable approach.* MIPA Institute.

Boltanski, L. (2019). *De la critique: Précis de sociologie de l'émancipation.* Gallimard.

Cantelli, F., Garon, F., & Schiffino, N. (2013). Participation et pouvoirs: Pour une lecture renouvelée. *Politique et Sociétés*, *32*(1), 3–19. https://doi.org/10.7202/1018718ar

Fillieule, O. (1997). Chapitre 3. Retour sur la participation politique. In *Stratégies de la rue* (pp. 127–162). Presses de Sciences Po.

Goeury, D. (2019, February 28). La déprise économique aux origines du Hirak de Jerada? *Le carnet du Centre Jacques Berque*. https://doi.org/10.58079/mut4

Iraki, A. (2021). Du syndicat au Hirak: Une évolution du conseil communal et de l'élite politique locale à Jerada. In A. Iraki (Ed.), *Vivre ou survivre après/avec la mine* (pp. 325–392). Institut national d'aménagement et d'urbanisme.

Iraki, A., & Zabadi, A. (2021). Décroissance urbaine et politiques de reconversion: Le cas de la ville de Jerada. In A. Iraki (Ed.), *Vivre ou survivre après/avec la mine* (pp. 45–80). Institut national d'aménagement et d'urbanisme.

Mayaux, P.-L., & Rousseau, M. (2021). Extraire la ressource, s'extraire du conflit. Réguler la surexploitation des mines et des eaux souterraines au Maroc. *Revue internationale de politique comparée*, *28*(3–4).

Tarrow, S. (2011). *Power in movement: Social movements and contentious politics*. Cambridge University Press.

Tilly, C. (2004). *Social movements, 1768–2004*. Paradigm Publishers.

Verba, S., Schlozman, K. L., & Brady, H. E. (1995). *Voice and equality: Civic voluntarism in American politics*. Harvard University Press

10 The Pathways of Green Hydrogen Production in North Africa

Mohamed Ismail Sabry

Introduction

The production of green hydrogen in North African countries has sparked considerable debate as negotiations to establish the necessary infrastructure continue to intensify. There are many potential benefits. Green hydrogen offers the opportunity for North African countries to become significant energy exporters. This could involve diversifying energy exports in Algeria, reinstating energy export capabilities in Tunisia, or establishing a new role as energy exporters for the first time in Morocco. EU investments are expected to follow with promises of capacity building and know-how transfer. EU schemes are not only designed to meet the demand as part of its green deal (European Commission, n.d.-b). Rather, some talk is uttered on the use of some of the produced hydrogen in the decarbonization of local industries and as an input for other important industries, such as green ammonia that could be used in the fertilizers industry (IRENA, 2018; Terrapon-Pfaff et al., 2021).

Yet this rosy picture is strongly challenged by social and environmental concerns raised by the same process thought to bring only blessings. Environmental threats include the intensive use of water for the generation of green hydrogen in a region that severely suffers from water deficiency, increased salination of seawater in the acclaimed scenario of using desalinated seawater in the process, as well as other concerns (Delpuech, 2022). On the other hand, social concerns mainly include the rights of local communities who share the ownership of vast lands in which green hydrogen projects (using renewable energy) are supposed to be located.

These issues present green hydrogen production as a potential new resource-based form of extractivism that could also have neocolonial dependency relations, whereby the resources of the periphery are being used for the benefit of the core (whether national elites or advanced economies). Extractivism refers to a development strategy that entails high reliance on the exports of mineral resources. The distribution of benefits is expected to be more politicized and guided by access to power (Philipps University of Marburg & University of Kassel, n.d.; Warnecke-Berger & Ickler, 2023). Against this perception are the claims of various interested parties, whether the EU or North African state officials, who assert that environmental and social impact assessment is taken seriously and that civil society's participation is guaranteed, thus denying the extractivist perception. There is a

DOI: 10.4324/9781003730750-10

possibility of a more inclusive pathway, where various actors would benefit, and the least, if any, would lose. This chapter investigates those important questions: which pathways are expected to be taken by North African countries? What are the prospects of their sustainability?

Green Hydrogen in Context

Hydrogen is widely used in different applications. This hydrogen, however, predominantly originates from fossil fuels (more than 95%), and thus, its production involves significant carbon emissions (IRENA, 2018, p. 13). In the widely used terminologies, such hydrogen is called grey or blue. Gray hydrogen releases carbon in the hydrocarbon input to the air in producing these fossil fuel hydrogen variants. In contrast, the more environment-friendly blue variant captures (although not entirely) carbon gases through the Carbon Capture, Utilization, and Storage (CCUS) technique (IRENA, 2020, p. 16). To the stated fossil fuel hydrogen variants, we could add the turquoise hydrogen in which solid carbon is stored. Other colors describe various forms, including brown for the hydrogen produced from coal (through gasification) and pink for that made from nuclear energy (Incer-Valverde et al., 2023). The production of hydrogen from the electrolysis of water and without any carbon emissions is widely referred to as green hydrogen. It is regarded as the source that would solve many problems facing the shift away from fossil fuels and accelerate the pace of the green transition. It was suggested as a storage and transmission option for renewable energy.[1] Hydrogen could be transported using the pipeline infrastructure that is currently used in transporting natural gas, where it could constitute up to 20% of the mix (natural gas and hydrogen mix) without major technical adjustments (although, in practice, a much lesser combination is allowed in many countries) (Terrapon-Pfaff et al., 2021, pp. 12–14, 66–68, 78). It could be used as a fuel for hard-to-decarbonize (hard-to-abate) industries and sectors. In the transportation sector, for instance, it could be utilized in fuel cell electric vehicles (FCEVs) for long-distance and haul and heavy-duty transportation such as trains and buses and is already (or planned to be) used in some railway services in several countries (IRENA, 2018, pp. 33–34; Terrapon-Pfaff et al., 2021, pp. 12–14, 66–68, 78). Hydrogen combined with carbon (captured from the air or carbon-emitting industries) produces synthetic fuels (e.g., methane, methanol, kerosene, diesel, and gasoline) chemically comparable to their corresponding conventional fossil fuels. These fuels are the best option to decarbonize some transportation means, such as freight ships and aircraft (IRENA, 2018; Terrapon-Pfaff et al., 2021, pp. 12–14, 66–68, 78).

Furthermore, green hydrogen could substitute fossil fuel-based hydrogen as an industrial input. One of the most important uses is ammonia production, achieved when hydrogen is combined with nitrogen through the Haber–Bosch process. The produced green ammonia could then be used to produce low-carbon fertilizers, where fertilizers are by far the most significant ammonia users. Ammonia is also used in chemical and pharmaceutical industries and could be utilized as fuel for maritime shipping. Green ammonia could be a cheaper option for freight transportation than liquified hydrogen, and the infrastructure for it (ammonia in general) already exists. Other uses of green hydrogen could include the iron and steel industry (direct reduction of iron ore process) and to a lesser degree the manufacturing of electronics, glass, and bulk chemicals (IRENA, 2018, pp. 13–15; Terrapon-Pfaff et al., 2021, pp. 12–14, 52–54, 93).

There are expectations that the hydrogen market will generally constitute about 18% of the total energy consumption in the world by 2050, and half of the demand will come from the industrial sector (IRENA, 2018, p. 31; Terrapon-Pfaff et al., 2021, p. 46). This further incentivizes the development of green hydrogen to competitive levels with fossil fuel-based hydrogen. The technology for producing green hydrogen already exists, such as the more long-lifetime alkaline electrolysis (ALK) and the newer and more flexibly operated technology of polymer electrolyte membrane electrolysis (PEM), with the potential for developing other technologies, such as the solid oxide electrolyzers (SOEC) (IRENA, 2018, p. 19; Terrapon-Pfaff et al., 2021, pp. 12–14).

The value chain of green hydrogen (see Figure 10.1) starts with renewable energy power plants, especially wind and solar power generation plants. Then comes electrolysis, which uses water in the production of hydrogen. The electrolyzers use different raw materials, processed materials, and subcomponents, depending on which module is used (U.S. Department of Energy, 2024, pp. 12–21). Downstream are the various uses of the produced hydrogen as a fuel for various sectors, an input for various industries, and the creation of synthetic fuel in combination with captured carbon. This links it strongly to the carbon capture industry and technologies (e.g., CCUS). A necessary synthetic fuel such as methanol could be further processed into intermediary products that are used in the manufacturing of a variety of important products such as plastics, paints, pharmaceuticals, and building materials (Terrapon-Pfaff et al., 2021, pp. 12, 60). We could also go upstream and consider the sectors that provide inputs for renewable power generation plants, from photovoltaic cell modules and windmill blades to critical and rare minerals. Thus, the hydrogen value chain is substantial, includes a wide range of economic sectors, and is circular for some industrial sectors. For instance, the iron and steel industry, which provides inputs to renewable energy generation plants and electrolyzers, could be a user of green hydrogen in its decarbonization and the production of green steel.

Yet the costs of green hydrogen, as well as all of its value chain, are still high (IRENA, 2020, p. 17). Skeptics are doubtful about the reduction of the costs of producing green hydrogen and that of electrolyzers. Export suggestions are more negatively scrutinized, given the estimated high losses (about 60%) from the use of hydrogen as a storage and transmitter of renewable energy electricity, the exceptionally high costs of shipping hydrogen, and the damage that the pipelines and the electronic equipment are exposed to while transporting hydrogen (Barnard, 2022). On the other hand, the enthusiasts acknowledge that green hydrogen will be more expensive than fossil fuel-generated hydrogen up to 2050. However, costs of production will fall with the learning curve dynamics as well as the global

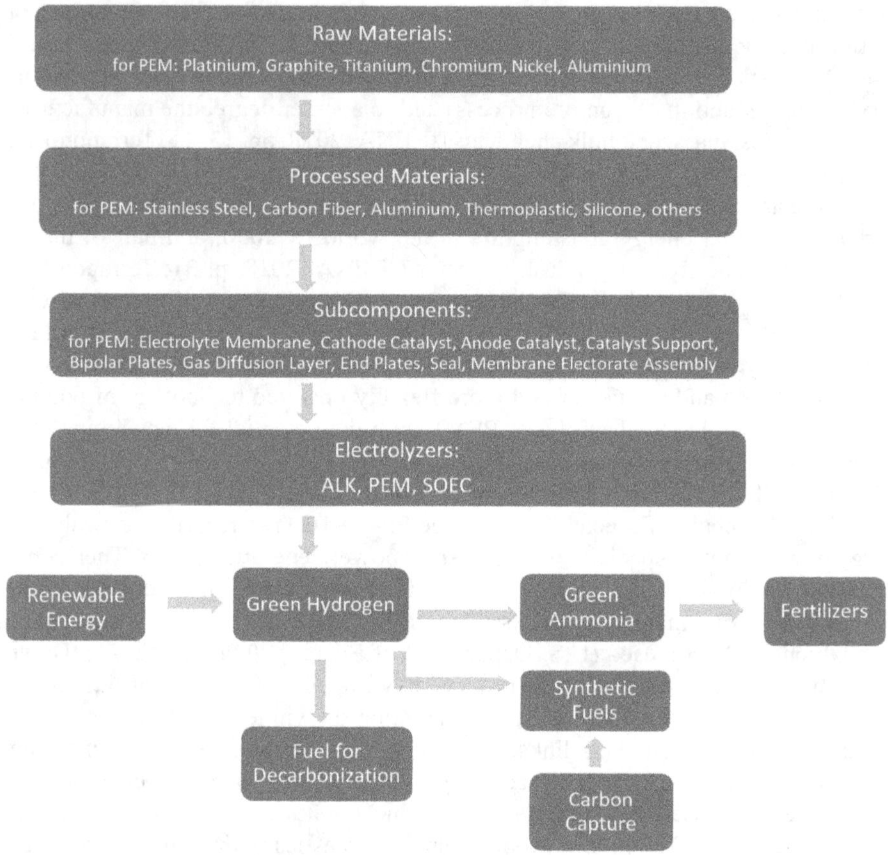

Figure 10.1 Supply chain for green hydrogen.

Source: Own elaboration based on data from the US Department of Energy (2024). More focus is put on the supply chain of the PEM electrolyzer

adaptation of decarbonization policies and international climate change agendas. Green hydrogen would be likely only used in the short term as a substitute for gray hydrogen as an industrial input. The medium term should witness the use of green hydrogen in the transportation sector (e.g., long-distance railway freight, trucks, and buses) (Terrapon-Pfaff et al., 2021, pp. 12–17, 64, 86–87). Yet this adds many uncertainties in modeling the economic viability of using green hydrogen and its derivatives.

Costs are not the only concern. The excessive use of water and land is another, although estimates vary (IRENA, 2020, pp. 40–41). Furthermore, there are concerns about the produced brine from the expected extensive desalination activities, how this brine could increase the salinity of the nearby seawaters, and affect the fishing activities of the local populations (Delpuech, 2022).

The significant economic power behind the great push toward green hydrogen is the EU, which has the world's most ambitious green hydrogen strategies (IRENA, 2020, p. 21). The "European Hydrogen Strategy," adopted in 2020, aimed at developing a hydrogen "investment agenda," proposing demand-side policies, establishing hydrogen infrastructure, supporting the value chains and innovations in hydrogen-related technologies, as well as strengthening EU global leadership and fostering "cooperation with Southern and Eastern Neighborhood partners" in the field of hydrogen (European Commission, n.d.-a). The drive was further reinforced with the REPowerEU plan to reduce Russian fossil fuel dependency following the Russian–Ukrainian War that broke out in February 2022 and accelerated the green transition (European Commission, 2022). The EU has identified different scenarios for its demand for hydrogen in 2050, widely ranging between 24% and 8% of its total energy demand. EU seeks the production of ten million tons of green hydrogen annually and importing a comparable figure (IRENA, 2020, p. 21; Terrapon-Pfaff et al., 2021, pp. 46–47).

This places North Africa at the center of EU green hydrogen schemes. Some plans assign that 80% of the EU needed green hydrogen imports to the south Mediterranean (including North Africa) (Sabido, 2022). The cost of electricity is the most significant component of hydrogen production. IRENA estimated that green hydrogen could be competitive with fossil-fuel-based hydrogen if cheaper renewable energy electricity is secured (IRENA, 2020, p. 15). The low costs of renewable energy from solar and wind sources in North Africa make hydrogen production less costly in the region. Also, geographic proximity reduces transportation costs (Terrapon-Pfaff et al., 2021, p. 15).

As is generally the case with renewable energy projects, the potential for creating jobs from hydrogen production remains limited if the process is not extended to the different activities in the value chain. Thus, using imported technologies and exporting raw green hydrogen would not match the hopes for more green jobs (Terrapon-Pfaff et al., 2021, p. 16).

Pathways to Green Hydrogen Production

The production of green hydrogen is an essential part of the bigger picture of the significant transformation that the world is witnessing and represented by the green transition. Structural changes always involve substantial changes that affect various actors differently. The opportunities green hydrogen offers and the massive scaling up of its production are significant. Still, the potential losses could also be high, primarily since the whole assessment is based on many uncertainties. How will the gains and losses be distributed in such a structural transformation?

Nobel Prize winners Daron Acemoglu and James Robinson introduced an inspiring distinction not long ago. They distinguished between extractive and inclusive institutions, attributing different developmental trajectories depending on the existence of those institutions. Extractive institutions are limited to the few, whether in the political field by limiting competition on and access to political power (dictatorship) or in the economic field by limiting benefits to those having access to rents. The opposite is true for inclusive institutions characterized by more democratic political institutions and productive and competitive economic institutions (Acemoglu & Robinson, 2019). Institutions shape the relationship between the various actors in each country, or what could be referred to generally as state–society relations. State–society relations, in turn, shape the developmental pathways of different societies, not only in terms of economic growth but also in terms of the distribution of that growth (inclusivity) and the environmental degradation that it causes (sustainability) (Sabry, 2022, 2023b). One could thus anticipate the presence of pathways that correspond to the existing institutions of society, and thus the presence of an extractive path favoring the elites and another inclusive whose benefits are shared among the wider population. However, one must investigate state–society relations more deeply to identify the beneficiaries of those proposed pathways.

Understanding state–society relations necessitates identifying the crucial actors in this relation as a first step. Collective actors are generally formed around a common interest, with an organizational form representing their common goal. If actors could be categorized into broad distinctive sets, those sets would be the state, businesspeople, labor, and civil society organizations (nongovernmental organizations not affiliated with businesspeople or labor). A common interest then carves out actors from among these four sets. Thus, distinctive collective actors could be shaped based on different interests in producing green hydrogen within the state, businesspeople, labor, or CSOs. The development of those actors is context-oriented and depends on perceived interests toward the major transformation under question, which would differ from one country to the other. It is important to stress that interest shapes actors; in other words, organizations and groupings of individuals with neutral or no (positive or negative) interest in green hydrogen production are not to be considered actors.

In North Africa, much of the earlier discussion on the benefits of green hydrogen becomes irrelevant until the long run, which could go as far as 2050. These are mainly the fields in which the costs are expected to be very high for domestic use, as is the case, for instance, with synthetic fuels and using green hydrogen in transportation. The most likely activities related to hydrogen in North Africa in the short, medium, and for some time in the long run are, first, the production of green hydrogen and its derivatives (green ammonia, synthetic fuels, etc.) for exporting mainly to the EU, second, the production of green hydrogen for the domestic use in energy-intensive industries that export to the EU and are included in the CBAM and required to pay higher taxes on their carbon emissions starting from 2026, and especially the fertilizers industry (through green ammonia), and third, the supplier industries to the electrolyzers. Accordingly, the likely interested actors in the production of green hydrogen would be state actors concerned about the generation of public revenues from export activities (e.g., generally the executive and more specific actors such as the ministries handling trade relations), the expansion of industrial activities (e.g., ministry of industry and/or mining), and it might represent a challenge or risk for actors concerned about the environment (e.g., ministry of environment, ministry of agriculture or natural resources), social consequences of structural change (e.g., ministry of human resources), or national sovereignty (e.g., nationalist or leftist majorities or factions in the legislative). For businesspeople, interested actors would be those whose business runs in the identified earlier industrial activities (e.g., exporters, suppliers, etc.), and threatened actors would be those with businesses strongly linked to fossil fuels and heavily dependent on grey hydrogen and its derivatives. Labor in the threatened industrial sectors would share the perception of the threat of the production of green hydrogen, especially if previous experiences in structural change retraining and compensation were not promising. Creating more or better-paid jobs would represent an interest for concerned labor. For CSOs, environmental or social threats to freshwater, seas, and land would represent an interest in the production of green hydrogen. Yet CSOs concerned about global climate change and climate change mitigation might be intensely interested in producing green hydrogen in North Africa. Figure 10.2 provides some possible actors who would be identified based on their interest in or opposition to green hydrogen production.

As a developmental project with economic, distributional, and environmental dimensions, the production of green hydrogen would follow different pathways depending on the existing state–society relations, which various institutions shape. Two broad pathways could be identified here. The first could be called the *extractive pathway*, whereby elites, interested state officials, or a coalition of state officials and local and foreign big business tycoons push the scheme forward, disregarding the interests of local communities and the population at large. The

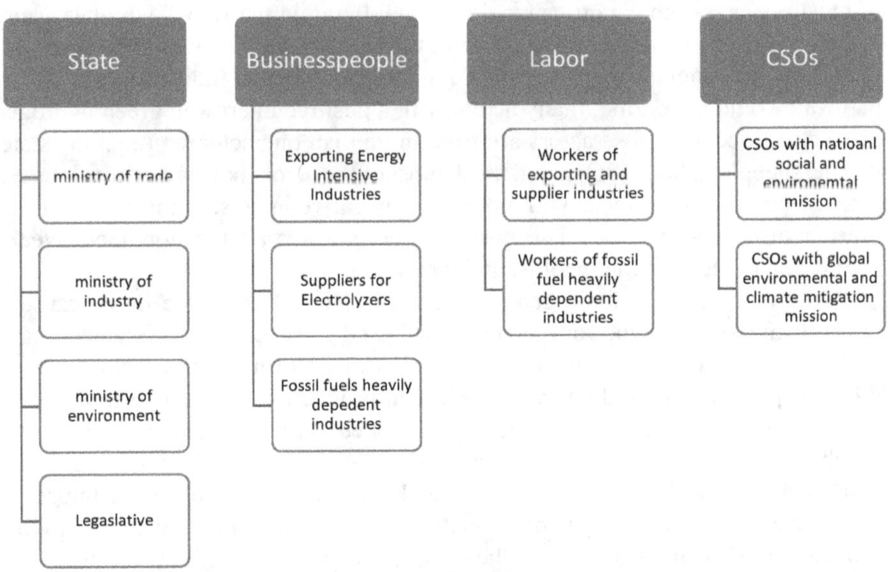

Figure 10.2 The sets of potential state and society actors.

Source: Own elaboration

second is a non-extractive and more *inclusive pathway* where a pro-green hydrogen production broader coalition is built, one that accounts for the interests of most of the concerned actors and balances between these interests. As Bebbington (2015, pp. 109–110) suggested, various channels could reflect inclusivity, such as job creation, supply chain linkages, social programs and spending, ownership sharing, actors' consultation, and environmental impact governance.

Pathways could be regarded as a continuum, the most extractive of which has the least beneficiary actors, while the most inclusive has the most beneficiary actors. A classic example of the former in the literature on resource-rich countries is Mobutu Sese Seko's Zaire (1965–1997). Mobutu controlled much of the country's rich mineral and agricultural resources. Officials also tried to secure resource loot, while social actors could not organize any remarkable resistance (Evans, 1989; Wedeman, 1997). Norway could be a good example of the latter, the most inclusive. The generous revenues of the oil resources discovered in the country in the late 1960s and early 1970s were used in creating a sovereign wealth fund. The resources available for this fund were used to support the development of the industrial sector, create strong linkages, and provide inputs for the oil sector while being technologically advanced and internationally competitive. The resources also helped the state to spend heavily on measures that create a more skilled labor force, such as education, human capital development, and social protection. Moreover, wages were guided by collective bargaining and setting labor wages to match the level enjoyed by the labor of internationally competitive industrial sectors (Magdich et al., 2021; Mehlum et al., 2012). Thus, a wide range of actors from different actor sets (e.g., the state, businesspeople, labor) benefited from the fossil fuel wealth. The experience of most resource-rich countries would likely fall within these two extremes, Zaire and Norway. The closer they are to one of them, the more they would be described as extractive or inclusive, respectively. As a methodological tool, a more inclusive pathway would have, first, many actors with a positive interest in green hydrogen production; second, those actors are from more than one actor set (e.g., the state, businesspeople, labor, CSOs); and third, most of the actors have a positive interest. Again, actors are only those with positive or negative interest in the process (e.g., green hydrogen production). The more these criteria are met, the more inclusive the path is and the less extractive it is, and vice versa.

In the case of green hydrogen production in North Africa, the initial cause is the EU's massive demand for green hydrogen and its schemes to implement many related projects in the region. The outcome is that North African countries have different pathways regarding green hydrogen production. According to a system understanding of mechanisms (see Beach & Pedersen, 2016), the process leading the cause into those different outcomes passes through the actions of different entities that act as mechanisms. Contextual conditions also shape the impact of those mechanisms. State and society actors could be the entities whose activities provide those mechanisms. Given the contradictory interests of the various actors, their activities and the mechanisms they produce often work in different directions. Contextual conditions then play a significant role in shaping the impact of these actors' activities, magnifying some while downplaying others. State–society relations specifically provide such primary conditions (see Figure 10.3).

Being inclusive or extractivist does not mean that the pathway is stable in the long run. A stable path is one in which the production of green hydrogen accelerates or fluctuates around a high level, while an unstable pathway is one in which the production diminishes through time to lower levels until it reaches a very low level that approaches the null level.

For a pathway to be stable, powerful actors or a coalition of powerful actors should support it in a way that overcomes any opposing coalitions and actors. Actors with similar beliefs form those coalitions where they coordinate their actions to influence policies (Fischer, 2015; Sabatier & Weible, 2007). Coalitions could be created based on the simple alignment of interests, where these interests must not be identical. The forming actors must not develop formal mechanisms or consciously act together, nor should their alliance be long term (Schmitz, 2017). A supportive policy coalition is generally needed for a significant transformation (Doner & Schneider, 2016).

The power of these coalitions is dependent on three main factors: first, the level of interest (utility) in (or against) green hydrogen production of the constituent actors; second, their comparative power; and third, the ability of actors in the same coalition to coordinate (see Figure 10.4). The intensity of interest of the various actors in green hydrogen production depends on the expected gains or losses that the process would entail, based on the promises and threats posed by green production schemes and the level of trust in those responsible for those schemes. The comparative power of actors vis-à-vis one another depends on broader state–society relations (Sabry, 2022, 2023b). Coordination also depends on state–society relations and the level of trust in and previous cooperation with other potential coalition

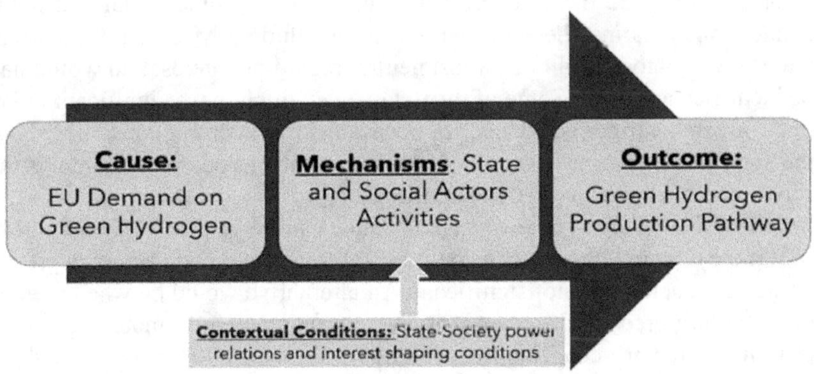

Figure 10.3 A system understanding of mechanisms for the process of green hydrogen production.

Source: Own elaboration

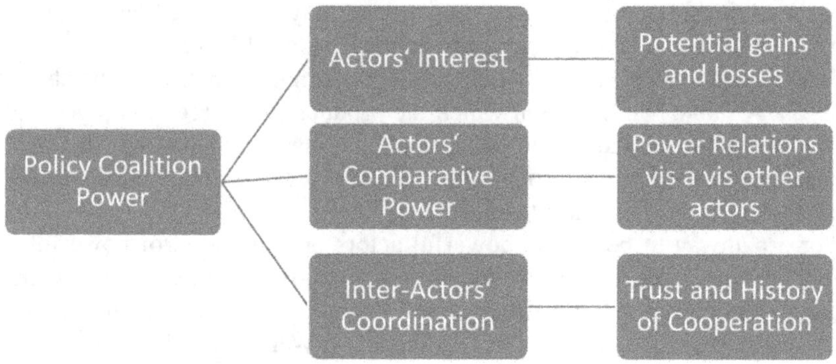

Figure 10.4 The factors shaping the power of policy coalitions.

Source: Own elaboration

partners. Inter-actors' coordination is crucial for establishing a coalition (Fischer, 2015; Sabatier & Weible, 2007, p. 196).

This suggests the presence of a matrix of four paths. Table 10.1 summarizes them.

- *An extractive-stable pathway*: This would likely be shaped by contextual conditions characterized by a more dominant state and possibly closer state-tycoons relations through deep networks of favoritism. The independent organizational power of other actors (e.g., labor unions, business associations, CSOs) would likely be insignificant. This would magnify the impact of the activities of the state and connected tycoons and suppress that of the other social actors. Regarding policy coalitions, the state-tycoons coalition would have the most influential actors. It would be firmly coordinated, given the possible social and political connections (sharing the same family, tribe, ethnic group, or political party). Other social actors might be almost neutral regarding interest and would hardly be identified as actors. Some of them, however, might have significant interests in the green hydrogen schemes. Yet, because of their relative weakness vis-à-vis the state and connected tycoons or their inability to coordinate among themselves, their actions would be insignificant.
- *An extractive-unstable pathway*: An unstable extractive pathway would be realized if the interests of powerful coalitions of state and tycoon actors in green hydrogen production are not significant. An alternative would be when the power of the contra-green hydrogen coalition is strong enough to match or even surpass that of the pro-coalition, which holds a few state and tycoon actors.
- *An inclusive-stable pathway*: This would likely be shaped by contextual conditions characterized by more balanced state–society relations. These relations exist when social actors enjoy strong and independent interest representation where no actor is significantly dominant (Sabry, 2022, 2023b). Such settings would boost the impact of various actors' activities as mechanisms that

Table 10.1 The Various Green Hydrogen Pathways

		Extractivity/Inclusivity	
		Extractive	*Inclusive*
Stability	Stable	Powerful state-tycoons coalitions have strong interests in green hydrogen production.	Interests in green hydrogen production for a wide range of actors.
	Unstable	Powerful state-tycoons coalitions do not have enough interest in green hydrogen production or the power of the contra-coalition matches or surpasses that of the pro-coalition.	In more balanced state–society relations, the interests of the various actors in the green transition would be less significant.

Source: Own elaboration

significantly shape the pathway. Providing interest for several actors and limiting the interests against the green hydrogen schemes would lead to this stable pathway.

- *An inclusive-unstable pathway*: If the green hydrogen production schemes failed to attract sufficient interest from a broad set of actors, this would be the case in a country with more balanced state–society relations.
- *A null-stable pathway*: This would be the case if the production of green hydrogen is insignificant and favorable policy coalition dynamics (as previously discussed) do not exist to kick start (or restart) the process once again.

The Green Hydrogen Pathways of North Africa

This section will study the pathways of different North African countries using a methodology that matches the previous theoretical discussion. The first step is to discuss each country's green hydrogen schemes briefly. A list of current and prospective projects of green hydrogen and its derivatives in North African countries is presented in Table 10.2. The second step is to identify interested actors from the different considered actor sets (e.g., the state, businesspeople, labor, and CSOs), the direction of their interests (positive or negative), and their intensity. This helps identify whether each country's pathway is more extractive or inclusive, depending on the three criteria highlighted in the previous section. The third step is to discuss state–society relations as contextual conditions shaping the pathway and assess the comparative power of the pro-green hydrogen policy coalition versus that of the contra-coalition. This would indicate the stability of the path of each country.

Algeria: A More Dominant State and Low Interests

With the globally tenth-largest natural gas and substantial oil reserves (Zoubir, 2020, p. xxiii), fossil fuel resources dominate the Algerian economy. They constitute about

Table 10.2 Hydrogen-Related Projects in North African Countries

Country	*Energy Source*	*Project*	*Capacity/Amount*	*Started/Planned*	*Investors*
Algeria	Carbon Capture	Bir Rebaa North	powered by 10 MW PV plant	2018	Italian Eni and Algerian Sonatrach
Algeria	Green Hydrogen and Green Ammonia	VNG Green Ammonia Plant	Pilot green hydrogen and green ammonia production	A declaration of intent signed in 2022	KfW financing the pilot Green Hydrogen plant, and German VNG (a subsidiary of German EnBW) will develop the pilot Green Ammonia plant
Morocco	Green Ammonia	OCP Green Ammonia Plant		Announced 2023	OCP
Morocco	Green Ammonia	Green Ammonia Project		A capacity of 183,000 tons by 2026	Irish-Portuguese Fusion Fuel
Morocco	Green Ammonia	Green Ammonia Plant at Jorf Lasfar port		Loan provided by Dutch government in 2022	Dutch Proton Ventures
Morocco	Green Ammonia	Green Ammonia Plant			Italian Saipem (controlled by Eni) and Italian Alboran Hydrogen
Tunisia	Green Hydrogen	H2 Vert	Pilot green hydrogen for the sake of producing 1,500 tons of green ammonia annually	2022	*Deutsche Gesellschaft für Internationale Zusammenarbeit*-German Society for International Cooperation (GIZ)

Source: Own elaboration based on (Martin, 2024; Sainati & Cornelio, 2024; Tanchum, 2024)

95% of Algeria's exports, 60% of budget revenues, and 30% of its GDP. There was a time when President Houari Boumediene (1965–1978) emphasized heavy industries and state-led industrialization financed by oil revenues (Testas & Karagiannis, 2012). Yet the economy has grown increasingly dependent on fossil fuels as public industrial complexes, and investments in heavy and light industries have dwindled because of financial hardships (Gribi et al., 2024).

Against this background, Algeria's National Hydrogen Development Strategy was announced in 2023. In this strategy, and unsurprisingly, the production of blue hydrogen was stated among the objectives. Still, green hydrogen received more emphasis where PEM electrolyzers would be used in its vast production. Desalinated water will be used, but the strategy mentions treated wastewater and, astonishingly, groundwater. By 2050, the annual production of green hydrogen should be around 50 TWh, 80% of which (40 TWh) should be exported, while 10 TWh should be available for domestic needs (Aboushady et al., 2024, pp. 7–9). In the short run, extending to 2030, setting the regulatory framework and pilot projects for domestic production would be the objective. Then, in the medium run (until 2040), scaling up of production will take place, benefiting from the rise in market demand, and later an "industrialization and export phase" for hydrogen will ensue where government funding will be no longer needed (Aboushady et al., 2024, pp. 7–9; Boudghene Stambouli et al., 2024). The Algerian state aims to meet 10% of the European demand for hydrogen, but this is not necessarily of the green variant (Tanchum, 2024, p. 28). The leading international partners for Algeria in these hydrogen schemes are EU countries, especially Italy and Germany. Some projects related to hydrogen production have already started the pilot phase. The presence of some of the needed infrastructure, such as desalination plants, gas pipelines, and LNG ships that could be adjusted to transfer hydrogen, adds to Algeria's strength as a potential significant green (and blue) hydrogen producer (Aboushady et al., 2024, pp. 16–18; Barnard, 2022, p. 15)—nevertheless, the abundance of fossil fuel resources still overcast green hydrogen schemes. The state plans to meet its objectives mainly by producing blue hydrogen and considers green hydrogen a long-term objective (Sainati & Cornelio, 2024, p. 98; Tanchum, 2024, p. 28).

The fertilizer sector could also benefit from the production of green hydrogen, given that Algeria annually exports around six million tons, about 29% of which is ammonia (Aboushady et al., 2024, p. 23). Fertilizers represent about 3% of Algerian exports, which is substantial if we disregard fossil fuel exports. Many of these exports are destined for European countries, especially France and Spain, which have about a third of these exports (Trading Economics, n.d.-a). Plans to develop phosphate production would further increase Algeria's benefits from the production of green ammonia (Barnard, 2022, p. 20). Yet, since the hydrogen currently used in ammonia production is generated from natural gas, questions could be raised on whether blue hydrogen (despite possible CBAM-related costs) could be a more viable alternative, at least in the short and medium runs. As for steel, Algeria is a significant world net importer (Taib, 2021); thus, green hydrogen would likely be of less help to the sector.

Thus, interested actors in the production of green hydrogen are mainly state actors. These are from the executive: the presidency, the Ministry of Energy and Mines, and the Ministry of Environment and Renewable Energy and from state-owned enterprises (SOEs) in the energy sector: Sonatrach and Sonelgaz as well as their created joint-venture SHAEMS. Businesspeople have limited interest in hydrogen production, at least in the short run (Aboushady et al., 2024, p. 11). The interest of the mentioned state actors is positive, yet not that strong. Algeria relies heavily on its fossil fuel resources. The alternative of blue hydrogen seems a more potent option for the state for the various applications, as revealed from the previous discussions. The pathway tends to be extractive because of the limited number of positively interested actors and because they come from almost one actor set (the state); this is regardless of how many actors have an adverse interest in green hydrogen production. Whether this pathway is stable necessitates an analysis of state–society relations.

State–society relations in Algeria have often been regarded as a crony capitalist. The *Pouvoir*, or the deep state, is at the center of the crony network, where army officers dominate the political system and their business cronies enjoy various economic privileges (Cammett et al., 2018, pp. 309–311). Political parties have been allowed to exist since the FLN lost its historical role in the post-independence single-party state. Still, the system was hardly democratic, and multiparty elections were mostly rigged (Zoubir, 2020, p. xxx). There were, however, some short-lived episodes in which a more open political environment prevailed. The most remarkable of these was in the late 1980s—following the 1988 mass riots—which ended with the military takeover of 1992 and cancellation of democratic elections; and the second was the one following the popular uprising of 2019 that forced President Abdelaziz Boutafliqa (1999–2019) to resign. Yet the *Pouvoir* continued to control the political system throughout the decades. Important decisions were made by "intra-elite negotiations" involving army and intelligence officers, senior bureaucrats, and major politicians (Rivetti & Cavatorta, 2018).

The central labor union in the country and the one that controls the industrial activity and significant public-sector firms, the UGTA, has been for long dominated by the state, despite its relative independence shortly after the establishment of the Algerian state in 1962 (Zobiri, 2015). There are not many independent business associations in Algeria. The Business Leaders Forum (FCE), for instance, was always supportive of Bouteflika's decisions and his presidential candidacy, and this was not much different for other business associations. Business associations hardly led business advocacy or criticized the state's policies (Rivetti & Cavatorta, 2018). The state still dominates the economy and controls the most important sectors. This is despite the privatization process witnessed in the 1990s following debt rescheduling and the negotiations with the International Monetary Fund (IMF). Privatizing public enterprises benefited the business cronies of the state in a way that surpassed some countries in the region, especially for banks and import–export enterprises. Accordingly, large enterprises are controlled by business cronies (Cammett et al., 2018, pp. 309–311). The number of SMEs, representing about 99% of the Algerian private sector, has expanded in the last decades, starting from the 1990s (Mosbah & Debili, 2014). Yet the rate of their annual creation lags behind the international average. They were overwhelmingly micro-firms, and their presence in the industrial sector was limited (15% in 2019) and even more limited (15% of industrial SMEs) in sectors with linkages with the renewable energy sector (e.g., electronic and electric, steel, mechanical, and metallurgical producers). The level of innovation in SMEs is too low, even compared to neighboring countries (Gribi et al., 2024). There are generally still high regulatory barriers to market entry (Aboushady et al., 2024, p. 12). On the other hand, CSOs were generally under the control of the Bouteflika's regime (Zoubir, 2020, pp. xxx–xxxi). The experience of the confrontations in the south of Algeria when the state authorized the shale gas extraction without consultation with local communities or public debate reveals the power imbalances between the state and CSOs. The environmental concerns because of fracking, which uses polluting chemicals and large quantities of water, induced local communities to protest through the "anti-fracking group." Despite the protests, the state did not abandon its extraction plans; it only postponed them (Rivetti & Cavatorta, 2018).

In conclusion, the state is the most influential player, and the oil rents from the country's extensive fossil fuel resources have historically fostered its power. The pro-green hydrogen coalition has the most influential actors, such as state actors, but it is limited to them, and their interests in the process are weak. Conceiving a contra-policy coalition to green hydrogen production will be mainly constructed from CSOs motivated by environmental concerns. The power of this potential contra-policy coalition is relatively weak in terms of the power of its actors, their coordination, and interests. Algeria's green hydrogen production pathway seems stable but tends to be a null pathway. Things might change in the long run, but the Algerian path tends to be an extractive, stable, and null pathway in the short and medium runs.

Morocco: A Dominant State, Powerful Societal Actors, and High Interests

Morocco has developed plans for green hydrogen production and is a regional pioneer in this field (see Table 9.2). The pipeline that previously transported Algerian natural gas to Spain could be repurposed (with modifications) to transport Moroccan green hydrogen. Additionally, existing harbors could facilitate the shipment of hydrogen and its derivatives.[2] In 2021, a green hydrogen cluster (GreenH2) was established to boost Moroccan private sector interest in hydrogen as a decarbonization tool and reduce firm costs through large-scale production. Various conditions generally foster the state's interest in green hydrogen production and the green transition. These conditions include the country's insufficient fossil fuel resources, political tensions with fossil fuel-rich neighboring Algeria, and geographical proximity to European markets. The executive is interested in the green hydrogen production schemes, especially the Ministry for Energy Transition and Sustainable Development. Yet the OCP—an SOE—is the leading player in the green hydrogen field. The OCP is the biggest producer of phosphate and the fourth biggest exporter of fertilizers internationally. This SOE brought about one-fifth of Morocco's export revenues in 2020. The company primarily benefits from the substantial phosphate reserves of Morocco, where nearly three-quarters of the world's phosphate rock reserves lie in Morocco (Tanchum, 2024, p. 22). The ammonia currently used in fertilizer is predominantly gray and mainly imported from Russia (Barnard, 2022, p. 10). Yet the OCP launched a green investment program that aims to boost OCP's mining and the company's capacity to produce fertilizers, stressing the commitment to realize carbon neutrality by 2040 (OCP, n.d.). The use and production of green ammonia is one of the critical means for the greening strategy of the company, and plans were already announced in 2023 for the construction of a green ammonia plant for the company (Tanchum, 2024, p. 22).

Many businesspeople are operating in industries that could have strong linkages with the electrolyzer sector. This includes input suppliers to the renewable energy sector needed to generate hydrogen (e.g., windmill blades, electric cables), which would likely serve the electrolyzer industry. Green hydrogen could also be used in the direct reduction process of iron to produce green iron that could be used as an input for the electrolyzer and further decrease the carbon imprint of the produced green hydrogen. Morocco's exports of iron and steel and articles of iron and steel are less than 1% of the country's total exports. Still, many of these are exported to EU countries, especially France and Spain (Trading Economics, n.d.-b), making shifting to green steel a reasonable strategy. Large or medium enterprises are more likely to operate in sectors linked to renewable energy generation and electrolyzer sectors, where these enterprises are controlled by local tycoons or multinational corporations (MNCs). On the other hand, SMEs would be more interested if more regional content for the renewable energy sector, especially hydrogen electrolysis, would be integrated. However, they are likely neutral regarding interests and could not be identified as collective actors.

Labor unions had doubts about the whole energy transition scheme based on past experiences with structural changes. Still, they lacked the drive to form a resisting block, expressing some support for the transition as beneficial and inevitable while seeking better terms and greater involvement in the decision-making process.[3] The most interested laborers are the workers of the OCP, given the substantial changes in its production processes in the fertilizer sector, such as replacing grey hydrogen with green hydrogen. Yet the OCP had successful cases with structural change concerning sustainability and structural training, thanks to strong relations between management and labor unions.[4] This might suggest the presence of a positive interest in the production of green hydrogen from public-sector labor and, more specifically, OCP labor and the labor unions that represent them. The social dialogue held by the OCP has national union delegates "of the most representative trade unions at OCP Group" (OCP Group, 2020). If the interests of labor actors toward the green transition could be identified as generally neutral in a way that denies their identification as active actors, the peculiarities of green hydrogen and the leading position of the OCP in the Moroccan case suggest the presence of potential interest in the production of green hydrogen of the labor unions representing OCP workers.

CSOs with a nationally oriented social and environmental mission are perhaps the only actors with a potential interest in the production of green hydrogen. For instance, there are concerns about the excessive use of water in renewable energy projects and the rights of local communities on the land used in existing and prospective projects. There were already local protests against renewable energy projects partly because of inadequate compensation for local communities, and these communities and those defending their interests were not adequately consulted.[5] The massive production of green hydrogen will significantly add to those concerns.

There is an agreement among many scholars that state–society relations in Morocco are characterized by a powerful state that is strongly connected to business family tycoons in what is often referred to as the *Makhzan* (Boussaid, 2010; Cammett, 2007), a rather crony capitalist setting (Saadi, 2016). Yet, compared to many MENA countries, state–society relations in Morocco are more open. Social actors, especially labor unions, have more organizational power (Cammett & Posusney, 2010), and they (e.g., business associations and labor unions) elect their representatives in the Chamber of Counselors (upper chamber) of the parliament (Achy, 2013). Nevertheless, the state, especially the King, is the dominant actor, and social actors' representation seems to be fragmented, especially for labor, whose representation is divided among various labor unions, many of which have political party affiliations (Anderson, 2016). CSOs were also fragmented, and a few of them prioritized environmental concerns.[6] They also lacked political access comparable to that of tycoons and labor unions.

The presence of various actors from different sets—from the state (mainly the executive and OCP), businesspeople (suppliers to the renewable power and electrolyzers plants), and labor (labor unions representing OCP workers) with interests that are pro-green hydrogen production—suggests the presence of a pathway that tends to be relatively inclusive. This is even if a different assessment could be done for the more general green transition pathway. Considering contextual conditions and policy coalitions, I suggest the following regarding stability. Pro-green hydrogen production has the strongest actors. The state faces minimal internal friction in supporting the green transition, with strong backing from the King, who provided significant impetus to the process.[7] The coordination between the state and interested business groups, especially domestic tycoons, is firm due to the presence of not only the Makhzan but also other channels, such as the strong relations with the most significant business association in the country, the *Confederation Generale Des Entreprises Du Maroc* (CGEM) and the considerable business representation in the parliament. Labor unions also potentially have some interest in the production of green hydrogen. Channels of coordination with the state exist, especially the strong channels existing with the OCP, which is the most interested actor in green hydrogen production. Thus, the pro-green transition coalition comprises the strongest state–society actors in Morocco (the state and tycoons), is highly coordinated, and has generally significant interests in green hydrogen production. In the contra-coalition, some CSOs would stand alone without significant actors from other actor sets and with little coordination among themselves to overcome their fragmented nature. Even if these CSOs evolved as a collective actor, imagining their contra-green hydrogen coalition would match the pro-coalition's power would be tough. Hence, the pathway characterizing Morocco's green hydrogen production is likely more inclusive and stable.

Tunisia: Powerful Societal Actors and Conflicting Interests

The production of green hydrogen in Tunisia is still in its initial phase. The EU, especially Germany, is active in the planned schemes and is expected to dominate investment in this field, lead training and capacity building, and generate much of the demand for the produced hydrogen. Green hydrogen is to be produced by the electrolysis of desalinated seawater. The produced hydrogen will be transported to Europe through the existing pipelines that transport Algerian natural gas to Italy.[8] The National Green Hydrogen Strategy target is to produce about 8.3 million tons, more than three-quarters of which will be destined for export markets (Tanchum, 2024, pp. 29–30).

Developing a new export commodity creates a high interest for the Tunisian state in green hydrogen, especially the executive and, more precisely, the Ministry of Industry, Energy, and Mines (MIEM) and the Presidency. The fertilizers industry, which would benefit from green ammonia, contributed about 3% of the total exports of Tunisia in 2022, where most of these exports were much of this production was destined for EU markets (Trading Economics, n.d.-b). This places two SOEs at the center of the interest in the production of green hydrogen. The first is the Gafsa Phosphate Company—*Compagnie des Phosphates de Gafsa* (CPG)—which extracts phosphate and, more importantly, the Tunisian Chemical Group—*Groupe Chimique Tunisien* (GCT)—in Gerbs which processes the extracted phosphate and produces various fertilizers.

As for business actors' interest, using green hydrogen in producing iron and steel is a worthwhile option. The iron and steel industry contributed about 1.5% of Tunisia's total exports, with most of the exports destined for EU markets, especially Italy (Trading Economics, n.d.-b). Regarding backward linkages, the supplier industry's contribution to Tunisia's renewable energy generation sector is relatively modest.[9] The same could be expected in the case of electrolyzers' inputs. Overall, business interest in green hydrogen does not seem strong enough or is not shared among strong business players.

On the other hand, labor has been critical to the green transition process, and nothing new should be expected concerning green hydrogen. The main concern for the labor unions in the country, or for instance, the *Union Générale Tunisienne du Travail*—Tunisian General Labor Union (UGTT)—originates from the energy sector and, more specifically, the *Fédération Générale de l'Electricité et du Gaz*—the General Federation for Oil and Gas (FGEG)—which is the labor syndicate of the *Société Tunisienne de l'Electricité et du Gaz*—Tunisian Company of Electricity and Gas (STEG). The UGTT (especially the FGEG) is alarmed by the prospects of private capital control over the energy sector (Louati, 2022) and wants the public sector to dominate renewable energy projects.[10] Finally, CSOs have various concerns about green hydrogen production and the green transition in general. The excessive water usage required for green hydrogen production in a water-scarce country and the lack of transparency and public information are critical points against green hydrogen schemes. However, these could be added to the state's neglect of its stated environmental commitments to renewable energy projects and the inadequate compensation for local communities affected by the construction of these projects on their lands.[11] The strong link between the fertilizers and phosphate industries increases environmental concerns about green hydrogen production, where many of the most decisive environmental confrontations took place in the country. GCT facilities were accused of being responsible for the spread of cancer, respiratory, and skin diseases among the hosting city inhabitants, and protests supported by CSOs managed to lock down a company facility for some time in 2020 (Sabry, 2023a).

This suggests that pro-green hydrogen production actors are mainly state actors, especially the MIEM, the head of the executive, the GCT, and some businesspeople actors in a few sectors (e.g., iron and steel producers and suppliers to the renewable energy and electrolyzer plants). Those feeling threatened by the production of green hydrogen schemes are the labor represented mainly by the UGTT and various CSOs. Among the actors with a positive or negative interest in green hydrogen production, those with a favorable interest are somewhat limited and come only from one actor's set, the state. Numerous actors have adverse interests (e.g., UGTT, CSOs). Hence, the pathway tends to be more extractive. But how stable is this pathway?

State–society dynamics have undergone several changes in Tunisia in the 21st century. A turning point was Kais Saied's constitutional coup on 25 July 2021, supported by the security apparatus (Khaddar, 2023). The new constitution passed a year after enormously strengthened the president's power and reduced that of the parliament (Petkanas, 2023). This change reconfigured the order of the democratic decade (2011–2021) in which the state was less dominant due to political polarization and instability, big business tycoons were more powerful, while other social actors' organizations gained some power, especially the UGTT. In the new order, businesspeople, especially tycoons, saw their influence wane in political parties and parliament. The president openly clashed with some of them under the pretext of an anti-corruption campaign, leading to arrests and pressuring others to invest in the economy as part of a reconciliation effort (Ben Salah, 2023; Zantour, 2023). Meanwhile, the UGTT maintained much of its power and sometimes openly challenged the state. Yet the president forced the FGEG to halt their resistance to PPP renewable energy projects. The UGTT did not take firm action, showing that it could give up support for the FGEG because of political considerations.[12] CSOs felt more threatened,[13] especially after the drafting of a law in 2022 that aimed at tightening state control over foreign funding of CSOs, requiring government pre-approval for their existence, facilitating the regulation of their activities, and allowing their dissolution without judicial oversight (Amnesty International, 2023). On the other hand, the president's consolidation of power and the end of cabinet fragmentation among political parties brought more cohesion to the state.

The post-25 July 2021, state–business relations became more restrained, limiting tycoons' political influence. The state showed less interest in social dialogues, weakening *Union tunisienne de l'industrie, du commerce et de l'artisanat* (UTICA)'s representation of business interests vis-à-vis the state.[14] Thus, coordination between the state and some businesspeople who might be interested in the production of green hydrogen has likely weakened. The coordination between the UGTT and CSOs remains generally limited on the contra-green hydrogen production potential coalition. Some mistrust exists between both sides, at least between the UGTT and many Tunisian branches of foreign-based CSOs. There was also less cooperation between both sides in important, relevant incidences, such as the protests against the GCT, where the union was in a dilemma between wanting to preserve jobs in this SOE and the environmental threats it caused (Sabry, 2023a). Some changes in the contra-camp are witnessed. The Working Group for Energy Democracy (WGED) was established as a CSO by FGEG syndicalists, promoting a broader discourse to rally environmentally and socially oriented CSOs. The WGED broadened its advocacy to include the demands of other actors beyond that of the FGEG. Yet the WGED is selective in its CSO partners (on ideological terms).[15] Consequently, the extractive pathway for producing green hydrogen is likely unstable. Even if coordination in the contra-coalition is not strong enough, the UGTT still has significant power, and CSOs have a wide margin of independence and a successful protest experience at times. The pro-green hydrogen production camp, on the other hand, is limited, even if it is more powerful because of the increase in the executive's power since 2022.

Conclusion

Different pathways for green hydrogen production are expected to dominate in several North African countries. Algeria would likely have an extractive, stable, but null path, wherein the short- and medium-run green hydrogen production is likely insignificant. Morocco's path seems to be the most inclusive and stable in North Africa. In contrast, the opposite is expected for Tunisia, where the pathway would tend to be more extractive and unstable.

The prospective massive production of green hydrogen would likely change many variables, carve other new actors, or force different actors to take sharper stances, whether in support or resistance to the process. In the long run, nothing is fixed, and all is variable, a fundamental economic assumption. The production of green hydrogen could be a project that most actors would defend if interests were readjusted and appropriate policies were set to accomplish this. Encouraging more local content and technology transfer through partnerships between FDI and domestic business, fostering retraining and human capital capacity building, enforcing stricter environmental and social impact assessment, and, as importantly, having broader and more effective public–private dialogues that should be more than consultative bodies could, all develop a more inclusive pathway. Sustaining such a pathway would provide no incentive to shift away from it in the short or long run. International actors, and on top of which, the EU, which forcibly pushes forward the green hydrogen production schemes in North Africa, should realize that such a pathway is not only a more stable but also a just pathway in which benefits are shared from such an envisaged significant transformation. Developmental assistance that enables more participatory and inclusive approaches should be prioritized.

Notes

1 Storage options are important given the temporal and spatial mismatch in the supply and demand of the electricity produced from renewable energy sources (Terrapon-Pfaff et al., 2021, p. 77).
2 Based on an interview with an employee at the German *Kreditanstalt für Wiederaufbau*—Credit Institute for Reconstruction (KfW) who was responsible for the green hydrogen project in Morocco.
3 Based on interviews with several members of a Moroccan labor union the Democratic Confederation of Labor (CDT).
4 Based on an interview with a member of a Moroccan labor union, the Democratic Confederation of Labor (CDT).
5 Based on an interview with a member of the Heinrich Böll Stiftung in Morocco.
6 Based on an interview with a Moroccan labor unionist.
7 Based on an interview with a KfW employee who was responsible for the green hydrogen project in Morocco as well as another interview with a member of a CSO active in the green transition.
8 Based on an interview with an engineer at *Société Tunisienne de l'Electricité et du Gaz* (STEG).
9 Based on interviews with a leading official at Agence Nationale pour la Maîtrise de l'Énergie- National Agency for Energy Conservation (ANME), a leading figure at the *Chambre Syndicale du Photovoltaïque de Tunisie*—Syndicate Chamber of Photovoltaic of Tunisia (CSPV), and KfW.
10 Several UGTT interviewees, one of whom is from the FGEG.
11 Based on an interview with a leading member of the *Forum Tunisien pour les Droits Economiques et Sociaux*—Tunisian Forum for Economic and Social Rights (FTDES).
12 Based on an interview with a leading figure at the FGEG and the WGED.
13 Based on an interview with a member of the *Heinrich Böll Stiftung* (HBS) in Tunisia.
14 Based on an interview with a leading member at the UTICA.
15 Based on an interview with a leading figure at the FGEG and the WGED.

References

Aboushady, N., Jaroudi, I., Boie, I., Dütschke, E., Kantel, A., Müller, V., Scherrer, A., Laasmi, M., Altenburg, T., Oyan, E., Stamm, A., Strohmaier, R., & Thoms, K. (2024). *Towards a green H2 economy: Algeria country report* (HYPAT Working Paper No. 11/2024).

Acemoglu, D., & Robinson, J. A. (2019). Rents and economic development: The perspective of *Why Nations Fail: Public Choice*, *181*(1), 13–28. https://doi.org/10.1007/s11127-019-00645-z

Achy, L. (2013). *Structural transformation and industrial policy in Morocco* (ERF Working Paper No. 796).

Amnesty International. (2023). *Human rights under assault two years after President Saied's power grab*. https://www.amnesty.org/en/latest/campaigns/2023/07/human-rights-under-assault-two-years-after-president-saieds-power-grab/

Anderson, A. A. (2016). *Going political: Labor, institutions and democratic unrest in North Africa*. Harvard University Press.

Barnard, M. (2022). *Morocco, Algeria, Egypt: Assessing EU plans to import hydrogen from North Africa*. Transnational Institute. https://www.tni.org/en/publication/assessing-eu-plans-to-import-hydrogen-from-north-africa

Beach, D., & Pedersen, R. B. (2016). *Causal case study methods: Foundations and guidelines for comparing, matching, and tracing*. University of Michigan Press.

Bebbington, A. (2015). Governing natural resources for inclusive development. In S. Hickey, K. Sen, & B. Bukenya (Eds.), *The politics of inclusive development* (pp. 86–118). Oxford University Press.

Ben Salah, F. (2023, February 25). Tunisia: Saied escalates power game with arrest of influential businessman. *Middle East Eye*. https://www.middleeasteye.net/news/tunisia-saied-escalates-arrest-businessman-fabricated-charges

Boudghene Stambouli, A., Kitamura, Y., Benmessaoud, M. T., & Yassaa, N. (2024). Algeria's journey towards a green hydrogen future. *International Journal of Hydrogen Energy*, *58*, 753–763. https://doi.org/10.1016/j.ijhydene.2024.01.119

Boussaid, F. (2010). *State–business relations in Morocco* (Knowledge Programme Civil Society in West Asia Working Paper No. 6).

Cammett, M. (2007). Business–government relations and industrial change. *World Development*, *35*(11), 1889–1903. https://doi.org/10.1016/j.worlddev.2007.01.003

Cammett, M., Diwan, I., Richards, A., & Waterbury, J. (2018). *A political economy of the Middle East* (4th ed.). Routledge. https://doi.org/10.4324/9780429492600

Cammett, M., & Posusney, M. P. (2010). Labor standards and labor market flexibility in the Middle East. *Studies in Comparative International Development*, *45*(2), 183–206. https://doi.org/10.1007/s12116-010-9062-z

Delpuech, A. (2022). *Who benefits from Tunisia's green hydrogen strategy*? Arab Reform Initiative & Heinrich Böll Stiftung.

Doner, R. F., & Schneider, B. R. (2016). The middle-income trap: More politics than economics. *World Politics*, *68*(4), 608–644.

European Commission. (2022, May 18). *REPowerEU: A plan to rapidly reduce dependence on Russian fossil fuels and fast forward the green transition*. https://ec.europa.eu/commission/presscorner/detail/en/ip_22_3131

European Commission. (n.d.-a). *Key actions of the EU hydrogen strategy*. Retrieved November 4, 2024, from https://energy.ec.europa.eu/topics/energy-systems-integration/hydrogen/key-actions-eu-hydrogen-strategy_en

European Commission. (n.d.-b). *The European Green Deal: Striving to be the first climate-neutral continent*. Retrieved October 30, 2023, from https://commission.europa.eu/strategy-and-policy/priorities-2019-2024/european-green-deal_en

Evans, P. B. (1989). Predatory, developmental, and other apparatuses. *Sociological Forum*, *4*(4), 561–587. https://doi.org/10.1007/BF01115064

Fischer, M. (2015). Institutions and coalitions in policy processes. *Journal of Public Policy*, *35*(2), 245–268. https://doi.org/10.1017/S0143814X14000166

Gribi, D., Amarouche, A., & Si Lekhal, K. (2024). Industrial policies in Algeria. *Journal of Economic Growth and Entrepreneurship*, *7*(2), 1–11.

Incer-Valverde, J., Korayem, A., Tsatsaronis, G., & Morosuk, T. (2023). "Colors" of hydrogen. *Energy Conversion and Management*, *291*, 117294. https://doi.org/10.1016/j.enconman.2023.117294

IRENA. (2018). *Hydrogen from renewable power: Technology outlook for the energy transition*. International Renewable Energy Agency.

IRENA. (2020). *Green hydrogen cost reduction*. International Renewable Energy Agency.

Khaddar, M. (2023). Tunisian democratisation. *The Journal of North African Studies*, *28*(6), 1324–1344. https://doi.org/10.1080/13629387.2023.2203465

Louati, I. (2022). *Tunisia: What is the energy transition about?* (RLS North Africa Research Paper Series No. 3). Rosa Luxemburg Stiftung, North Africa Office.

Magdich, A., Szenderák, J., & Harangi-Rákos, M. (2021). Economic diversification in resource-based economies. *Pressburg Economic Review*, *1*(1), 27–36. https://doi.org/10.5281/zenodo.7517205

Martin, A. P. (2024). Grid and bear it. In M. Tanchum (Ed.), *Renewable energy and electricity interconnection megaprojects in North Africa* (pp. 68–91). European Institute for the Mediterranean.

Mehlum, H., Moene, K., & Torvik, R. (2012). Mineral rents and social development in Norway. In K. Hujo (Ed.), *Mineral rents and the financing of social policy* (pp. 155–184). Palgrave Macmillan. https://doi.org/10.1057/9780230370913_6

Mosbah, A., & Debili, R. (2014). Development of Algerian SMEs. *Journal of Business and Social Development, 2*(1), 37–48.

OCP. (n.d.). *Our green investment program*. Retrieved October 12, 2024, from https://www.ocpgroup.ma/Strategy/Commitments/Green-Investment-Program

OCP Group. (2020). *Social dialogue policy*. https://ocpsiteprodsa.blob.core.windows.net/media/2021-11/23_OCP%20Social%20dialogue%20policy.pdf

Petkanas, Z. (2023). Kais Saied and the demise of democracy. *The Journal of North African Studies, 28*(4), 733–740. https://doi.org/10.1080/13629387.2023.2211838

Philipps University of Marburg, & University of Kassel. (n.d.). *Extractivism*. Retrieved January 22, 2024, from https://extractivism.de/en/#project

Rivetti, P., & Cavatorta, F. (2018). Algeria: Oil and public opinion. In I. Overland (Ed.), *Public brainpower* (pp. 23–40). Springer. https://doi.org/10.1007/978-3-319-60627-9_2

Saadi, M. S. (2016). *Moroccan cronyism: Facts, mechanisms and impact* (No. 1063). Economic Research Forum.

Sabatier, P. A., & Weible, C. M. (2007). The advocacy coalition framework. In P. A. Sabatier (Ed.), *Theories of the policy process* (pp. 189–222). Westview Press.

Sabido, P. (2022). *L'hydrogène d'Afrique du Nord*. Transnational Institute. https://www.tni.org/fr/hydrogène-vert

Sabry, M. I. (2022). The institutional origins of state–society relations. *Fulbright Review of Economics and Policy*. https://doi.org/10.1108/FREP-05-2022-0032

Sabry, M. I. (2023a). State–society relations and industrial sustainable growth. *Sustainable Development, 32*(3), 1792–1810. https://doi.org/10.1002/sd.2746

Sabry, M. I. (2023b). *The growth paths of state–society relations*. Emerald Publishing.

Sainati, T., & Cornelio, J. R. J. (2024). The impacts of energy megaprojects in North African countries. In M. Tanchum (Ed.), *Renewable energy and electricity interconnection megaprojects in North Africa* (pp. 92–117). European Institute for the Mediterranean.

Schmitz, H. (2017). Who drives climate-relevant policies? *New Political Economy, 22*(5), 521–540. https://doi.org/10.1080/13563467.2017.1257597

Taib, M. (2021). *The mineral industry of Algeria*. U.S. Geological Survey.

Tanchum, M. (2024). Pathways to power. In M. Tanchum (Ed.), *Renewable energy and electricity interconnection megaprojects in North Africa* (pp. 16–47). European Institute for the Mediterranean.

Terrapon-Pfaff, J., Prantner, M., Zelt, O., Missaoui, R., Ghezal, A., & Toumi, M. (2021). *Study on the opportunities of "Power-to-X" in Tunisia*. Deutsche Gesellschaft für Internationale Zusammenarbeit (GIZ) GmbH.

Testas, A., & Karagiannis, N. (2012). Towards an alternative industrial and trade profile for Algeria. *The Journal of North African Studies, 17*(4), 631–652. https://doi.org/10.1080/13629387.2012.686299

Trading Economics. (n.d.-a). *Algeria exports*. Retrieved November 20, 2024, from https://tradingeconomics.com/algeria/exports

Trading Economics. (n.d.-b). *Morocco exports*. Retrieved November 22, 2024, from https://tradingeconomics.com/morocco/exports

U.S. Department of Energy. (2024). *Water electrolyzers and fuel cells supply chain: Supply chain deep dive assessment*. U.S. Department of Energy.

Warnecke-Berger, H., & Ickler, J. (Eds.). (2023). *The political economy of extractivism*. Routledge.

Wedeman, A. (1997). Looters, rent-scrapers, and dividend-collectors. *The Journal of Developing Areas*, *31*(4), 457–478.

Zantour, K. (2023, December). Arrest of business tycoon Marouane Mabrouk sends shockwaves across Tunisia. *Al-Majalla*. https://en.majalla.com/node/306261/business-economy/arrest-business-tycoon-marouane-mabrouk-sends-shockwaves-across

Zobiri, H. (2015). State, sovereignty, and labor movements in Algeria. *The Arab Studies Journal*, *23*(1), 274–294.

Zoubir, Y. H. (2020). *The politics of Algeria: Domestic issues and international relations*. Routledge.

11 Contentious Imaginaries of Energy Transition in Tunisia

Between Inclusive Energy Futures and Transnational Green Extractivism

Nathalie Ferré, Philipp Wagner, Alessandra Bonci, and Aron Buzogány

Introduction

The post-revolutionary Tunisian energy sector underwent major legislative changes, leading to partial privatization of energy production and transnational investments. Encouraged by international donors and the lobbying of private companies, these changes are usually framed in terms of support for Tunisia's lagging clean energy transition and national energy security and receive further support through the European Green Deal. At the same time, social mobilization against socioeconomic and territorial inequalities—often caused by extractivist activities such as the phosphate industry—is among the central struggles of post-revolutionary Tunisia.

The TuNur project, our main focus in this chapter, is a prominent and contentious example of solar energy initiatives in Tunisia. Spearheaded by the Tunisian-British company TuNur, the project aims to harness solar energy in southern Tunisia and export it to Europe via high-voltage cables across the Mediterranean. Likewise, different multilateral development banks and international organizations (IOs) envisage the construction of the Elmed interconnector between Tunisia and Sicily. In December 2022, the European Commission pledged to allocate 307 million euros from a total budget of 850 million euros (including contributions from the World Bank, the European Bank for Reconstruction and Development, and *Kreditanstalt für Wiederaufbau* (KfW)) to construct high-voltage cables across the Mediterranean. This mega-infrastructure project aligns with the broader strategy of the EU, known as the "European Green Deal" which aims to decarbonize the European economy by 2050. To achieve this goal, the European Commission emphasizes the widespread electrification of the economy and mobility, resulting in a substantial increase in the demand for metals such as copper and lithium for energy transmission and storage. This strategy gained renewed urgency following the Russian–Ukrainian conflict, as European strategies sought to reduce dependence on Russian gas. The RePowerEU strategy proposes to rely on the import of renewable energy from countries outside the EU, including Tunisia.

These developments in European energy strategies and the TuNur project, which is among the most visible infrastructure projects concerning energy export

DOI: 10.4324/9781003730750-11

from Tunisia, raise one central question: do they pave the way for new forms of extractivist economies, which would enable the continued accumulation of benefits for the Northern countries through the exploitation of the natural resources of the Southern countries, including both minerals and renewable resources, such as wind and sun?

To address this question, we draw upon Eduardo Gudynas's definition of extractivism, which describes an asymmetric system of exchanges involving the exploitation and exportation of minimally processed natural resources within the context of less diversified economies (Gudynas, 2009). Updated through the concept of neo-extractivism, research now considers the politics of national postcolonial states, coalitions of transnational actors such as firms, and the role of other dominant state actors such as China to analyze the persistence of an asymmetric exchange system since independence (Boutaleb & Brisson, 2022). We also draw on research that extends the concept to renewable resources such as sun and wind to encompass "green extractivism." The critique associated with the term denounces the structural conditions of the green-technological energy transition, perpetuating global inequalities and exploitation on a worldwide scale (Dietz, 2023). In this chapter, we further the idea that such a concept is useful if adapted and used reflexively to study contexts different from Latin America, and we focus on the actors involved in promoting and contesting extractivism in Tunisia.

Rather than analyzing asymmetric exchanges at the international level, in this contribution, we look at sociotechnical imaginaries of energy futures. Renewable energy exportation from Tunisia to Europe is currently still in a visionary and uncertain stage. This implies an examination of the sociopolitical visions of what a desirable energy future should entail as well as the alternative imaginaries that contest green energy exportation. In doing so, we use the "sociotechnical imaginaries" concept from science-technology studies (STS), which has been developed to describe the nexus of technology, science, and democracy by focusing on the production of power and social order. Sociotechnical imaginaries mean projecting these relations into futuristic desired utopias (Jasanoff & Kim, 2013). Social imaginaries are "collectively held, institutionally stabilized, and publicly performed" and "animated by shared understandings of forms of social life and social order attainable through, and supportive of, advances in science and technology" (Jasanoff & Kim, 2015, p. 4). While temporally contingent and culturally particular, sociotechnical imaginaries are not limited to the level of nation-states but can also be explicitly propagated by corporations and organized groups, including communities or social movements (Jasanoff & Kim, 2015). What makes sociotechnical imaginaries particularly relevant for our case is that future expectations have the power to structure present developments and determine expectations toward new market dynamics (Beckert, 2016)—even if the material manifestation of projects deviates from this or even fails.

Using the TuNur case as an example, we develop an actor-centered approach that considers how imagined energy futures perpetuate extractivist imaginaries and how the concept is used in mobilization strategies. First, we focus on actors involved in promoting extractivist strategies. We do not restrict our interests merely to governments of a postcolonial country but also include transnationally operating corporations, legal professionals, and national economic elites. Second, we show that in our case study, the concept of extractivism is simultaneously a tool for denouncing and politicizing power relations within the global economy. As Allain and Maillet (2022) have demonstrated, this concept was forged through the work of scholars and activists and has circulated within these circles:

> the use of the concept of extractivism allows activists to politicize their situation by creating links between different national situations and enables researchers to situate these processes of exploitation in time and space to understand them as forms of exercise of capitalist, patriarchal, anthropocentric, and postcolonial power.
>
> (Allain & Maillet, 2022, p. 12, authors' translation)

It is a concept that enables the denunciation of existing power relations and serves to rally struggles against the exploitation of natural resources by foreign firms or through the politics of postcolonial states (Boutaleb & Brisson, 2022). Existing literature on activism using the concept of extractivism shows that these struggles often rely on transnational networks and strategies (Rahman & Hasan, 2022; López et al., 2015). On the contestation side, we show that this will likely emerge from various, often unconnected actors, such as trade unions, members of civil society, local interest groups, and transnationally active networks of resistance.

We, therefore, study the transnational configuration that considers the mutual dependencies and interactions between actors involved in developing "green energies" and those that develop tactics to counter transnational energy projects. Our "configurationist" perspective builds on the French tradition of anthropology of the state, which analyzes, for instance, "developmentalist configuration" as

> an essentially cosmopolitan world of experts, bureaucrats, NGO staff, researchers, technicians, project chiefs, and field agents, who make a living, so to speak, out of developing other people, and who, to this end, mobilize and manage a considerable amount of material and symbolic resources.
>
> (Olivier de Sardan, 2005, p. 25)

Seen from this perspective, the boundaries between domestic and external actors are far from being clear—and we are particularly interested in the configurations of various, and often changing, groups of actors in the climate and energy field.

This chapter argues that transnational actors, union workers, local communities, NGOs, professional organizations working in the field of solar energy, or local affiliates of the global climate movement imagine contradictory energy futures and that this leads to contentious collective action. Our findings show that sociotechnical imaginaries are complex and multilevel and that they perpetuate the history of extractive practices by playing a role both in designing legal and infrastructure systems and in contesting them (Jenss & Bonci, 2025; Schuetze et al., 2024). This is especially interesting for scholars studying the making of large energy infrastructures, the legal and ideational systems they are embedded into, and the state–society relations that shape them. Our perspective implies a shift from state practices only and calls for an inclusion of non-state actors and their agency below and beyond the scale of the state.

This chapter is based on field research conducted in 2022 and 2023. Working on different but overlapping projects, the authors have conducted 35 semi-structured interviews with domestic stakeholders (trade unionists, staff of local energy agencies, business representatives, non-profit members) and international development agencies based in Tunisia, including both the capital, Tunis, and the Southeast of Tunisia, where trade unionists contested connecting solar plants to the grid.

The first part of this chapter delves into the transnational energy configuration that develops neoliberal and extractivist sociotechnical imaginaries. Although the infrastructure still has to be built or might even fail, the ideas they advocate for have fundamental repercussions on Tunisian legislative developments. Subsequently, in the second part, we demonstrate that the concepts of "extractivism" and "just transition" serve to make political claims contesting these energy projects, often in collaboration with transnational allies. We aim to show that these concepts have different meanings in various contexts and at different scales.

Extractivist Sociotechnical Imaginaries and Their Effects

Previous research has underscored the centrality of imaginaries and discourses in shaping energy system transformations. For instance, Rignall (2016) and Moore (2018) examined the development of solar energy in Morocco, demonstrating that sociotechnical imaginaries play a central role due to their structuring effects on energy production systems. During the conceptualization phase of energy projects, sociopolitical conflicts become particularly visible as political and economic actors take positions either to reform the energy system or to safeguard their positions within the existing system. Energy systems, as the literature on energy humanities argues convincingly (Szeman & Boyer, 2017), are characterized by not solely technical aspects but also sociotechnical, encompassing both the "hardware of the system (e.g., power plants, transmission lines, transformers) and the political, social, and institutional aspects of systems (e.g., regulatory institutions, political frameworks, activist groups, citizens, engineers, and financiers)" (Moore, 2018).

The TuNur Imaginary: A Colonial Legacy for the Desert

In Tunisia, the ongoing development of infrastructure and the legal frameworks for energy export to the EU are still in the visionary stage—and are marked by significant contestation. One prospective project for Tunisia's energy future draws upon an extractivist imaginary, relying on market laws to facilitate the decarbonization of the European economy and address Tunisia's energy dependency issues (El Amine, 2023). Like the Desertec project for the broader Mediterranean region, which inspired TuNur, this vision entails harnessing an energy source deemed infinite from the desert for the European market, overlooking the materiality of renewable energies and their land and resource requirements. Such imaginaries of the energy future are far from being novel. Since the 19th century, various scientists, whether supported by colonial powers or not, have envisioned exploiting solar energy from the Sahara while making the desert fertile (Henry et al., 2011). Although projects like these were not realized, they fostered the idea that the Sahara's sunlight could provide sufficient energy for the European continent, a notion echoed in the Desertec project and German state strategies for importing green hydrogen from Africa. Therefore, current projects for the future draw upon extractivist imaginaries.

Energy export ambitions through large-scale infrastructure projects across the Mediterranean are actually not new. As Alexander Stumm (2020) shows, resource exports from North Africa to Europe through Desertec were imagined using ecomodernist and techno-political narratives dating back to the colonial era of the 19th and 20th centuries. Extractivist projects, therefore, stand in a colonial tradition and materialize primarily in mega-infrastructure projects that are inherently tied to the emergence and functioning of the modern world order (Allain & Maillet, 2022). The underpinning imaginaries for transregional trade express visions of territorial adjustment that go hand in hand with ideas of modernization and civilization.

Infrastructural adjustment programs have manifested themselves in different contexts in Tunisia. French colonizers used discourses on industrialization and development to justify the construction of transport or energy infrastructures (Belaïd, 2018). After Tunisia reached independence in 1956, President Habib Bourguiba also engaged in projects of national modernization through infrastructural undertakings, which were closely linked to discourses on nation-building and progress (Sofi, 2018). In addition, international financial institutions such as the World Bank and donor organizations started engaging in structural adjustment programs within the Tunisian economy, particularly from the 1980s on (Blin, 2009). These different periods highlight how state-led and international interventions in Tunisia's economic infrastructures have created path dependencies that continue to shape the diverse governance practices on liberalization and potential forms of contestation until today. Although the infrastructure has not been built, these projects have tangible consequences for changes in Tunisian legislation and investments. Until recently, the state-owned STEG (*Société tunisienne de gaz et d'électricité*, French for Tunisian Company of Electricity and Gas), founded in 1962 in the aftermath of Tunisian independence of 1956, held a quasi-monopoly on the production, transmission, and distribution of electricity and gas. The legislative system governing the sector has evolved considerably over the past decade.

How Business and International Organizations Shape Energy Politics in Tunisia?

Considering the joint action of a transnational energy configuration that comprises EU policy-making actors and financial institutions like the EBRD, international financial institutions (IFIs) organizations such as the World Bank and the IMF, member state organizations, national political and economic elites, it becomes clear that the legislative evolutions are strongly linked to the joint action of these stakeholders. The evolution of the Tunisian legislation on renewable energies is closely connected to EU support and bilateral cooperation of EU member states, particularly through the German–Tunisian partnership (see Louati, 2022). EU institutions, IOs such as the IMF and World Bank, and German development agency *Gesellschaft für Internationale Zusammenarbeit* (GIZ) all pushed to attain similar evolutions of the Tunisian energy system: the removal of energy subsidies, an evolution toward "real energy prices," the liberalization of the energy market, the introduction of authorization and concession regimes, and the establishment of an independent regulator of the energy market (Louati, 2022, p. 21). In addition, transnational private foundations such as Renewable Energy Solutions for Africa (RES4Africa) engage in advocacy actions and training programs for public and private actors to support the implementation of these legal reforms.

GIZ is a main stakeholder in the energy sector in Tunisia and regularly acts as a subgrantor for EU green projects. Starting in the 1980s, it supported the first solar projects to electrify remote rural areas (interview with one of the first public officers of the *Agence nationale de maîtrise de l'énergie* (ANME), May 2023, Tunis). GIZ was also one of the main actors supporting the creation and the action of the ANME in 1985, in charge of implementing government initiatives regarding renewable energies and energy efficiency. GIZ provided dozens of experts to work within the agency and directly participated in reforming the legislative framework for solar electricity (Rocher & Verdeil, 2014, p. 288). The direct work with public officials, such as with the Tunisian Ministry of Industry, proves the utility of breaking up the dichotomy between "national" and "international" actors as if the latter were exterior to national policy-making. This crucial role of GIZ in policy-making in Tunisia's energy landscape also highlights how the development agency acts as a door opener for German business interests: Especially in the field of solar energy, Germany has been constructing the image of a soft power and standard-setter (Quitzow & Thielges, 2020). In doing so, German industries also seek to open up new sales markets for renewable energy technologies.

Also, the ANME was a central actor in launching the Tunisian Solar Plan in 2010, which was directly linked to the EU's Mediterranean Solar Plan and the ambitions of the Desertec export project. The Plan developed within the Union for the Mediterranean aimed to develop regional energy projects and export green energy to the EU (Louati, 2022). With EU support in the framework of the Tunisian–German energy partnership, the ANME launched a study on renewable energies and an action plan for 2014–2020. The recent decision in 2022 of the EU Commission, supported by the member states, to commit funds to a 1bn Euro project (with EIB, EBRD, KfW, and the World Bank) to construct the high-voltage cable Elmed in the Mediterranean is the infrastructural materialization of the EU support to developing renewable energies through an export and neoliberal approach.

Private business actors, supported by law firms, also influenced Tunisian energy politics. The two main Tunisian employer organizations, namely the UTICA and the *Confédération des Entreprises Citoyennes de Tunisie* (CONECT), have specialized federations for firms working in the solar energy sector. The Ministry of Industry invited representatives from both organizations to give their opinions or even participate directly in drafting the laws cited earlier. For large solar projects such as TuNur, developers are also assisted by international law firms that both advise private companies about the national legislation and investment possibilities in Tunisia and simultaneously, try to influence the government to adopt legislation in favor of private investment:

> *We worked [on the 2015 law], it's not us, but we participated, because we, with our London office, we worked with the partners, who wanted to whisper to the State certain provisions, certain practices on how to prepare a law on renewable energies and all that. So, we came up with quite a few ideas. And it's going well. And we're continuing, even with the Tunisian authorities, to bounce ideas off each other, to arrange things, to improve things. But this law has been improved by new laws, for example this authorization for change of vocation [from agricultural land to industrial land], the acceleration of the procedure and all that, not by the 2015 law on renewable energies, but by another law on the acceleration of investment projects.*
>
> *(Interview, transnational law firm, Tunis, May 2023)*

The business representatives not only directly participated in drafting the laws but also led a media campaign to try to influence public opinion. Indeed, in reaction to the discourse of trade unionists and critical responses to the liberalization of the energy market, business and employers' representatives organized media campaigns and strategies to foster social acceptability. UTICA and CONECT built a counter-discourse to the trade unionists' claims to protect the public energy sector. This involved building an astroturf citizen communication campaign, in coordination with large transnational firms, called "#Sayeb triciti" ("#Free electricity") and giving interviews in national media:

> *We did contracts with communication agencies, yeah, we got everybody involved. Out of our own pockets, the members. I remember everyone paying 3000 dinars out of their own pockets to do PR work. Because listen, at a certain point, you find the unions talking in the media, scaring the population about these private companies coming in and all that and all that. . . . We faced up to this slogan and we worked hard and it worked very well. All the media, they invited us, all the media talked about it, several actors talked about it, whether in debates, we stayed with it for about six months and it worked very well.*
>
> *(Interview, CONECT, Tunisian employer's organization, May 2023, Tunisia)*

To counter social movements, particularly the contestation led by STEG trade unionists, employers' federations led their own campaign using national and social media. The previous elements argue for the necessity to go beyond the national/transnational divide to understand the shaping of contemporary Tunisian energy politics. The process involves government members, national economic elites, international law firms, international financial institutions, and technical agencies, such as the GIZ.

Legal Effects of Sociotechnical Imaginaries

Sociotechnical imaginaries have yet to be translated into material infrastructures, but the actors advocating for them have prepared the ground for the recent major changes in the Tunisian legislation. In particular, Law No. 12–2015 significantly changes the Tunisian energy sector, making private investment possible through self-consumption, concession (projects of over 10MW), and authorization (projects of 10MW) regimes. Individuals and private firms are allowed to produce energy primarily for their own use and sell the energy surplus to the STEG. In 2019, Law No. 2015–2012 was amended by Transversal Law 2019–2047, which makes it possible for energy producers to sell energy directly to consumers without going through the STEG but using the national grid for distribution. This legislation is supposed to attract foreign investments in the energy sector and make exports possible.

The business actors advocating for the TuNur project were particularly influential in changing Tunisian legislation. Since 2008, TuNur promoters have planned to export energy to Europe and seek to change the legislative system to enable this. While setting up the project, the US-American initiator of TuNur contacted the World Bank to find reliable allies in Tunisia to develop the project. He sought out a business representative in the field of solar energy who also worked within public institutions, had very close ties with the Tunisian Ministry of Industry, worked with the GIZ since the 1980s, and was an active member of the Tunisian–German energy partnership. The multi-positionality of certain actors hence creates several links between public and private organizations in developing the legal framework. The Tunisian TuNur partner was crucial in meeting all the main stakeholders of the energy sector and organizing high-level meetings with the Tunisian President:

> *So we did the whole tour of the big decision-makers, STEG, the Ministry, and so on. And we started to put together the concept and propose the big project, which initially was 2000 MW, initially it was CSP, because photovoltaics was expensive at the time. . . . There were no laws to produce and export. I think, thanks to TuNur, the 2015 law was born, because there were discussions at a very high level with Ben Ali's former government, then the new one, and the foundations were laid.*
>
> *(Interview with the TuNur Tunisia partner, UTICA, May 2023, Tunisia)*

The same TuNur partner has often declared that the legal framework is "essential" for the private sector to attract foreign investments. Indeed, during a focus group on concentrated solar panel at the second edition of the SITE,[1] he stated:

> *"Tunisia alone could be enough to satisfy the European energy needs, so we must act fast!". . . . The Germans have been really focusing on Tunisia lately.*
>
> *(SITE, 2023, reported by the author)*

The businessman refers to his frequent business trips to Germany, where he maintained contacts with German and German–Tunisian businesses working to ease the Tunisian legal framework for foreign capital. The transnational entanglements between businesspeople in the private sector are, therefore, crucial to understanding the reconfigurations of Tunisia's legal framework.

This section showed how the discursive and material levels interact with and partly constitute each other. Discursive imaginaries might prefigure the actual material construction of energy infrastructures, while the latter contribute to constructing narratives of modernity, progress, and power. Also, the fact that infrastructural projects that are not there yet have failed or are uncertain also produces their own sociotechnical imaginaries. For example, the structural incertitude around the TuNur project produces a mismatch between the official projections of the TuNur group and the European Network Transmission System Operators for Electricity (ENTSOE) and reality. Indeed, according to the ENTSOE, TuNur's project[2] should have been commissioned in 2020. Conversely, when asked a Tunisian engineer working at the ANME about the TuNur project in 2023, they answered:

> *The TuNur project has been rejected multiple times . . . it won't work . . . it has some very specific needs such as land and water, and these are sensitive issues.*
>
> *(Interview with ANME engineer, February 2023, Tunis)*

This shows that in professional circles, the TuNur project is regarded at best as an unfinished business and, at worst, as a failed project. Nevertheless, the effects of this uncertainty seem to be reflected in increased lobbying to change the legislative framework and inspire more investment in its model.

Contesting Extractivist Sociotechnical Imaginaries: Toward an Inclusive Energy Future?

The sociotechnical energy futures outlined earlier are grounded in extractivist imaginaries and ongoing competition between countries and economic actors for access to renewable resources or mineral deposits. A heterogeneous set of actors mobilize around energy export projects from Tunisia to Europe to denounce the extractivist nature of these energy projects for Tunisia. They advocate for a just transition and seek to construct a discourse proposing an alternative to a transition focused on privatization and foreign investments. The main resistance to projects that aim to foster private investment in renewables emanates from the FGEG, the STEG (Tunisian Gas and Electricity Company) trade union.

Since its creation after the Tunisian independence, the STEG has had a specific role as it is seen as a main actor in achieving both energy independence from the colonial power and electrification of 99% of the country, in both rural and urban areas (Rocher & Verdeil, 2014). Within the STEG, a strong trade union federation (the *Fédération Générale de l'Electricité et du Gaz* (FGEG)) developed early strategies to defend the monopoly over the production, transport, and distribution of electricity. In the history of the FGEG, it was efficient in blocking previous projects of subgranting of distribution and private investment in producing renewable energy (Rocher & Verdeil, 2014, p. 285). For instance, the FGEG voiced opposition to the planned legislation to liberalize the energy sector in 2014 under the Jomaa government, as the drafting of the law No. 2015–2012 did not involve trade unionists or STEG managers and engineers (Louati, 2022, p. 19).

According to the key laws of 2015 and 2019, authorization and concession regimes allow increasing private investments in renewable energy production. Beyond export projects, private investments from Tunisian and international companies are, therefore, targets of contestation to oppose the perceived loss of popular control. For instance, STEG's trade union FGEG fears that producing renewable energies will undermine the public company's central role in the energy market and might be limited to the transport and distribution of electricity. The emerging framing focuses on the quality of public service, the availability of jobs, and the need to defend accessible energy for citizens. After passing the Transversal Law 2019–2047, the FGEG has been blocking the Tataouine plant, built by the Italian firm ENI under the authorization regime, for over two years. The occupation was meant to put pressure on the government during the negotiations and to oppose the obligation of the STEG to transport energy from private energy producers while bearing the maintenance costs for the grid (interview with STEG trade unionist, June 2023).

However, STEG has no consensus on how to develop the renewable energy sector.[3] Some fringes of the FGEG (the trade union federation for STEG workers) call for investments in local energy communities and energy autonomy for marginalized areas. They created a group called WGED, which tries to influence the STEG by developing alternative strategies for Tunisia. It also transnationalized its activities by collaborating with think tanks such as the Amsterdam-based Transnational Institute (see, e.g., the following report by Ben Ammar, 2022). Some of its members also support initiatives conducted by local associations, such as the *Plateforme tunisienne des alternatives* (the Tunisian platform for alternatives), which organized local debates on energy sovereignty in Segdoud. In the oasis village located in a southwestern region with low employment opportunities, water scarcity, and severe drought episodes, a Franco-Moroccan solar plant is planned to be built on agricultural land.[4] Instead of developing solar energy for private profit, the *Plateforme* advocates for energy projects supporting local development and including inhabitants in their design. The *Observatoire tunisien de l'économie* (the Tunisian observatory for the economy), a Tunisian think tank, is also active in producing reports on the energy transition, depicted as an "unjust transition" and organizing public talks inviting trade unionists (Ben Rouine & Roche, 2022; Hamouchene, 2022; Hamouchene & Sandwell, 2023).

The claims raised by these actors reintroduce the political dimension to the energy transition and counter the neoliberal discourse framing the solution for the energy transition as being the private sector and foreign investments. In the following, we will briefly sketch out the alternative solutions they propose for a "just energy transition" on the local and transnational levels (Ben Rouine & Roche, 2022; Ben Ammar, 2022). This network frames energy not as a technical but as a political question. Energy politics, therefore, raise questions about redistribution, power relations, and democratic control:

> *For instance, who will benefit and who will lose from this transition? Who controls the knowledge and technology that will be used to implement this transition and to what extent will the transition deepen Tunisia's historical dependency on imperial powers? Will this energy transition open the door to liberalization and the privatization of the energy sector? To what extent will this energy transition help to address the issues of structural unemployment and inequality in the country? Will this transition facilitate an increase in democratic control over natural resources or will it exacerbate capitalistic land-grabbing at the expense of local communities?*
>
> *(Ben Rouine & Roche, 2022)*

The visions of alternative energy transition share the aspiration of demanding energy democracy, namely citizen participation in decentralized energy cooperatives rather than a centralized vertical structure like the STEG or private businesses. "This alternative must allow peoples and communities to recover their right to take control of their natural resources and to reshape energy systems" (Extract of the founding document of the Working Group for Energy Democracy, Ben Ammar, 2022, p. 28).

In Tunisia, the project to export Tunisian solar energy to the EU is framed as a continuation of colonial relations of domination and green resource grabbing. Instead of exporting energy to Europe, these movements prioritize securing national renewable energy production and meeting national goals for reducing CO_2 emissions. They advocate for energy sovereignty and politics that break away from the extractivist use of natural resources and from importing natural gas primarily from Algeria. Energy sovereignty also entails developing industrial policies to produce equipment for renewables in Tunisia rather than importing it. Expert reports criticize the government authorization and concession regimes favoring international firms rather than Tunisian ones. Indeed, for the tenders between 2017 and 2019, under the authorization regime, 22 projects have been approved. Only half of the projects included Tunisian firms, and only four were carried out solely by Tunisian firms. Under the concession regime, all five projects approved were awarded to foreign companies (Louati, 2022, p. 18; Ben Rouine & Roche, 2022).

Criticisms against connecting the Tunisian grid to the European one also concern inequalities between both regions. Instead of having an "unrestricted flow of cheap natural resources (including solar energy) from the global South to the rich North," the alternative scenario advocates for taking into account the needs of local communities so that energy transition brings resources where energy is produced (Ben Ammar, 2022, p. 5). The risk of the energy transition leading to deepening structural development inequalities is also raised with regard to inequalities between Tunisian regions. When considering the companies eligible to install solar panels for self-production, the companies are predominantly based in wealthier and more industrialized regions. Out of 380 Tunisian firms, only 40 are based in the areas targeted for installing solar panels. Sfax and Tunis are those where the most employment and benefits are being created at the expense of the regions that need them most (Ben Rouine & Roche, 2022). At the transnational and national scales, these projects risk continuing the logic of "accumulation by dispossession" (Harvey, 2004; Rousselin, 2018) by extracting land and capital resources from the most marginalized regions without contributing to local development and generating shared benefits.

Conclusion

This chapter focused on the entanglements between the local and transnational levels that seem to act separately but are, in fact, deeply entangled in practice. The interaction between these scales allows us to observe specific energy futures by connecting the sociotechnical imaginaries *and* the material conditions rather than studying them discursively and abstractly. Using a configurationist perspective, this chapter showed that the frontiers between domestic and external interests and actors are not that clear-cut. Indeed, we observed how various groups of actors imagine sociotechnical futures within the realm of energy, according to their interests and goals, and can shape Tunisian energy politics.

Based on the concept of sociotechnical imaginaries (Jasanoff & Kim, 2013) in the context of energy transitions, we find two parallel transnational imaginaries of an energy transition in Tunisia. The first imaginary extends an extractivist colonial imaginary of the Sahara Desert as an infinite solar energy source for the European continent. It aims toward a market liberal opening of the energy market, export orientation via integration in the European energy grid, and modernization based on the inflow of technology and "de-risked" capital, supported by the EU and International Financial Institutions. The second imaginary—which is politically marginal—uses the term extractivism to denounce "green grabbing" and postcolonial unequal power relations. Our findings show how local associations, non-state actors, unions, and NGOs try to think, imagine, and plan a more inclusive energy future for Tunisia. The diverse social movements advocate for a fair energy transition, support state, and community ownership of energy projects, and oppose export orientation in the face of local needs. This narrative is equally embedded in transnational discourse networks, as is the first one. However, the ideological and sociotechnical imaginary gap between various non-state groups and the state, IOs, and private investors appears unbridgeable, and these actors are marginalized in the policy-making process. The multilevel conflicts over the energy transition raise serious questions about the inequalities and hierarchies being perpetuated in this complex process.

Our case study-based analysis comes with some important limitations. Indeed, mainly due to lack of space, we could not fully address the regional inequalities within Tunisia, which are also crucial to understanding the complexities of

Tunisian politics and the politics of energy management at large. We also note that job preservation within STEG is the main source of contention to the 2015 law and the mobilization for the public sector. Indeed, the larger discourse against extractivism in Tunisia is also a socially situated one, which is mobilized by local NGO actors that have access to transnational resources (academic reputation, training abroad) and are part of transnational networks. This approach is not dominant within STEG and rests mainly on alliances between the local and the transnational civil society organizations.

We conclude that the concept of extractivism is relevant to study *multiple* sociotechnical imaginaries in North Africa, and between Africa and Europe. The extractivist nature of the projects, wherever in the world, produces multiple and complex scenarios whereby different actors such as NGOs, unions, industrial players, and think tank professionals push for diametrically different energy futures.

Notes

1 *Salon International de la Transition Énergétique*—International Fair for Energy Transition in Tunis (25–27 October 2023)

2 ENTSOE TuNur project https://eepublicdownloads.entsoe.eu/clean-documents/tyndp-documents/TYNDP%202016/projects/P0283.pdf.

3 The STEG has itself been severely criticized for the way it developed renewable energy projects in 2009 in Borj Salhi by grabbing the inhabitants' agricultural lands, partly destroying their livelihood, and not offering appropriate compensation (see a report by the FTDES; Labiadh & Attar, 2021).

4 Delpuech Aïda & Arianna Poletti, "C'est notre soleil": à Segdoud, la lutte pour la souveraineté énergétique, 22 April 2022, https://inkyfada.com/fr/2022/04/22/segdoud-lutte-souverainete-energetique-tunisie/.

References

Allain, M., & Maillet, A. (2022). Les mobilisations autour de l'extractivisme: Circulation et potentiel heuristique d'un concept en voie de globalisation. *Revue internationale de politique comparée*, *28*(3), 7–29.

Beckert, J. (2016). *Imagined futures: Fictional expectations and capitalist dynamics*. Harvard University Press.

Belaïd, H. (2018). Éléments pour une histoire de l'énergie en Tunisie pendant la période coloniale (1894–1954). In M. Corriou & M. Oualdi (Eds.), *Une histoire sociale et culturelle du politique en Algérie: Études offertes à Omar Carlier*. Éditions de la Sorbonne.

Ben Ammar, I. (2022). *Towards a just energy transition in Tunisia*. Tunisian Platform for Alternatives; Working Group for Energy Democracy; Transnational Institute.

Ben Rouine, C., & Roche, F. (2022). *'Renewable' energy in Tunisia: An unjust transition*. Transnational Institute. https://longreads.tni.org/renewable-energy-in-tunisia

Blin, M. (2009). The political economy of IMF and World Bank interventions: Is Tunisia really a model student? In J. Harrigan & H. El-Said (Eds.), *Aid and power in the Arab world* (pp. 105–147). Palgrave Macmillan.

Boutaleb, A., & Brisson, T. (2022). Exploitations extractivistes? In *Écologies* (pp. 405–412). La Découverte.

de Sardan, J.-P. O. (2005). *Anthropology and development: Understanding contemporary social change*. Zed Books.

Dietz, K. (2023). La transition verte européenne, tremplin de l'extractivisme latino-américain. In *Transition "verte" et métaux "critiques"* (pp. 71–87). Éditions Syllepse.

El Amine, Y. (2023). *Tunisia's energy sector: A just transition analysis*. Arab Reform Initiative. https://www.arab-reform.net/publication/tunisias-energy-sector-a-just-transition-analysis/

Gudynas, E. (2009). Diez tesis urgentes sobre el nuevo extractivismo. *Extractivismo, política y sociedad*, 187–225.

Hamouchene, H. (2022). Extractivism and resistance in North Africa. In *The Oxford handbook of economic imperialism*. Oxford University Press.

Hamouchene, H., & Sandwell, K. (2023). *Dismantling green colonialism: Energy and climate justice in the Arab region*. Pluto Press.

Harvey, D. (2004). The "new" imperialism: Accumulation by dispossession. *Socialist Register*, *40*, 63–87.

Henry, J.-R., Marçot, J.-L., & Moisseron, J.-Y. (2011). Développer le désert: Anciennes et nouvelles utopies. *L'Année du Maghreb*, *7*, 115–147.

Jasanoff, S., & Kim, S.-H. (2013). Sociotechnical imaginaries and national energy policies. *Science as Culture*, *22*(2), 189–196. https://doi.org/10.1080/09505431.2013.786990

Jasanoff, S., & Kim, S.-H. (2015). *Dreamscapes of modernity: Sociotechnical imaginaries and the fabrication of power*. University of Chicago Press.

Jenss, A., & Bonci, A. (2025). Political practices between internal colonialism and global inequality: Energy infrastructures in Tunisia and Costa Rica. *Political Geography*, *119*, 103321.

Labiadh, I., & Attar, H. (2021). *Borj Salhi ou la face cachée des énergies renouvelables*. FTDES. https://ftdes.net/borj-salhi-3/

López, E., Vértiz, F., & Olavarria, M. (2015). Extractivism, transnational capital, and subaltern struggles in Latin America. *Latin American Perspectives*, *42*(5), 152–168. https://doi.org/10.1177/0094582X15588169

Louati, I. (2022). *Tunisia: What is the energy transition about?* Rosa Luxemburg Stiftung.

Moore, S. (2018). *Sustainable energy transformations, power, and politics: Morocco and the Mediterranean*. Routledge.

Quitzow, R., & Thielges, S. (2020). The German energy transition as soft power. *Review of International Political Economy*, *29*(2), 598–623. https://doi.org/10.1080/09692290.2020.1813190

Rahman, A., & Hasan, M. (2022). From local to global: Networked activism against multinational extractivism. *Review of Communication*, *22*(3), 231–255. https://doi.org/10.1080/15358593.2022.2076588

Rignall, K. E. (2016). Solar power, state power, and the politics of energy transition in pre-Saharan Morocco. *Environment and Planning A: Economy and Space*, *48*(3), 540–557.

Rocher, L., & Verdeil, E. (2014). Energy transition and revolution in Tunisia: Politics and spatiality. *The Arab World Geographer*, *16*(3), 267–288.

Rousselin, M. (2018). A study in dispossession: The political ecology of phosphate in Tunisia. *Journal of Political Ecology*, *25*(1), 20–39. https://doi.org/10.2458/v25i1.22825

Schuetze, B., El Khazen, E., Mueller, C., & Wagner, P. (2024). Facilitating energy flows, containing humans: Authoritarian energy transitions in the Middle East and North Africa. In N. Buxton (Ed.), *State of power report* (pp. 109–118). Transnational Institute.

Sofi, M. D. (2018). The Tunisian Republic and the restructuring of socio-economic institutions. *Islamic Studies*, *57*(3–4), 245–259.

Stumm, A. (2020). Neo-colonial continuities in the Mediterranean infrastructure projects of Atlantropa and Desertec. *Ardeth*, *7*, 127–140.

Szeman, I., & Boyer, D. (Eds.). (2017). *Energy humanities: An anthology*. Johns Hopkins University Press.

12 Conclusion

Geopolitics, Green Rents, and Emerging Cleavages in the Maghreb

Hannes Warnecke-Berger and Rachid Ouaissa

Myth of Development: Rent Remains the Key to the Maghreb's Present and Future

Across the chapters of this volume, a first conclusion emerges with striking consistency: rent remains the central analytical category for understanding the Maghreb's political economy. Historically, external rents anchored Algeria, Morocco, and Tunisia in a hierarchy of unequal specialization, supplying hydrocarbons, phosphates, low-value manufactures, and tourism to external markets while importing capital-intensive equipment, high-technology goods, regulatory frameworks, and, increasingly, migrant remittances. Growth, where it occurred, was therefore externally induced and structurally constrained, tied to sectors that generated rents without generating broad-based productive transformation.

This rent orientation is also deeply rooted in colonial legacies. Under French rule in Algeria, Morocco, and Tunisia, economic structures were deliberately organized around extraction and export toward the metropole. Infrastructure, property regimes, and administrative institutions were designed to facilitate resource extraction rather than endogenous industrialization. Postcolonial states inherited these patterns of unequal specialization and centralized bureaucratic control. As a result, rent-based accumulation was not created anew after independence but reproduced and adapted from colonial economic structures, embedding external dependence and extractive logics at the core of postcolonial political economy.

As several contributions demonstrate, postcolonial state classes sought to convert these rents into instruments of rule by embedding them in a nationalist and progressive imaginary of development. Governments presented rent-based growth as a pathway to sovereignty, modernization, and social advancement, cultivating what can be described as a myth of development (Warnecke-Berger & Ickler, 2023a, p. 1): the promise that control over resources and external revenues would eventually translate into industrialization, employment, and welfare for the broader population. This imaginary was politically powerful and socially resonant, particularly in the aftermath of decolonization and during periods of high commodity prices (Elsenhans, 1991).

Economically, however, this narrative collided with what we call the seduction of rent (Warnecke-Berger & Ickler, 2025). Rather than being used to overcome

DOI: 10.4324/9781003730750-12

unequal specialization, rents were increasingly deployed for political stabilization: to finance selective redistribution, unproductive public employment, clientelistic networks, and prestige projects that symbolized progress without generating sustained learning effects. Productive diversification remained limited, while dependence on imported capital goods and technologies deepened. In this way, national appropriation of rent coexisted with the persistence of externally articulated production structures.

The result was a distinctive development trajectory marked by structural heterogeneity. High-rent sectors and enclaves coexisted with vast low-productivity segments that absorbed the majority of the labor force. Persistent labor surpluses, blocked middle classes (Ouaissa, 2018), and recurrent cycles of protest were not anomalies but systemic outcomes of a development model unable to transcend its rent-based foundations (Ouchichi, 2025). The Maghreb thus experienced a paradoxical combination of progressive developmental rhetoric and enduring economic constraint: states appeared sovereign and developmental in discourse, while remaining locked into patterns of unequal specialization that limited their capacity to transform rent into mass welfare and productive alternatives.

This historical contradiction did not disappear with the exhaustion of fossil-led growth; it re-emerges today in transformed form. The green transition does not arrive in a vacuum but enters political economies already shaped by the dependence on rents, unequal specialization, and the enduring tension between developmental promise and structural constraint. What is new is not the logic of rent itself, but its current and emerging material and geopolitical configuration. Solar radiation, wind corridors, phosphates, and hydrogen infrastructures now occupy the position once held by oil, gas, and mining, while the surrounding narratives echo familiar claims of sovereignty, modernization, and national upgrading, as various chapters in the book underline.

The risk, as the sections that follow in this conclusion will demonstrate, is that green rents replicate the very contradictions that characterized earlier phases of rent-based development trajectories. Progressive language, national ownership schemes, and climate-oriented development strategies may coexist with continued enclave formation, limited domestic linkages, and persistent reliance on imported technology and external markets. At the same time, the green transition opens a genuinely new political terrain: it multiplies external actors, intensifies geopolitical competition, and creates new sites of contestation over land, labor, and infrastructure. The question is therefore not whether the Maghreb is entering a post-extractive era, but whether the reconfiguration of rent under green conditions will finally enable a break with unequal specialization—or stabilize it under a new, sustainable guise.

Rather than treating these developments primarily as surface manifestations of external dependency or renewed neocolonialism, the more consequential analytical question lies elsewhere. Whether green extractivism in the Maghreb is driven by external domination, as some authors highlight (e.g., Hamouchene & Sandwell, 2023), or endogenous modernization gaps underlined by others (e.g., Schiffbauer et al., 2014) is ultimately secondary to recognizing the structuring power of rent itself. It is the dominance of rent as a mode of surplus generation and political mediation that systematically links international hierarchies with domestic class relations, institutional arrangements, and development trajectories. Understanding the region's green transition, therefore, requires moving beyond dichotomies of external versus internal causation and toward an integrated analysis of how global power relations and intra-societal, domestic dynamics are co-produced through rent. Once rent is analytically recognized as the structuring principle of political economy, the decisive issue is not the "greenness" of new projects, but the political effects of a changing surplus structure.

Taken together, the volume shows that the Maghreb's central development problem is not resource scarcity but the political economy of rent: a surplus structure that repeatedly converts progressive imaginaries into distributive stabilization, while reproducing patterns of unequal specialization and thereby blocking internal political transformation as well as deepening dependencies on external actors. It is precisely here that the transition from fossil to green rents becomes analytically revealing.

Green Rents Between Transformation and Reproduction

Our hypothesis was that the arrival of green rents does not automatically disrupt this configuration. As the chapters on renewable energy projects, phosphates, hydrogen strategies, and post-extractive spaces demonstrate, solar and wind megaprojects, hydrogen roadmaps, and green ammonia initiatives can easily reproduce extractivist logics under a sustainable label. When embedded in narrow state–corporate alliances and externally designed value chains, they tend to reinforce enclave structures, intensify land and water conflicts, and deepen technological dependency.

At the same time, green rents possess genuine transformative potential. One could argue that—if deployed productively—they could contribute to the establishment of an internal, consumption-capable market: through employment-intensive investments in green infrastructure, the development of local manufacturing niches, entrepreneurial ecosystems, and domestic supplier networks, as well as through the deliberate strengthening of mass purchasing power. Such a strategy would absorb labor surpluses, expand effective demand, and thereby lay the foundation for a self-sustaining domestic market.

Crucially, rising incomes must not primarily translate into elite consumption rents or capital flight, but be reinvested into productive sectors. In line with Elsenhans' (2004) argument, increasing the purchasing power of broad social strata would generate profits not from rent extraction, but from the expansion of real markets—thus creating a rational incentive for affluent actors to invest in productive activities rather than to preserve rents or externalize their assets. Whether this potential is realized depends less on physical endowment than on politics. As the volume shows repeatedly, outcomes hinge on the sequencing and combination of policies, on the capacity to integrate industrial, fiscal, labor, and social strategies, and on how geopolitical pressures are refracted into domestic struggles.

At this point, Europe enters the picture not merely as one external actor among others, but as the Maghreb's most consequential economic counterpart. As the region's largest trading partner and as a political project committed to rapid decarbonization, the EU is structurally dependent on access to energy, raw materials, and strategic infrastructure from North Africa. Europe's ambition to remain competitive in a decarbonizing global economy—across batteries, hydrogen, fertilizers, and renewable electricity—cannot be realized without stable, large-scale cooperation with the Maghreb (Tanchum, 2024). This (inter-)dependence fundamentally reshapes the region's geopolitical position.

For the Maghreb, this constellation is deeply ambivalent. On the one hand, asymmetries of power remain pronounced. Europe's regulatory capacity, technological dominance, and financial leverage allow it to shape value chains, standards, and investment frameworks in ways that can rapidly translate dependency into political constraint. Green cooperation can thus become a new channel through which subordination is reproduced, this time justified by climate urgency rather than development necessity.

On the other hand, precisely this European dependence opens new arenas of negotiation. The green transition creates a situation in which North Africa is no longer marginal but structurally indispensable. Access to solar radiation, land, phosphates, and geographic proximity cannot be substituted easily or cheaply elsewhere. This gives Maghreb states leverage—albeit uneven and politically contested—to renegotiate terms of cooperation, influence project design, and link energy exports to broader developmental objectives. Which alliances are pursued, with Europe, the Gulf, China, or hybrid constellations, is therefore not predetermined. It is the outcome of political struggles within state classes, between elite factions, and across society.

Crucially, green rents thus do not merely enable new external bargaining positions; they also open the possibility of domestic transformation. If strategically deployed, they could support progressive reforms of domestic political economies: reorienting industrial policy, upgrading skills and vocational training, strengthening public investment capacities, and recalibrating social contracts away from pure distributive stabilization toward productive inclusion (Bresser-Pereira et al., 2019; Meckling, 2025). Yet realizing this potential requires more than political will. It presupposes the development of a scientific and policy-oriented understanding within the Maghreb itself of how the negative effects of rent—clientelism, enclave formation, technological dependence, and labor exclusion—can be neutralized and under which conditions rents can be harnessed for progressive transformation rather than merely contributing to the political reproduction of existing power relations.

In this sense, the green transition confronts the Maghreb not only with a geopolitical challenge but also with an epistemic one. The question is no longer whether rent can be avoided but whether it can be governed differently: transformed from a mechanism of political stabilization and unequal specialization into a lever for structural change. Whether such a reorientation succeeds remains an open political question, and one that will be decided as much in domestic debates over development strategy and social priorities as in negotiations with Europe and other external partners.

From Policy Instruments to Political Sequencing

Analytically, the policy instruments required to use green rents productively are well known. Industrial policy can support domestic value chains in renewables, storage, and green industrial inputs (Evenett et al., 2024; Lebdioui, 2024). Trade and investment policy can protect nascent industries and negotiate technology transfer (Bradlow & Kentikelenis, 2024). Fiscal policy can channel rents toward long-term public investment rather than current consumption (Fehling & Burchardt, 2023). Labor market, vocational training, and education policies can align skills with emerging sectors, while social policies can cushion distributional conflicts and provide political legitimacy for structural change (Grabowski, 2017).

The challenge, as several chapters emphasize, is not the absence of instruments but their sequencing under conditions of the dependence on rents and geopolitical asymmetry. Industrial policy without fiscal reform risks captures by existing elites. Protection without credible upgrading strategies entrenches inefficiency. Infrastructure spending without labor and education reforms reproduces enclave dynamics. Conversely, austerity-oriented consolidation undermines the very investment and compensation mechanisms needed for transformation.

Sequencing, therefore, becomes a political problem rather than a technocratic one. It requires state classes to accept short-term constraints on patronage and prestige in order to build longer-term productive capacities. It requires opening negotiation spaces to municipalities, small and medium enterprises, local producer groups, and segments of the middle classes. And it requires external partners—above all the EU—to recognize that a sustainable Euro-Mediterranean energy order cannot be built solely on import security, private risk minimization, and narrow cost–benefit calculations.

From this perspective, the primary objective cannot be the elimination of rent as such, but its political neutralization (Warnecke-Berger, 2024), specifically, the neutralization of its adverse political and economic effects. Rent emerges as surplus within global hierarchies of specialization; its existence is not in itself pathological. The problem lies in the way rent structures incentives, power relations, and expectations, crowding out productive alternatives and stabilizing distributive rather than transformative coalitions (Warnecke-Berger, 2025).

Rents can, in principle, be mobilized to create economic alternatives, above all through employment (Elsenhans, 2004). Under conditions of rent dominance, however, employment cannot be assessed solely through the lenses of productivity, profitability, or market incentives. As Keynes already recognized, markets fail to function as allocative mechanisms when structural conditions suppress effective demand and distort relative prices (Keynes, 2009/[1936], p. 110). In economies which surplus structure is dominated by rent, this failure is not cyclical but structural. Employment creation, therefore, becomes an explicitly political task—one that must be institutionally embedded and politically insulated from short-term distributive pressures (Warnecke-Berger, 2021). This shifts the analytical focus toward the institutional settings through which rents can be transformed into productive capacities. The question is not whether rents exist, but under which institutional and political conditions they can be redirected toward employment-intensive activities, learning effects, and long-term diversification.

Our analysis underscores that class configuration is central in this regard. Historically, lower and middle strata in the Maghreb have remained dependent on state-led distributive logics—public employment, subsidies, and clientelistic access—rather than being integrated into autonomous productive structures (Ouaissa, 2023). As the Arab uprisings vividly demonstrated, this dependence severely constrains their capacity to emancipate themselves economically and politically from rent-based governance and from a clientelistic state–society relations (Ouaissa, 2014).

In this context, targeted cooperation with external partners becomes increasingly important as a strategic lever. External alliances can provide access to technology, finance, and markets that are otherwise unavailable, but only if they are embedded in institutional frameworks that prioritize employment, capability-building, and domestic linkages. Without such frameworks, external cooperation risks reinforcing dependence on rents; in joint and strategically designed alliances, by contrast, it may contribute to the gradual neutralization of rent's structurally distortive effects.

Exclusion, Social Valves, and the Political Conditions of Green Transformation

Before green rents can be understood as a potential lever of transformation, it is necessary to revisit the structural conditions under which the Maghreb has historically grown. Across the region, rent-based development has produced not only unequal specialization but also systematic exclusion from productive integration. Large segments of the population, particularly young cohorts and peripheral regions, have remained structurally detached from stable employment, industrial upgrading, and upward mobility. This exclusion is not accidental; it is the functional counterpart of a political economy organized around rent capture rather than productive expansion.

Historically, this exclusion has been managed through a limited set of social and political valves. One has been state-led co-optation: unproductive public employment, subsidies, and selective redistribution have absorbed parts of the labor surplus and stabilized regimes without altering underlying economic structures (Ferrié, 1999; Martinez, 2009). Another has been migration (Herbert, 2022). Emigration has operated as an external safety valve, exporting surplus labor while importing remittances that sustain domestic consumption and social reproduction (Farzanegan & Hassan, 2020). In recent years, remittances have become an increasingly central pillar of household survival and macroeconomic stability around the world (Warnecke-Berger, 2022), and particularly in North Africa, even as they further decouple social reproduction from domestic productive transformation.

These mechanisms of stabilization have reached their limits. Fiscal constraints, demographic pressure, and declining capacity for public-sector absorption reduce the effectiveness of state co-optation. At the same time, migration is increasingly securitized and politicized. European strategies that link energy cooperation to migration control embed the Maghreb's social question directly into Euro-Mediterranean geopolitics. State classes may trade border management and mobility restrictions for financial inflows and green investment, reinforcing their role as gatekeepers between surplus populations and external opportunities. Yet this dynamic risks deepening frustration among younger generations whose horizons are shaped by blocked domestic mobility and increasingly closed external borders. Migration remains a vent—but an increasingly contested and unstable one.

It is against this background of exhausted social valves that green rents enter the scene. Green energy, hydrogen, and phosphate-based transition strategies are accompanied by a progressive developmental discourse emphasizing national appropriation, resource sovereignty, and inclusive growth (Amouzai & Haddioui, 2023). Governments highlight rising export revenues, local content clauses, and the symbolic break with fossil dependency as evidence that green energy opens a new developmental horizon. In this narrative, solar fields, hydrogen corridors, and green industrial inputs appear as instruments of modernization capable of combining climate responsibility with national industrial ambition. While green industrial policies are often theoretically well justified, they can fail because they do not directly address the underlying market failure (Harrison et al., 2017).

Yet this discourse coexists with a persistent structural contradiction. While green rents may increase aggregate revenues and expand the room for maneuver of state classes, they do not, by themselves, alter the underlying pattern of unequal specialization. As the empirical chapters demonstrate, the Maghreb's insertion into global green value chains remains concentrated in low-value segments: the provision of land, energy flows, and raw materials, while technology, equipment, standards, and system integration are imported. Even where green assets are formally nationalized or tightly regulated, production remains externally articulated. Rent capture may be nationalized; productive capacity is not.

This contradiction generates a distinctive form of green rent dependence. Higher rent inflows coexist with limited learning effects, weak domestic linkages, and continued reliance on imported capital goods and know-how. Rather than overcoming rent-based development, green rents risk stabilizing it under new conditions (Sim, 2020). The state gains fiscal and geopolitical leverage, but this leverage is often channeled into distributive coalitions oriented toward managing rents rather than transcending them. Progressive rhetoric and persistent structural constraints thus coexist uneasily, and this outcome is not accidental but structural.

At the same time, the green transition opens a genuinely new political terrain. Unlike earlier rent phases, it multiplies potential actors, scales, and arenas of contestation. Green infrastructure intersects with labor markets, regional development, vocational training, and industrial policy in ways that create space for new coalitions linking workers, municipalities, local communities, segments of productive capital, and parts of the middle classes. Such coalitions are increasingly visible across the cases analyzed in this volume yet remain under-theorized in both development and geopolitical scholarship.

This emergence is paradoxical. The green transition unfolds in a global context marked by rising nationalism, hardened borders, and the reassertion of top-down state power (Hauge et al., 2025). Global blocs, security logics, and geopolitical rivalries increasingly structure economic relations. In such a world, the importance of transnational coalitions—linking domestic actors with external partners, knowledge networks, unions, and civil society—appears almost anachronistic. Yet, precisely because national strategies alone are insufficient to overcome rent dependence, such coalitions become indispensable counterweights to both external domination and domestic rent stabilization.

Their weakness, however, is equally structural. Global precarity, fragmented labor markets, and asymmetric access to resources limit these coalitions' capacity to consolidate. The green transition, therefore, confronts the Maghreb with a double challenge: neutralizing the exclusionary effects of rent while simultaneously building new forms of political coordination under increasingly adverse global conditions. Whether green rents become a mechanism for renewed stabilization or a lever for structural change will depend on how these fragile coalitions evolve and on whether they can gain sufficient institutional and political traction within rent-dominated societies.

At its core, the question is whether the green transition generates new societal coalitions—and whether these coalitions are capable of acting as an effective counterweight to entrenched power structures. The issue at stake is not merely the technological reconfiguration of the energy system but the broader political–economic redistribution of resources, influence, and institutional authority that accompanies the emergence of new value chains, investment flows, and regulatory regimes. A genuinely socioecological transformation would thus require the formation of new alliances among segments of the state apparatus, economic actors, local communities, trade unions, and civil society organizations. Crucially, such coalitions would need to achieve sufficient institutional embeddedness and political leverage to at least partially disrupt the logic of rent-based governance.

Empirical developments in Algeria, Morocco, and Tunisia suggest continuity rather than rupture. In all three cases, actors with privileged access to state resources and decision-making arenas have emerged as the main drivers of the green transition. These include state-affiliated elites, powerful and politically connected families, segments of the military, large domestic conglomerates, regime-linked business groups, and international financial institutions. Rather than generating new configurations of social power, the transition thus risks reproducing—and potentially consolidating—existing structures of authority within rent-based political economies (Moustakbal, 2023).

Against this backdrop, the green transition appears less as a catalyst for structural transformation than as a new arena for strategic reconfiguration within rent-dominated political economies. The central analytical challenge, therefore, lies not only in identifying whether new coalitions emerge but also in assessing whether they possess sufficient political autonomy, organizational density, and societal legitimacy to challenge established rent-based alliances—or whether they are ultimately absorbed into pre-existing clientelist and state-centric arrangements.

Crucially, however, such coalitions do not emerge in a vacuum. They are embedded in shifting power relations between global actors, competing development models, and rival energy and resource regimes. Once rents become the object of international competition, external alliances cease to be merely technical or economic arrangements; they become geopolitical projects that reconfigure domestic power balances. It is at this point that geopolitics enters the analysis not as an external backdrop but as a constitutive dimension of domestic political economy.

Geopolitics as a New Domestic Cleavage

Hence, we do not treat "geopolitics" as a descriptive label for interstate rivalry, nor as a background condition that merely "constrains" domestic politics (see, for an overview, Nickel, 2024). We use the term as an analytical concept to capture how global struggles over energy systems, infrastructure, standards, and strategic materials are translated into domestic conflict lines through the mediation of rent. Geopolitics, in other words, is the political organization of space and interdependence around rent-generating capacities—around who controls them, who gains access, and who bears the social and ecological costs (for competing approaches to geopolitics and geo-economics, see, e.g., Alami et al., 2022; Babic, 2025; Schindler et al., 2024). Our perspective matters because the Maghreb's green transition is not simply a technological shift but also a re-allocation of geopolitical relevance in a world economy where energy and raw materials again define strategic hierarchy.

The green transition intensifies external competition for access to the region's rent-generating assets: land, solar irradiation, wind corridors, phosphates, strategic infrastructure, and geographic proximity to Europe. The EU, driven by its Green Deal and post-Ukraine energy-security concerns, seeks long-term access to hydrogen, electricity, and critical minerals to stabilize its decarbonization trajectory and maintain global competitiveness. Gulf monarchies project capital and influence through sovereign wealth funds and renewable investments, often seeking portfolio diversification rather than structural transformation. China expands its footprint through infrastructure, technology provision, and trade within the Belt and Road Initiative framework, embedding the region in hybrid energy and industrial systems that combine green and fossil elements. The United States and other actors introduce layers of security, counterterrorism, and great-power rivalry, reinforcing the region's strategic density.

From this perspective, the conclusion's central claim can be stated more precisely: the green transition transforms external alignment into a domestic cleavage, because competing external projects and blocs do not present themselves to Maghreb societies as neutral opportunities. They become resources in domestic struggles—within state classes, between elite factions, and between state and society—over the capture and use of emerging green rents. The question is therefore not only which partner the Maghreb chooses but also how external alignment reorganizes domestic coalitions: which ministries and agencies gain leverage, which business groups become indispensable intermediaries, which regions are targeted for infrastructure investment, and which social groups become "winners" or "absorbed costs" of the transition.

This mechanism becomes particularly visible at the present global conjuncture, which is best understood as a bifurcation point in world energy and resource politics. One trajectory points toward a genuinely post-fossil regime: a new world-surplus structure organized around renewables, critical minerals, and green industrial inputs. The other trajectory points toward a fractured and uneven outcome: the parallel persistence of fossil dominance (most visibly in the United States under Trump), hybrid energy regimes combining fossil and green rents (most visibly in China), and a large periphery of countries that either remain locked into fossil pathways because they cannot finance their energy transition or are integrated into green value chains only as low-value suppliers of land, energy flows, and raw materials. Under both trajectories, however, one feature remains constant: rent becomes more—not less—central to geopolitical positioning, because geopolitical leverage increasingly rests on controlling *rentier nodes* of the emerging energy order: infrastructures, corridors, certification regimes, standards, financing channels, and strategic inputs. By *rentier nodes*, we refer to strategically positioned sites—material, regulatory, technological, and financial—where rents are generated through the control of access, standards, and circulation rather than through direct production, which function as geopolitical chokepoints structuring dependency (Bridge & Bradshaw, 2017).

It is under these conditions that the Maghreb's geopolitical relevance rises. Yet the book's empirical point is that this rise does not necessarily imply a structural realignment away from Europe. Instead, the volume's evidence suggests a more paradoxical pattern: new geopolitical competition is layered onto an old architecture of external anchoring. This can be shown through three interrelated dimensions—trade, investment, and finance—which together approximate the Maghreb's effective "geopolitical embedding" in the world economy.

Exports and the geography of external demand: Export data highlight a strong and persistent European orientation in North African exports across most product categories, particularly for green-related raw materials (see Figure 12.1). Even where China's role has increased, most visibly in fossil fuels and selected primary commodities, this expansion remains largely additive rather than transformative. Overall, the export structure indicates selective diversification rather than structural realignment. China emerges as an important marginal destination in specific sectors, but the EU continues to anchor North Africa's export geography, especially in emerging green-material baskets. This pattern supports the chapter's central claim: the green transition reshapes the composition of rents, but it does not fundamentally overturn the region's historically entrenched external orientation and unequal specialization.

FDI and the geography of ownership and project governance: Figure 12.2 shows that inward FDI in the Maghreb remains structurally dominated by European investors, particularly in Morocco and Tunisia, where the EU27 accounts for the majority of FDI stocks throughout the period. The United States plays only a

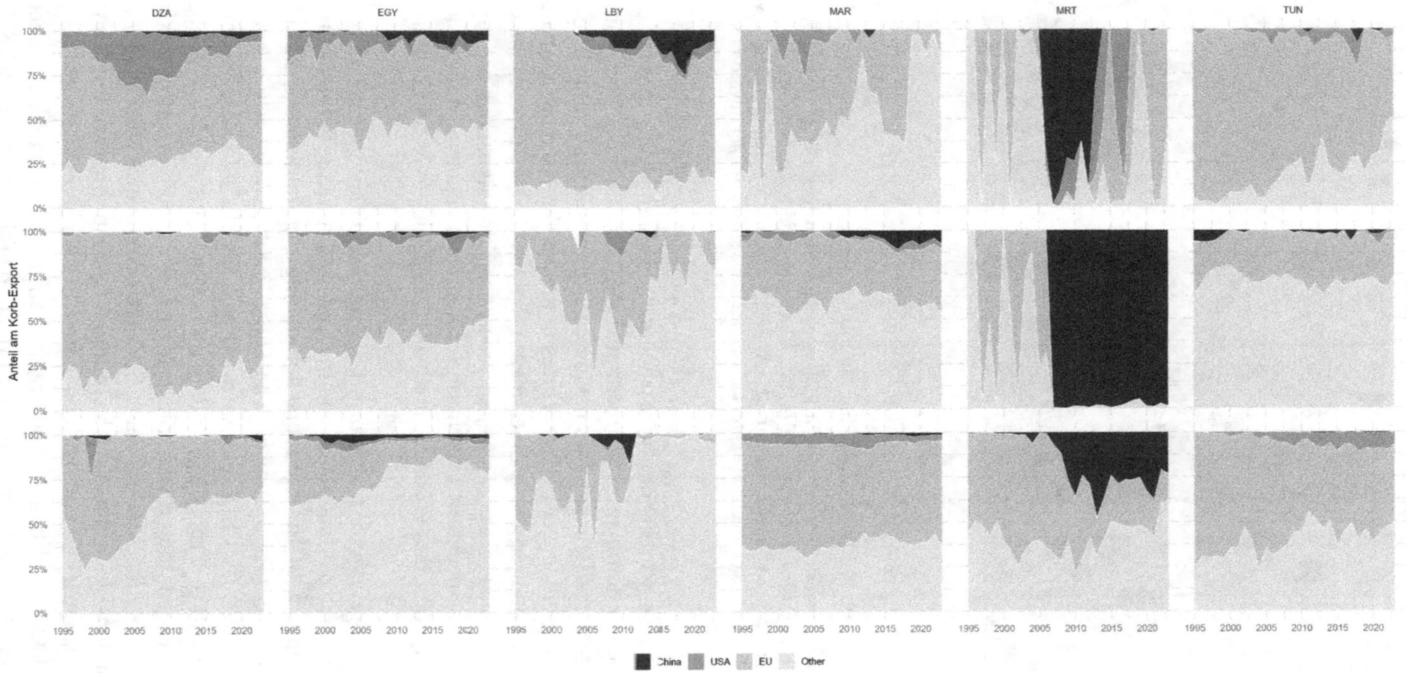

Figure 12.1 Geopolitical trade orientation.

Note: Own calculations based on UN Comtrade trade data. The figure shows the destination structure of exports from North African countries (Algeria, Egypt, Libya, Morocco, Mauritania, Tunisia) by geopolitical trading partner (China, USA, EU, and Other). Exports are disaggregated by product baskets (fossil fuels, green-related raw materials, and their primary commodities) and expressed as percentage shares of total exports in each basket and year.

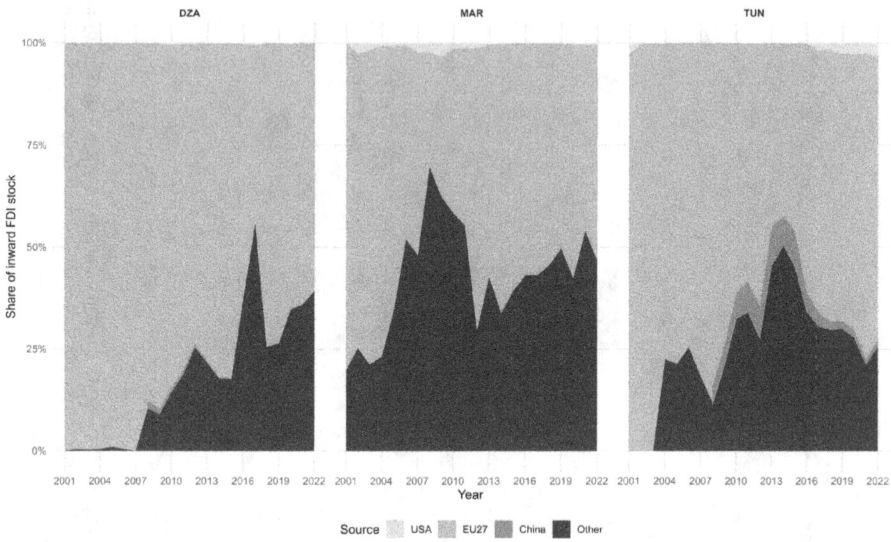

Figure 12.2 Composition of FDI stocks in the Maghreb.

Note: Own calculation. Source: Bilateral inward FDI stock data from Kox (2025), *World Bilateral FDI Statistics: A Time-Consistent Database, 2001–2022*. The figure reports shares of total inward FDI stocks in Algeria, Morocco, and Tunisia by origin (USA, EU27, China, and residual "Other"). Values are aggregated at the country-year level and expressed as percentage shares of total inward FDI.

minor and volatile role, while China's presence remains limited and does not translate into a sustained or dominant investment position. Overall, the pattern points to continuity rather than realignment. Despite increasing geopolitical competition and narratives of shifting influence, FDI structures in the Maghreb remain anchored in long-standing Euro-Mediterranean investment relations. This reinforces the chapter's core argument: new geopolitical and green transition dynamics are layered onto existing patterns of external anchoring rather than replacing them—and it is precisely this layering that produces intensified struggles over rent capture and project control.

*Debt and the geography of financial discipline and policy sp*ace: Figure 12.3 shows that the Maghreb's bilateral and commercial debt structures remain strongly anchored in Europe, with EU creditors dominating non-multilateral PPG debt across Algeria, Morocco, and Tunisia. The United States plays only a marginal and episodic role, whereas China has emerged as a visible but clearly secondary creditor since the 2000s. Crucially, the data do not indicate a decisive geopolitical realignment. Instead, they reveal a layering of new creditors onto an existing rent-based financial architecture, in which European dominance persists alongside a growing role of non-Western and Arab creditors. Once multilateral finance is excluded, Maghreb countries do not exhibit a pattern of China-centered debt dependence. Instead, bilateral and bank-based creditor structures remain dominated by European creditors, Arab state lenders, and private banking channels, with China

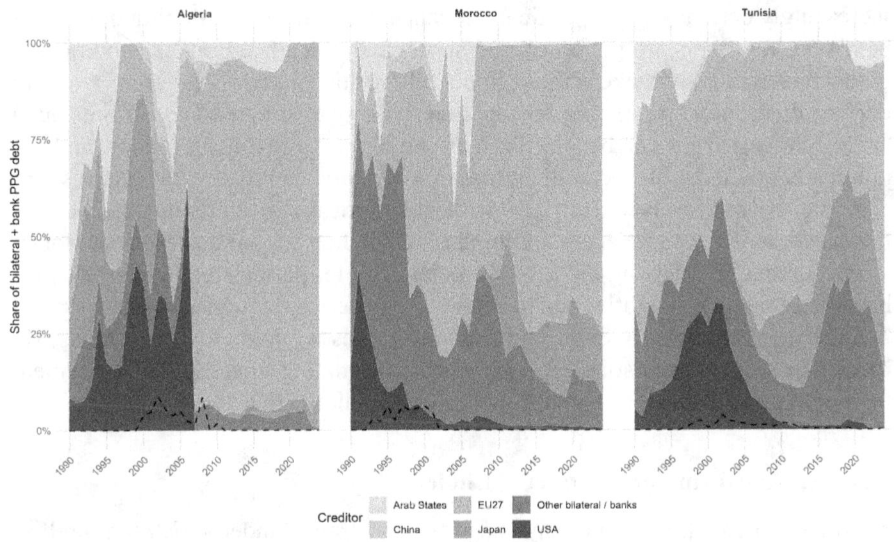

Figure 12.3 Bilateral debt of Maghreb states.

Note: The figure uses World Bank *International Debt Statistics* (IDS) data and reports shares of public and publicly guaranteed external debt owed to bilateral creditors and commercial banks only. Multilateral loans, bonds, and other market instruments are excluded. Creditor groups include the EU27, USA, China, Japan, Arab states, and other bilateral or bank creditors. Values represent country-year shares of total bilateral and bank PPG debt.

playing a marginal and episodic role. The implication is analytical: geopolitics operates not only through "choices" but also through financial structures that preform policy space, shaping which industrial and social strategies are feasible under green transition conditions.

Taken together, these three dimensions clarify the "new" geopolitical configuration: the Maghreb is not merely "caught" between blocs; rather, it is being repositioned within a world economy in which access to and distribution of rent determine geopolitical relevance. This repositioning is not external to domestic politics. It produces domestic winners and losers, reorganizes elite competition, and reshapes state–society relations. Geopolitics thus becomes a domestic cleavage because external alignment is simultaneously a distributive struggle over the control and use of rents, and because green rents multiply the arenas (e.g., land, infrastructure, standards, finance) through which these struggles unfold. It is within this fractured global landscape that the Maghreb's geopolitical position must be understood.

In this emerging geopolitical configuration, rent becomes a central analytical category. Control over rent-generating capacities, rather than mere ownership of resources, defines bargaining power, shapes alliance choices, and structures both international positioning and domestic coalitions.

The Maghreb is not merely reacting to external pressures; it is being repositioned within a global order in which access to energy, raw materials, and surplus increasingly determines geopolitical relevance. How this repositioning unfolds depends on how rents are governed and strategically deployed under conditions of global uncertainty. At stake is the region's role within an emerging "green world order." In this context, rentier nodes function not only as structural constraints but as strategic assets. They can be mobilized as bargaining capital in diplomatic and economic negotiations. Morocco illustrates this dynamic clearly: energy and resource agreements are closely intertwined with geopolitical considerations, particularly the question of Western Sahara, as emphasized by Foreign Minister Nasser Bourita in the context of renewing the EU–Morocco fisheries partnership agreement when he stated that "The negotiations to renew the fisheries partnership agreement . . . include the Moroccan Sahara, and this constitutes a stage that strengthens Morocco's position as the sole interlocutor for negotiating international agreements that include the Sahara"(cited in Amouzai & Haddioui, 2023).

Europe, Constraint, and Strategic Choice

International coalitions ultimately shape the constraints under which Maghreb actors operate, but Europe occupies a distinctive position within this landscape. As the region's largest trading partner and a political project committed to rapid decarbonization, the EU is structurally dependent on access to energy, raw materials, and strategic infrastructure from North Africa. No credible scenario for Europe's green transition and global competitiveness can be realized without the Maghreb. At the same time, this interdependence is profoundly asymmetrical. Europe commands superior technological capabilities, financial instruments, and regulatory power. CBAMs, hydrogen certification regimes, and critical-mineral strategies therefore carry the risk of locking the Maghreb into low-value segments of green supply chains unless they are explicitly embedded in broader developmental arrangements.

What follows from this is not merely a policy challenge, but a strategic one. Europe must recognize the pre-formative role of rent in structuring both geopolitical relations and domestic political economies in the Maghreb. Green cooperation that ignores rent dynamics risks reproducing the very instabilities it seeks to contain. Equally important, Europe must take the internal social and political dynamics of Maghreb societies seriously. Conflicts over employment, land, migration, and social justice are not externalities to energy cooperation; they shape the sustainability of any geopolitical arrangement.

For Maghreb governments, the current moment opens a narrow but significant window. They can accept a role as the green periphery—an export corridor for clean molecules and electrons, coupled with migration control and security cooperation—or they can leverage Europe's dependence to negotiate a more ambitious agenda centered on industrial upgrading, regional integration, and social investment. Which path is taken will depend not only on domestic coalition-building but also on Europe's willingness to move beyond a narrow conception of energy security.

A durable Euro-Mediterranean partnership requires the deliberate construction of broad-based winner coalitions. This implies granting the Maghreb partial and conditional access to European markets in ways that stimulate industrial upgrading rather than merely resource extraction. It also entails enabling the region to benefit from transfer mechanisms—whether through agricultural market access, climate finance, or industrial cooperation—that relax external constraints and support the creation of domestic employment. Over time, such arrangements could initiate an upward spiral in which productive capacity, employment, and social inclusion expand in tandem, gradually narrowing the welfare and political stability gap between Europe and its southern neighbors.

This strategy, however, demands a shift within Europe itself. Supporting development and stability in the Maghreb cannot be achieved without adjustments in Europe's own political economy. Higher real wages, stronger domestic demand, and a renewed commitment to employment-centered growth are not obstacles but preconditions for a more balanced external relationship. Europe must once again assume the role of a demand and employment locomotive—less as a low-cost producer, more as a market, a technological partner, and a site of social upgrading in which other regions can be productively integrated.

In this sense, raw material and energy policy cannot remain detached from questions of global social policy. Linking Europe's green transition to broader objectives of employment, redistribution, and structural convergence is not an act of altruism, but a condition for overcoming the structural heterogeneity that has long defined Euro-Mediterranean relations. Only by confronting these underlying conditions can green cooperation move beyond extractivism and contribute to a more stable and equitable geopolitical order.

References

Alami, I., Dixon, A. D., Gonzalez-Vicente, R., Babic, M., Lee, S.-O., Medby, I. A., & de Graaff, N. (2022). Geopolitics and the "new" state capitalism. *Geopolitics*, *27*(3), 995–1023. https://doi.org/10.1080/14650045.2021.1924943

Amouzai, A., & Haddioui, O. (2023). *Green hydrogen in Morocco: Just transition or greenwashing neocolonialism? The case of Guelmim-Oued Noun* (Flex Crops & Commodities Report). Transnational Institute.

Babic, M. (2025). *Geoökonomie: Anatomie der neuen Weltordnung*. Suhrkamp.

Bradlow, B. H., & Kentikelenis, A. (2024). Globalizing green industrial policy through technology transfers. *Nature Sustainability*, *7*(6), 685–687. https://doi.org/10.1038/s41893-024-01336-4

Bresser-Pereira, L. C., Oreiro, J. L., & Marconi, N. (2019). *Developmental macroeconomics: New developmentalism as a growth strategy*. Routledge.

Bridge, G., & Bradshaw, M. (2017). Making a global gas market: Territoriality and production networks in liquefied natural gas. *Economic Geography*, *93*(3), 215–240. https://doi.org/10.1080/00130095.2017.1283212

Elsenhans, H. (1991). The great depression of the 1930s and the Third World. *International Studies*, *28*(3), 273–290. https://doi.org/10.1177/0020881791028003003

Elsenhans, H. (2004). Overcoming rent by using rent: The challenge of development. *Intervention. Zeitschrift für Ökonomie*, *1*(1), 87–115.

Evenett, S., Jakubik, A., Martín, F., & Ruta, M. (2024). *The return of industrial policy in data* (IMF Working Paper WP/24/1). International Monetary Fund.

Farzanegan, M. R., & Hassan, S. M. (2020). How does the flow of remittances affect the trade balance of the Middle East and North Africa? *Journal of Economic Policy Reform*, *23*(2), 248–266. https://doi.org/10.1080/17487870.2019.1609357

Fehling, P., & Burchardt, H.-J. (Eds.). (2023). *Taxation and inequality in Latin America: New perspectives on political economy and tax regimes*. Routledge.

Ferrié, J.-N. (1999). *La démocratisation limitée en Afrique du Nord: De la "société civile" à la participation politique* (Études et Documents 7). CEDEJ.

Grabowski, R. (2017). Premature deindustrialization and inequality. *International Journal of Social Economics*, *44*(2), 154–168. https://doi.org/10.1108/IJSE-07-2015-0197

Hamouchene, H., & Sandwell, K. (Eds.). (2023). *Dismantling green colonialism: Energy and climate justice in the Arab region*. Pluto Press.

Harrison, A., Martin, L. A., & Nataraj, S. (2017). Green industrial policy in emerging markets. *Annual Review of Resource Economics*, *9*, 253–274. https://doi.org/10.1146/annurev-resource-100516-053445

Hauge, J., Houtzager, B., & Hörmann, A. J. (2025). The new economic nationalism: Industrial policy and national security in the United States, China, and the European Union. *Geoforum*. Advance online publication. https://doi.org/10.1016/j.geoforum.2025.104382

Herbert, M. (2022). *The challenge of coordinating border management assistance between Europe and the Maghreb*. Migration Policy Institute.

Keynes, J. M. (2009). *Allgemeine Theorie der Beschäftigung, des Zinses und des Geldes* (Original work published 1936). Duncker & Humblot.

Lebdioui, A. (2024). *Survival of the greenest: Economic transformation in a climate-conscious world*. Cambridge University Press.

Martinez, L. (2009). *Maghreb: Vaincre la peur de la démocratie* (Cahier de Chaillot 115). Institut d'Études de Sécurité de l'Union européenne.

Meckling, J. (2025). The geoeconomic turn in decarbonization. *Nature*, *645*(8082), 869–876. https://doi.org/10.1038/s41586-025-09416-x

Moustakbal, J. (2023). The Moroccan energy sector: A permanent dependence. In H. Hamouchene & K. Sandwell (Eds.), *Dismantling green colonialism* (pp. 220–232). Pluto Press.

Nickel, C. (2024). What do we talk about when we talk about the "return" of geopolitics? *International Affairs*, *100*(1), 221–239. https://doi.org/10.1093/ia/iiad295

Ouaissa, R. (2014). *Die Rolle der Mittelschichten im Arabischen Frühling: Ein Überblick*. Springer VS.

Ouaissa, R. (2018). Classes moyennes algériennes, rente et stagnation politique. *NAQD*, *36*, 123–145.

Ouaissa, R. (2023). Rents hinder capitalism: The rentier middle classes in the Middle East. In H. Warnecke-Berger & J. Ickler (Eds.), *The political economy of extractivism* (pp. 199–214). Routledge.

Ouchichi, M. (2025). *Political economy of Algeria: Extractivism, rents and populism*. Routledge.

Schiffbauer, M., Abdoulaye, S., Hussain, S., Sahnoun, H., & Keefer, P. (2014). *Jobs or privileges: Unleashing the employment potential of the Middle East and North Africa*. World Bank.

Schindler, S., Alami, I., DiCarlo, J., Jepson, N., Rolf, S., Bayırbağ, M. K., Cyuzuzo, L., et al. (2024). The second Cold War: US-China competition for centrality in infrastructure, digital, production, and finance networks. *Geopolitics*, *29*(4), 1083–1120. https://doi.org/10.1080/14650045.2023.2253432

Sim, L.-C. (2020). Low-carbon energy in the Gulf: Upending the rentier state? *Energy Research & Social Science*, *70*, 101752. https://doi.org/10.1016/j.erss.2020.101752

Tanchum, M. (Ed.). (2024). *Renewable energy and electricity interconnection megaprojects in North Africa: Prospects for Euro-North Africa cooperation*. European Institute of the Mediterranean.

Warnecke-Berger, H. (2021). Fixing the labour surplus in existing economic structures. In N. Wilcock & E. Federzoni dos Santos (Eds.), *Not paying the rent: Imagining a fairer capitalism* (pp. 157–166). Palgrave Macmillan.

Warnecke-Berger, H. (2022). Rents, the moral economy of remittances, and the rise of a new transnational development model. *Revue de la régulation*, *31*(2). https://doi.org/10.4000/regulation.20809

Warnecke-Berger, H. (2024). Rohstoffe, Renten und ungleiche Spezialisierung: Über die Chancen einer neuen Weltwirtschaftsordnung. In A. Veit & D. Fuchs (Eds.), *Eine gerechte Weltwirtschaftsordnung?* (pp. 317–338). Transcript.

Warnecke-Berger, H. (2025). Surplus, rent and unequal development: Raw materials and remittances as the motor of rent societies in the Global South. In B. Sanghera (Ed.), *Global rentier capitalism* (pp. 210–224). Routledge.

Warnecke-Berger, H., & Ickler, J. (2023a). Introduction: The political economy of extractivism. In H. Warnecke-Berger & J. Ickler (Eds.), *The political economy of extractivism* (pp. 1–16). Routledge.

Warnecke-Berger, H., & Ickler, J. (Eds.). (2023b). *The political economy of extractivism: Global perspectives on the seduction of rent*. Routledge.

Warnecke-Berger, H., & Ickler, J. (2025). The political economy of extractivism. *Exploring Economics*. https://www.exploring-economics.org/en/discover/the-political-economy-of-extractivism/

For Product Safety Concerns and Information please contact our EU
representative GPSR@taylorandfrancis.com
Taylor & Francis Verlag GmbH, Kaufingerstraße 24, 80331 München, Germany

www.ingramcontent.com/pod-product-compliance
Lightning Source LLC
LaVergne TN
LVHW010548300926
849162LV00002B/272

* 9 7 8 1 0 4 1 2 2 1 2 6 5 *